Changing Your Stripes

The Social Psychology of Situation, Self, & Solutions

Matt Moody Ph.D.

www.ChangingYourStripes.com

2 Ed.

Cover:
Original oil paintings by Virginia Finlinson Moody, 1912-1994

Cover Design:
Devin Finlinson Moody, b. 1987

ISBN:
1-4276-0057-0

Dedicated to the memory of
my mother, Virginia Finlinson Moody,
a model of selfless compassion and patience;
and to my dearly departed sister, Patricia Moody White
who, like mom, made you feel like a person
of importance and worth
when in her presence;
and to my dad, Milo Crestfield Moody:
respected and honored by those he generously served
as a medical doctor and a church leader—
purely positive about life
to the age of ninety.

Contents

3 Solutions: Recovering the True You

THE JOURNEY

by Reed H. Bradford

For this is the Journey that men make:
To find themselves. If they fail in this, it matters little
whatever else they may achieve: Money, Fame, Revenge.
When they end the Journey, they can put them all into
a bin marked "ashes." They mean nothing.
But if one has found that he has within him
a divine soul, if he has discovered the principles
upon which the fulfillment of that soul is based, and
if he implements those principles, then he has a mansion
within which he can live with dignity
and joy each day of his life.

PREFACE

"The woods would be very silent if no birds sang . . . except those who sang best." These words by John Audubon are encouraging to all, to sing the song that is in them and to sing it as best they can, in their own unique way—pushing aside comparisons. In writing this book, I am singing!

Part of my unique "singing" style is expressed through my use of *italics*, "quotation marks," and Capital Letters. So when you come across an emphasized word . . . or three, just imagine I'm talking to you personally and I'm animating my voice. Being emphatic and dramatic is a family tradition (and his last name was?). Further, I have used "quotation marks," *italics*, and Capital Letters to *bring out* words and ideas . . . so you can better "see" parallels and comparisons, and to *point out* terms that will have a special meaning within the context of this book.

Throughout the book, you will also observe that I make use of the ellipsis: "three dots" . . . that will invite you to pause and pay attention. To better convey the cadence of my normal speaking voice was one motive, and another intent was to lend greater force and focus to key conclusions. Killing two birds with one stone, I sometimes used the ellipsis *(and even italics)* to keep my auto-hypenator from chopping certain words in two.

As you pass your eyes over the ink, I hope you will allow my unique way of *symbolizing* to constrain you to deeper and richer meaning, . . . for there IS method to my madness.

How to read this book: You have my permission to *jump in* anywhere you'd like. Now doesn't that sound fun? If you spend a few moments perusing the table of contents and the index, I am confident you will find many topics that will capture your curiosity.

I remember when I began my Master of Education program, and to my complete surprise all my professors were actually "teachers." So instead of simply droning on with some sleep-inducing lecture, my professors actually did more than merely "profess." Because they were truly teachers, . . . they "taught."

In a most delightful learning experience, part of my education included the bestowal of *responsibility* to craft my own curriculum. Wow! After decades of being dictated "what to do" I was given the weight of responsibility to decide what I was going to learn. I soon realized that if I didn't do a good job of this, I would be cheating myself! Thus, within the broad parameters of a course topic, my wise teachers would ask: "What is it you would like to learn . . . and how can I help you?"

From firsthand experience, I've learned that doing your "own" assignments is much more motivating than doing the ones dictated by the dictator! This is precisely why I'm giving YOU the *responsibility* to enter these writings "anywhere you'd like!" Master teachers have taught me that your own motivations and honest intuitions will faithfully lead you to the greatest depths of learning.

While you're following your own questions and curiosities, you will eventually *discover* that some concepts are best understood by grasping previous explanations, but I will leave that up to you to discern for yourself. Hint: *Cause versus Constraint* in the "Situation" chapter, *Emotion as Energy-in-Motion* in the "Self" chapter, and *Memory as Re-Membering* in the "Solutions" chapter — all these all foundational concepts, just to name a few.

When you eventually climb into the middle of this book, you will stumble upon a concept called *The Looking Glass Self* which explains the emergence of self-identity—not to be confused with *who you are.* In a nutshell, the theory contends that you don't really know *who you are* till somebody tells you. Some people stubbornly kick at this idea: "Hey, I know who I am . . . and I don't need anyone to tell me." But *what you have in your head* is really a "myth" called self-identity (see page 92).

Even so, people persist in *thinking* they have the best access to themselves, but this is not true, . . . others have the best view; at least the best view of the self I call "being"—which is the most important aspect of self, *because* this is where "character" is located.

Character is not a *physical attribute;* character transcends the boundaries of the body and is expressed in *how you are being* with others. Because "being" is located in relations, you can only become aware of your *way of being* in reflections coming from the social mirror: Other people tell you *how you are being;* they let you know *who you are.* At which point, you construct a "myth" in your mind . . . which sounds like a bind, but the book suggests *solutions.*

Some people don't want to see their reflection in the mirror, especially those who suspect that they will not like what they see. Have you ever met a cranky old codger . . . who was completely oblivious to *being* cranky? Such crusty codgers are clueless precisely because nobody *dares* reflect back to Mr. I. M. Crotchety the fact that he IS . . . crotchety.

Can you imagine the kind of reception you would get if required to confront some abrasive Ogre: *"Pardon me, your Maniacal Majesty, . . . but you're a very cranky, crusty, cantankerous sorta fella, has anyone ever shared that with you Mr. Dictator, Sir? May I make a humble suggestion? I think you'd win more friends and influence more people if you would try de-emphasizing the "oppression" thing, and maybe concentrate on learning a few first names, and talking about other people's interests!"*

It's actually pretty much "standard operating procedure" for diabolical dictators to behead the bearer of bad news; thus, sharing constructive criticism with demoniacal despots has been largely avoided for a few millennia. The fact is that some people—like toxic tyrants—make themselves *unapproach-able* because they don't want to see *who they are* in the social mirror. This means that unapproachable types . . . don't get approached, and don't get *much-needed* feedback (see page 155).

Just as we don't really know *who we are* till somebody tells us, similarly, I don't *know* the impact of what I've written in this book until reflective feedback returns from those who read. When the readers speak, it is then I come to *know* how my words "come across." Therefore, as you read this book, I am eager to hear . . . what's not clear and what's not correct?

I'd like to know what's working and what inspires, and what may be falling flat on its face? Some might *fear* such feedback, but in writing, as in Life, it is the feedback that helps us adjust, clarify, and become! If you have a helpful suggestion to offer, please contact me through my website: www.ChangingYourStripes.com

Our Lives are works in progress. Each new day extends a fresh opportunity to learn and grow. Every new day offers refining moments to knock off the rough edges of our character and become smooth and polished in purpose. In like manner, this book is a work in progress. There are parts that may need improvement, but as the days roll by and I keep at the task, my words will become wiser as I adjust to fair feedback.

I welcome comments that can make the explanations in this book more effective and fluent. These writings are committed to the process of Change. In the mean time, I present to you . . . my *last abandoned draft.* I invite you to read these words with the same kindly attitude expressed by Dinah M. Kraig:

* * * * *

Oh, the comfort,
The inexpressible comfort of feeling safe with a person,
Having neither to weigh thoughts nor measure words,
But to pour them all out, just as they are,
Chaff and grain together.
Assured that a faithful hand will take and sift them,
Keep what is worth keeping, and then,
With the breath of kindness,
Blow the rest away.

* * * * *

In 475 B.C. Heraclitus declared: *"It is in changing that we find purpose."* Finding your Purpose . . . and living up to that Purpose IS the reason these words are written. So, I would say "good luck" as you read *Changing Your Stripes* . . . but I know that *luck* is the residue of *persistence effort.* The lucky ones are the people who *faithfully endure* in the journey. So press forward, for your *luck* is about to Change.

Matt Moody, August 12, 2006

INTRODUCTION

A Superior Premise for Satisfying Solutions. Many therapies for solving life's ever-appearing problems come from the traditions of secular psychology; perspectives that foster an inferior starting point, a poor premise:

> *What is it about my bad biology, my bad brain chemistry, and/or my bad upbringing that "causes" the misery in which I am mired?*

Because the origins for human problems are assumed to be "caused" by physical factors in the body . . . or by a bad environment, I call this kind of science: It's-Not-Your-Fault Psychology. There is great popular appeal for the "you're-not-responsible" paradigm: Yahoo! You don't have to OWN any bad behavior!

Ironically the very institution that you look to for healing and happiness often enables you to reject personal response-ability, and instead encourages people to blame emotions and actions on their bad upbringing or their bad biology. Convenient excuses come via dubious diagnoses of disorders—Bi-Polar, A.D.D., P.T.S.D., O.C.D., etc.—that people purportedly "come down with" like physical diseases. And if a disorder . . . is not in order, excuse-making psychology will assist you in blaming your misery of mind and emotion upon the influence of unfit parents or inappropriate peers. Regardless of the diagnosis, the bottom-line for this kind of science is: It's not your fault!

Nevertheless, some troubles you encounter in life *will* occur by no fault of your own. Indeed, many misfortunes happen beyond your direct control: The movements of Mother Nature, physical diseases and disabilities, mechanical failures, accidents caused by the inattentive acts of others, and abuses brought on by intentional mistreatment—all these scenarios *cause* what I call "Situational Suffering." Yet even amid such situations—that are NOT caused by you—there remains one thing that is completely caused by you: Your *response* to "whatever happens" at the level of heart, mind, and emotion.

Instead of beginning with *blame* and *fault* (see page 20), a superior entry into the issues of life begins with the question of *Response-Ability* (check out this topic in the Index). So even when physical ailments or aggravating environments tug and tear at your flesh, you remain free to choose your *responses* of heart and soul. This means you get to OWN ALL that comes out of you in terms of mind and emotion; a notion that receives a positive nod from the populous in *theory*, . . . but is far less popular in *practice*. Unfortunately, the lure of It's-Not-Your-Fault Psychology wins many more followers.

We live in an excuse-making society that entices us to blame someone else or something else, for the irritable and sometimes insane reactions that come out of us. The truth is that personal happiness is found in the exact opposite direction from blame and excuse (refer to page 17). When you can fully own your responses of mind and emotion, you can live free from the self-imposed prison of a *victim's mentality*—even when victimized.

As you Change Your Stripes, even amid bodily ailments and environmental adversities, you will enjoy the *victor's view;* and you will increase in strength of character directly *because* of tough times—not just in spite of them.

Instead of dwelling upon yesterday's bad news, a superior premise begins by focusing upon the dynamics of the present moment; what is happening NOW in terms of your Response-Ability: Your ability to choose Love instead all other responses that *fall short* of Love; your ability to respond in ways that will build *your* strength of character, instead of make *you* "something less" (see page 196). The raw reality of life is this: Any response coming out of you that is Less-Than-Love is a response that will diminish your personal peace and limit your best life as a human being.

Becoming a New Kind of Creature. The Saying goes, "You can't change a tiger's stripes!" That may be so, as long as a tiger remains a tiger. But what if that striped animal could be changed into a new kind of creature? What if people could change *who they are* fundamentally, and not just superficially or cosmetically . . . what if people could change their stripes?

The truth is that you will be *who you are* until you become someone different. Until you Change Your Stripes, you will bring the *old animal* with you wherever you go! And as you encounter *new situations,* you will tend to act according to the *old patterns* of the *old creature,* . . . repeating *old ways* that may not work and may not bring happiness.

The common cure for dealing with a tiger-like disposition, explosive and ferocious, is to ship the ornery animal off to a different place—relocate to a new zoo! Or if the tiger is especially tenacious, another cure is to simply leave the cranky creature. Either way, as long as that tiger remains a tiger . . . cutting claws are liable to leave their mark upon new prey . . . in a future day, and the false remedy of *relocation* will eventually be repeated.

When stubborn creatures resist fundamental change from their core, . . . root problems remain the same even though superficial scenery and personal appearance may change. So as remedies go . . . better than *relocation* is *recovery*.

At our first of many meetings, Alice announced, "I've married the same man three times." What she meant by this was that she had really married three different men, . . . but because the same nagging issues cropped up in all three marriages, she concluded that the problem was the "type" of man she had married. In her view, these three men were "broken" in the same way, . . . making them essentially the "same man" three times over.

Initially, it did not occur to her that the common denominator in all three failed marriages was . . . Alice! Though her husbands certainly made their *unique* and *negative* contributions to the quagmire, they were basically responding to the menacing advances of an untamed tiger. When human beings are attacked by a tiger, they tend to respond in similar ways: with defense and self-protection. For Alice, all three husbands cowered and defended from her cutting claws in the "same" protective pattern. What a coincidence!

The ultimate answer for Alice was not to get de-clawed or to take tiger etiquette lessons, . . . but to *change her stripes* completely and become a new kind of creature. Instead, Alice opted for *relocation* over *recovery*, and moved to a new zoo. She divorced number three and married number four! For Alice, a regrettable lament is forecast: Without a fundamental change in Alice from her core, it's only a matter of time till her new man gets mauled . . . also. And when husband number four cowers and defends in the same predictable fashion, Alice will exclaim: "I've married the same man four times!"

* * * * *

You can try to run from your troubles,
but you cannot run from yourself.
Wherever you go, . . . you will
bring yourself with you.

* * * * *

Within each of us are unresolved problems *waiting to happen*. Old unresolved issues that are like *land mines* longing to be stepped on, . . . anxiously waiting to explode. And these same old issues arise because of *who we are!* All our problems are portable; we bring them with us wherever we go! Without a fundamental change from our core, . . . a change from the heart, our *built in* troubles will eventually surface as we face future situations we have yet to master. Hence, the same *old creature* relocates to a *new situation*, or a *new relationship*, with energetic hopes and optimistic anticipations, only to find the same *stale issues* arising again . . . and again. This broken-record routine will tend to play its annoying tune over and over until you . . . Change Your Stripes!

* * * * *

Mastering a challenging situation
is ultimately a matter of mastering yourself!

* * * * *

You must not expect that things will get better simply because tough times decrease via avoidance. Life is to be lived with gusto! Challenges are to be met head on, . . . for it is directly "in" our challenges that we find our ultimate destiny. In the ever-appearing adversities of life, we can increase in strength of character; a character that at mortal death is the only possession of which it can be said: *"you took it with you."* What you will take into the eternal world is . . . what you become!

* * * * *

The greatest prize
for Life's labors is not
in material possessions or
impressive accomplishments,
but in the progress of personal character.
You labor for your own becoming,
this is your richest reward.

* * * * *

Ironically, it is often the case that untamed tigers will actively participate in the very creation of a problem in the first place, and then paradoxically perpetuate it by *reacting poorly* to the very situation they set up! *Alice brought herself and her tiger-like disposition* to each new relationship, and what she saw coming back was mostly a function of *who she was,* . . . she was *setting up* her own troubles! She had not sufficiently increased in strength of character by *changing her stripes.*

Similarly, we can behave like cantankerous tigers, and inflame the very struggles we complain about—the struggles we wish would go away. Whether large or small, we play our part in making difficulties worse than they would be, . . . if only we would *change our stripes;* and thereafter, respond in new ways, . . . loving ways, according to the attributes and natural inclinations of a new kind of creature. The process of *Changing Your Stripes* is promoted as you understand:

* The nature of the "Zoo" you live in, . . .
  seeing the realities of your **Situation**.
* The makeup of the "Animal" you are, . . .
  understanding your **Self**.

~ 1 ~

Situation:

The Zoo You Live In

Life is a Set Up!

Have you ever experienced the frustration of being set up? Have you ever found yourself in a situation where there was little wiggle room to choose a winning response: The old *damned-if-you-do-or-damned-if-you-don't* dilemma?

Consider this *set up* scenario: Someone cries "fire" in a crowded theater—when there really is no fire. This is a sure *set up* for some sour responses! Visualize the chaos created by this false alarm. Sounds of sobbing and shrieking ring out as frantic people push towards exit doors, causing others to trip and fall. Bodies are bruised and even broken. All these noxious consequences because one mischievous *creep* cried "fire," and all in the crowded theater reacted as if the warning was reliable; each responding in their own way, depending upon the kind of creature they are.

In the same way, you can *expect* life to present many unexpected and unwanted moments that will be a *set up* for frustration! Life is a *set up* because others can independently choose courses of action that impinge upon your personal path, just as you also impinge your *preferences* and *prejudices* upon others; thus, life is a *set up* for frustration especially as people show little regard for the welfare and best interests of others, and instead act to further selfish agendas. Life is a *set up* because some egocentrically seek for profit, pleasure, power, and promotion at the expense of others.

Situational Set Ups. There are four fundamental sources that supply *situations* with frustration and possibly devastation to our lives. As these unwanted events occur, we are *set up* for misfortune and heartache:

* The Inconsiderate or Abusive Acts of Others,
* Accidents that happen due to Human Error,
* The untimely movements of Mother Nature, and
* Consequences of Mechanical Failures.

Making a firm commitment to Changing Your Stripes means continually asking this essential question:

* * * * *

As bad things happen to me,
and I am Set Up by Situations beyond my control,
how will I respond to these trials and troubles
to further my greatest growth of character?

* * * * *

This is a most critical question because the way you respond to whatever life *throws at you* determines whether life IS a drudgery or a delight! In the end, your happiness is not determined by *what happens to you,* but by *how you respond to what happens to you.*

So . . . Life is a Set Up: welcome to earth! Get used to it, get over it, and get on with it! However you respond—whether gracious or grumpy—you will act according to the *disposition* of the *animal that you are,* presently. Anyone might respond well when surrounded by loving and patient people, but what comes out of you when the going gets tough? (And by the way, the going *will* get tough . . . that's life.) The way you respond to unkind or abusive acts, the way you respond to unexpected events of accident, nature, or mechanical failure . . . reveals *who you are at the heart.* How you handle hardships exposes *the very core of your character.*

"Changing Your Stripes," means becoming the kind of creature that can and will respond with calm and clarity even amid commotion. It means responding to life's toughest challenges with compassion, rather than contempt. Being the kind of creature that will respond well to adversity IS a key to contented and rich living.

CAUSE VERSUS CONSTRAINT

In the previous scenario, where the *creep* cried "fire" in a crowded theater, many would conclude that this mischief-maker "caused" the resultant damage to person and property. Certainly, this person is morally responsible and legally liable for his instigating offense. It is also a fact that had this deceptive act NOT occurred . . . the havoc would not have happened; this *relationship of contingency* is the idea commonly associated with the word *Cause.* There is no question that the people in the theater were absolutely *Set Up* for a losing set of responses! Sometimes life happens just like this *false-alarm* scenario. *Life IS a Set Up!*

To the goal of Changing Your Stripes, it is important to remember that all the people in that crowded theater responded according to their personal perception and choice, decisions they made according to the *kind of creature they are* currently. The way each person reacted was neither a fixed or mechanical response, nor was it a necessary reaction; each person could have done things differently, especially if he or she were a *different kind of creature.*

Accepting the way I define "cause" herein, the kid who cried "fire" did not technically or directly *cause* the specific reactions of each person in the theater; rather, the false alarm *constrained* those reactions. This means the cry of "fire" placed perceptual limits upon the people and in response, each person made last second decisions within more narrow interpretive boundaries—according to *who they are from their heart, the kind of creature they are from their core.*

Definitions. A "constraint" is that *meaningful* and interpretive impact upon people that tends to narrow and limit a range of responses; yet the returning *response* has room to reflect the individual disposition, perception, and choice of the impacted. Constraints apply to beings that can perceive situations in a variety of ways, and then choose variable responses according to their values and rationale. When I use the word *meaningful,* this is not a synonym for *significant,* rather it signifies: meaning-full . . . full of meaning. This is the nature of linguistic relations called communication: it is *full of meaning* and it also has *impact,* thus . . . it is *constraining.*

In contrast, the word "cause" describes a *mechanical* interaction between two physical things. A *causal* impact always produces a *necessary* outcome, which is a *consistent* outcome occurring beyond perception and choice. The result of a causal impact is called . . . *effect,* whereas the answer to a constraint is termed . . . *response. Effects* are not chosen, and *responses* are always chosen.

However, there are some responses that flow from us that feel very "un-chosen." I call them *knee-jerk reactions.* These particular responses are NOT chosen in the *moment.* While they do flow from us in the *now*, they *were chosen* in prior days, weeks, and months. The *knee-jerk reaction* is a type of response that is the cumulative result of a repetitive pattern of choices made in the past, that *sets in motion* an automatic and "unthinking" reaction to emerge in the moment.

Like a land mine, *knee-jerk reactions* are set to explode at some future time as explode-able people are stepped on; therefore, irritating situations are a Set Up for an explosive kind of creature. Not all human responses are consciously chosen in the moment, but may burst out of us unthinkingly by virtue of a prior pattern of choices; reactions *squirt out* of us unconsciously like a reflex twitch.

If you are going to Change Your Stripes, it is supremely important to realize and remember that YOU are the ultimate author of all your *knee-jerk reactions.* Each choice you make is like shooting an arrow into the air, it must land somewhere and at some time; once they are launched, *decisions made/arrows shot* cannot be called back, and choices—like arrows—will always have a landing consequence. The knee-jerk reaction that erupts today is the landing of yesterday's "shot arrows" (for more about reactions see Provoke-Ability Quotient, page 48, and Energy-in-Motion, page 131).

* * * * *

My choices are determined by my present disposition:
I am not completely free to choose any choice,
nor am I free from the consequences of my choosing.
Consequences unfold according to Governing Laws of Life.

* * * * *

In summary, a *Cause* evokes a necessary *Effect* that occurs between physical things, whereas *Constraints* create limiting boundaries within which a *Response* is chosen. Causes occur in the physical realm of your world, whereas Constraints manifest within the behavioral and meaning-full realm. The phrase, "Life IS a Set Up," means that the world constrains you in every moment. Constraints are every impact that impinge upon your life; they can be helpful or hurtful, they can encourage or discourage. Constraints can intervene within your life as softly as a small pebble tossed into your pool of consciousness, or they may manifest as an abrupt impact that crashes into awareness. While constraints do *cause you to pay attention* for a time, . . . they do not *cause your eventual responses* in terms of subsequent thoughts, actions, motives, or emotions—such are determined by *who you are* from your core.

* * * * *

While a Constraint may "Cause" me to pay attention for a time, it cannot "Cause" my ultimate Response.

* * * * *

Communicative Constraints. Constraints press upon us in the common communications of everyday life. Constraints come in the form of spoken or written expressions, including the full range of nonverbal gestures and actions. Communicative *constraints* exist in a *meaningful* realm, as opposed to *causes* that occur entirely in a *mechanical* realm. Again, the word "meaningful" refers to the interpretive and expressive ways we relate with one another: talking, listening, speaking and responding, using both verbal and bodily expressions. Human discourse is full of meaning; the *meaning that is made* in daily dialogue and the *interpretive replies* that come in response, present mutually constraining impact.

Communicative constraints may tempt, tease, entice, lure, coax, cajole, or persuade the recipient of a meaningful impact; however, such expressive and influential constraints always fall short of *necessary mechanical* causation. Constraints may confront you in compelling ways, but you always have interpretive wiggle room to respond variably; the chosen responses that answer a constraining impact will take on the color of the *creature* being constrained; in other words, you will act according to the Animal You Are . . . until you Change Your Stripes and Become a New Kind of Creature.

* * * * *

The tone and temper of all Reaction and Response inevitably depends upon the disposition of the perceiver—the core of one's character.

* * * * *

This is why Changing Your Stripes is such a vital project: Your own *disposition of character* is a constraint to obtaining your own best interests in life—it's the old "you-are-your-own-worst-enemy" dilemma.

Though the rhetoric of "free to choose" runs rampant in pitches of *positive mental attitude* and *"I'm here to pump you up"* paradigms, the stark reality is that people are only partially free to choose (see page 43). The truth is you can only make choices within the constraints of your current character; your proactive choices in life and your reactions to *what happens* are both limited by your disposition. Curiously, you are a constraint to yourself: You really can be *your own worst enemy*, but if you Change Your Stripes, you can be *your own best friend* and a delight to others.

Besides the barriers you personally bring to a situation via ignorance and incompetence—your lack of wisdom to *know* and inability to *do*—situational constraints place limits upon perceived and real options, further narrowing your choose-able range of responses. As you become more aware of the *animal that you are*, and more in-tune with the givenness of this *earthly situation*, you can begin to find freedom within your "box" of constraint.

* * * * *

I begin to think outside the box, once I realize
I am living IN a box of continual constraint.
This is my Mortal Situation: Life is a Set Up!

* * * * *

In the end, it *mostly* doesn't matter whether the constraints that press upon you are real or imagined, as W. I. Thomas maintained, "That which a person perceives as real, is real in its consequences"—said succinctly, Perception IS Reality! But this idea misses the mark in one very big way: Independent of a person's perceptual constructions of reality, there are physical realities that stubbornly assert their existence regardless of how you perceive them. Herbert Blumer, author of Symbolic Interactionism theory, calls this stubborn nature "the obdurate reality of the empirical world." The word *obdurate* means "unyielding and obstinate."

The tangible aspects of reality can unexpectedly whack you hard in the head; for instance, even if "perception" does not acknowledge the reality of a low-hanging branch, the tree will tell you of its existence in a very firm and memorable manner—ouch! Therefore, perception is NOT purely all of reality; rather, perception leads you to the consequences that you experience in reality, and consequences confirm whether your perceptions of reality are adequate. The world in which we live is both perceptually *meaning-full* and tangibly *material;* thus, in addition to *communicative constraints* that influence us within a meaningful world, there are also *physical constraints* that impact us within a material world.

Physical Constraints. People are also constrained by the realities of a tangible world, the physical presence of both *things* and other *beings.* The physical world constrains us by low hanging branches, jutting rocks, cracks in concrete, etc.—constraints that may trip us up if we're not aware. Every object in sight is a potential influence that can shape our choosing: swinging doors, slippery floors, dirty walls, bouncing balls, moving cars, or sticky bars—all these and a million more, are physical *things* that constrain the world of human *beings.* Further, because human *beings* are embodied, the tangible reality of human bodies is also a constraint to individual human action.

Physical constraints occur in both positive and negative ways; they can be pleasant and desirable, or intrusive and unwanted. A desirable kind of physical constraint occurs when people experience bodily closeness or physical touch, inviting an amicable moment; conversely, when others crowd space, or block paths of entry or escape, such are examples of unpleasant physical constraint. Because our tangible world includes millions of physical *things* and embodied *beings*, mortal life presents a plethora of constraining possibilities; for the purposes of this topic, primary focus is upon physical constraints within human relations—person to person.

There is a point at which physical *constraint* crosses over a line to become physical *cause*. Physical approaches that fall short of *forceful* bodily contact remain in the category of constraint; when those who are physically constrained can still choose a range of preferred physical responses, then, the dividing line between *cause* and *constraint* has not been crossed. However, when physical force becomes oppressive and over-powering—as to inflict *effects* upon one's body beyond the input of perception and choice—this impact is classified as Cause. Within living relations, Cause occurs through physical impacts that are sufficiently forceful as to eliminate all options; further, such physical *cause* will produce necessary *effects* to the body of the impacted.

In addition to physical *effects* of scratches, cuts, bruises, or breaks, physical *cause* also includes *forceful* bodily contact that pushes or pulls people in unwanted ways—causing *effects* to bodily movements. But even if confronted with physical impacts that *cause* necessary *effects* to one's body or body movements, these same physical impacts *cannot cause* the movements of heart and soul. In other words, even though a body may be bound, restricting physical movements, and even though an intrusive impact may bruise or break a body, still the responses of heart and soul are never *mechanically* caused, but instead are *meaningfully* constrained by the same physical impacts.

* * * * *

Effect is a word to describe necessary outcomes,
Causes create mechanical Effects;
Response is a word to describe chosen outcomes,
Constraints present real & perceived boundaries to Response;
Cause & Effect occurs Mechanically,
Constraints invite and invoke Responses Meaningfully.

* * * * *

Given the definitions of Cause and Constraint herein, causal impact only occurs between physical things. Since the human body is both a physical thing as well as living being, your tangible body can be necessarily *effected* by intentional or accidental physical impacts; and from the other side of impact, YOU can *cause effects* to other tangible things and embodied beings.

Understanding the distinctive manifestations of Cause, Constraint, Body, and Be-ing is a key that can free people from unnecessary suffering. For example, *suffering of soul* is a chosen response that manifests *meaningfully* according to the character of the person impacted; where as, *bodily pain* is a *mechanical* outcome of physical injury, occurring beyond the perception and choice of the impacted.

Even if unwanted forceful bodily contact occurs, while *effects* to the body may be *caused* . . . still *responses* of heart and soul remain constrained; hence, the saying "pain is necessary, but suffering is optional." When correctly understood and applied, the principles detailed in this book will eliminate *unnecessary* heartache and suffering that is ironically *self-inflicted* rather than *caused* by external forces (see page 237).

* * * * *

Bodily Pain is a necessary
Effect Caused by forceful physical contact;
whereas, Suffering of Heart and Soul is optional and chosen
according to the character of the person impacted,
within the meaningful boundaries of Constraint.

* * * * *

Cause and Constraint are commonly confused. Distinctions between Cause, Constraint, Body, and Be-ing are not easily explained or readily conceived. Much confusion comes from misunderstanding the nature of being human. *Human being* and *human body* are often erroneously equated; thus, multiple aspects that make up YOU—body, being, mind, emotion, action, intention, heart, and soul—are all lumped together into one *generalized conception* of self.

Because of this conceptual lumping, some incorrectly conclude that responses of heart, mind, and emotion are *caused* by the same impacts that *cause effects* to a body; in other words, given a physically intrusive impact, it is supposed that all *mechanical effects* and *meaning-full responses* associated to an intrusion are necessarily caused by that intrusion. The false logic goes like this: It was YOU that was harmed, and your mind and emotions are all part of YOU, right? Hence, the confusion is created because an overly general conception.

There are multiple and distinct facets to the Human Self, and while there is unity between each aspect of *who you are*, still each facet has its own unique way of reacting and responding. With a clear understanding of the multiple aspects of being human—and how each aspect functions and manifests—you can better understand the subtle distinction between *necessary pain* and *optional suffering* (what luck, the aspects of Self are explained in chapter 2).

Finally, a most important point bears repeating: Even amid outer abuses, inner liberty remains; this is the principle that Viktor Frankl learned through his experiences of extreme abuse while incarcerated in Nazi death camps.

* * * * *

Inner Liberty means
that no outward abuse can cause
Inner Responses of Heart,
Mind, and Soul.

* * * * *

* * * * *

The same intrusive impacts that cause effects to my body, can only constrain Responses of Heart, Mind, & Soul. At the level of "Be-ing," ALL impacts that confront me, both physical and communicative, are Constraints . . . and never Causes.

* * * * *

Recall that low-hanging branch that whacked you hard in the head: This intrusive impact may have left a necessary *mark* that was caused, but thereafter, how you respond to the tree . . . is entirely up to thee. In other words, the way you make meaning about *what happened* is constrained—not caused. Causal impacts that forcefully harm your body, do not also *mechanically cause* your subsequent responses of mind, motive, or emotion. Discerning the distinctions between *cause vs. constraint* and *effect vs. response* will facilitate the goal of Changing Your Stripes!

OUTER BONDAGE, INNER LIBERTY

The dividing line between *cause* and *constraint* is illustrated in Viktor Frankl's book, "Man's Search for Meaning." During World War II, Viktor Frankl was a prisoner of a Nazi death camp where he witnessed horrific human suffering and abuse. Of his arduous experience Frankl observed:

> *"If there is a meaning in life at all, then there must be a meaning in suffering. Suffering is an ineradicable part of life . . . The way in which a man accepts his fate and all the suffering it entails, the way in which he takes up his cross, gives him ample opportunity—even under the most difficult circumstances—to add a deeper meaning to his life . . . Here lies the chance for a man either to make use of or forego the opportunities of attaining the values that a difficult situation may afford him."*

In every adversity . . . there is opportunity: the chance to obtain *value* and *deeper meaning* in Life. Even under appalling abuse, there is liberty within; you are the ultimate author of your inner responses. Of this liberty, Frankl noted:

> *"Only a few kept their full inner liberty and obtained those values which their suffering afforded, but even one such example is sufficient proof that man's inner strength may raise him above his outward fate. Such men are not only in concentration camps. Everywhere man is confronted with fate, with the chance of achieving something through his own suffering."*

In distinguishing the sometime subtle line between Cause versus Constraint, it is important to recall the difference between physical *effects* that are forcefully *caused* upon a human body, as opposed to the *responses* that come from one's heart, mind, and soul—responses that can only be *constrained.* Effects caused by *physical impact* to a physical body occur completely beyond a person's perception and choice, whereas expressions of heart, mind, and soul, though constrained by the same intrusive *physical impact*, still enjoy what Frankl calls "inner liberty."

* * * * *

Even as physical injury and pain is Caused,
You are Free to choose Responses of Heart and Soul.
You are able to "make use of" what a
difficult situation can teach.

* * * * *

Inner Liberty is always available; you are ever free to embrace it! Responses of your heart and soul cannot be caused by external impact. The way you express yourself during trying times of life reveals *who you are* from the heart. As an Old Testament proverb teaches: *"If thou faint in the day of adversity, thy strength is small."*

* * * * *

Character is tested at the Edge of Adversity:
the way you Respond when the going gets tough,
Reveals the Core of your Character.

* * * * *

Kahlil Gibran recognized that human beings express Inner Liberty. Not only did he maintain that we are free to choose Love *in spite* of life's tragedies, but further, we are more able to amplify that Love directly *because* of our tragedies. Gibran taught that the expanded space that pain *carves out* . . . creates potentials for greater compassion:

* * * * *

"The deeper that sorrow
carves into your being, . . .
the more joy you can contain"

* * * * *

Said another way: *Our pain carves out a larger space for love to fill.* Filling the space excavated by pain and suffering with larger amounts of love hits at the heart of what it means to live richly and celebrate Life! On the other hand, we are "at choice" to embrace the opposite aim, for pain also carves out a larger space that can be filled with hateful emotions. Inner Liberty is lost as we allow our souls to be poisoned with anger and resentment. By harboring hateful emotions, we become shackled by chains of our own choosing.

As we choose *contempt* instead of *compassion*, we lose the liberty to enjoy contentment and peace that naturally comes with compassion. By choosing *compassion* over *contempt*—embracing positive emotions over poisoning emotions—we become free to enjoy the heights of happiness! Each person decides whether painful trials will be a continuous *Tormentor* or a persistent *Teacher*. Every human being is *at liberty* to remain *bitter* . . . or become *better!* The very afflictions that may *enrage* us, can also *enlarge* us!

Faced with affliction, Life perpetually presents two opposing paths: become *poisoned by* oppression . . . or find *opportunity in* oppression. By tasting the *bitterness* of suffering, we learn to appreciate the *sweetness* of Life—and in this knowledge lies immense opportunity!

Again, the downward outcome can also be chosen: We can become *sour* by yielding to self-made misery. Those who choose not to discover the *"values that a difficult situation may afford"*—choosing *bitter* over *better*—are destined to retain a *sour* taste even as *sweetness* is abundantly available. What twisted reasoning is held in our heads, that makes wallowing in angry emotions the preferred alternative? Why would anyone choose to drag the heavy weight of yesterday's misery into the brightness of a new day?

* * * * *

From the Oppression of Pain arises Opportunity:
As we keep Inner Liberty, there awaits the
Euphoric Energies of Love and Compassion;
Our Pain carves out a larger space for Love to fill.

* * * * *

Some who choose the slippery course of *contempt*—and its attendant misery—might argue that their particular tragedy is *exceptional;* they may contend that their abuse is so *egregious* that "getting over it" is a mountain too tall to climb. Here's the truth: the severity of a situation is not the determining factor for becoming *bitter* or *better*, as Frankl noted:

> *"Even though conditions such as lack of sleep, insufficient food, and various mental stresses may suggest that the inmates were bound to react in certain ways, in the final analysis it becomes clear that the sort of person the prisoner became was the result of an inner decision, and not the result of camp influences alone."*

How we respond to accident, oppression, or abuse IS the result of "an inner decision." This is not merely a good-sounding theory, but what Frankl discovered from his arduous experience of suffering. Frankl learned that the ability to make this inner decision is mankind's *"final freedom."* No situation, no matter how tragic or terrible can keep us from this choice, this freedom.

* * * * *

It's not What Happens to you in Life, but how
You Respond to "What Happens" that matters most;
oppressive people may compel your flesh, but no power
on earth can force you from Inner Liberty—
it is yours to lose or keep.

* * * * *

In life, the color and character of your response is all important. The way that you react is a reflection of *who you are* from your core; your reactions reveal the depths of heart and soul. Learning to respond well to life's most challenging moments leads to contented living. *Who you are* from the heart defines whether *poisoned* or *positive* emotions will flow from you in a pressing moment. For this reason, Changing Your Stripes is a project of paramount importance.

Can you see the intrinsic *trap* before you? The very condition of your disposition is naturally self-perpetuating. You tend to reinforce *who you are* today . . . because *who you are* presently IS the one doing the thinking, perceiving, responding . . . and choosing! This is why people behave in consistent patterns of habit. How can you possibly think *fresh new* thoughts using *your stale old* mindset? (see page 175).

How can you choose compassionate responses when your disposition is not presently compassionate? Breaking out of this self-perpetuating *bind* requires that *you* become a new creature from your core, *today!* The kind of creature that can be calm, patient, and compassionate even amid compelling constraints of confusion and distress. Becoming the kind of creature that will consistently keep Inner Liberty is enhanced by understanding . . . Response-Ability.

THE DIVISION OF RESPONSE-ABILITY

If you want to know what you're made of . . . watch what comes out of you under pressure! When Life squeezes you with trials and troubles, how do you respond? The *Division of Response-Ability* is drawn: "If it comes out of you . . . it is yours." You are the author of all your responses: the good, the bad, and the ugly. Embracing this principle is empowering! For if you are the ultimate author of your behaviors, motives, and emotions, then you also possess the final veto vote; otherwise, you're stuck in stale stories of how others or your circumstance is victimizing you.

If It Comes Out of You . . . It is Yours

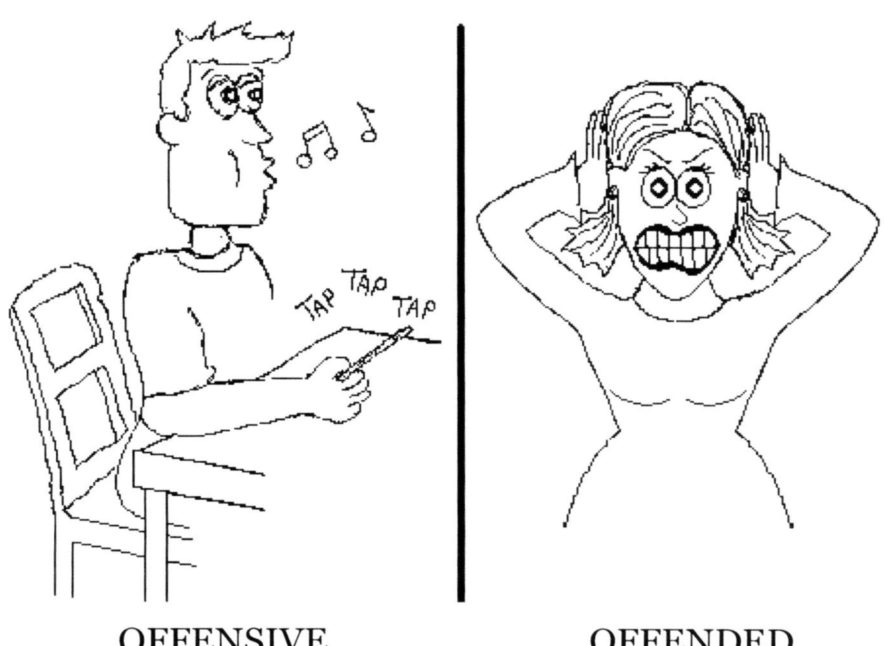

OFFENSIVE OFFENDED

You are the author of your responses. Only when you own Response-Ability for Actions, can you change them.

* * * * *

The irritating behavior of others presents a Constraint to which you respond, and while that bothersome behavior may necessarily capture your Attention, the obnoxious actions of others cannot cause the particular style or character of your Response.

* * * * *

With a distinction between *cause* and *constraint* in mind, recall the scenario of the creep who cried *fire* in the crowded theater. All reacted according to the current condition . . . of their disposition. Some people were pushing as opposed to calmly moving out the exits, because of *who they are.* They reacted according to their individual excite-ability, . . . the *pre-disposition* that they brought with them to the theater *before* the dunce did his dirty trick; the same *self-perpetuating* disposition they've been shaping since childhood through a consistent pattern of chosen responses. This means, some people are more *prone* to froth with frenzy when constrained by a pressing event; such people might be termed: frenzy-able!

Technically speaking, the scrapes, cuts, and bruises experienced by the theater patrons were directly *caused* by frenzied people pushing from behind, and not by the bone-head who blurted out the false alarm—this was *constraint.* To be clear, *cause* requires physical connection.

So, who's *responsible* for the chaotic tangle that occurred in the hypothetical theater? This question would normally put the average mind into a complex and confusing analysis of cause and effect—to include a lot of blaming and finger pointing. The analysis is really quite simple, and answers come clear according to this principle: The Division of Response-Ability: *If It Comes Out of You . . . It is Yours!*

Let's agree to put the *creep* who cried "fire" in jail for disturbing the peace, and require restitution for damages, too. But it would be well for all the *frantic* and *pushy people* in the theater to consider Changing Their Stripes and become the kind of creatures that can remain calm even amid frenzy and frothing. Because *Life is a Set Up*, those who would live life to its fullest will become completely *Response-Able* and prepare their character for Life's next tough test—coz it's on its way, ready or not?

The Division of Response-Ability:
If It Comes out of You . . . It is Yours

HURTFUL HURT

While offensive behavior may necessarily Capture your Attention, the hurtful actions of others cannot Cause the Character of your Response.

Who's to Blame? In response to the *accusing* query, "Who's to Blame?" I've got two words: Wrong Question! When you ask a wrong question, . . . you will get a wrong answer! I recall a client who tried to put a percentage to the blame he bore for creating the marital mangle in which he was mired; he figured his contribution was about *66%.*

Trying to divide blame between relational combatants by percentage—*70-30* or *60-40,* etc.—may make the lower percentage partner feel better, but in the end, the question of blame is unhelpful—it doesn't practically improve anything. Such thinking simply plays into an excuse-making mentality: *"I may be bad, but at least I'm not THAT bad!"*

The best question to ask is: Who's Response-Able? And the answer is: Everyone! Everyone is Able to Respond; hence, everyone is personally Response-Able for the stuff that they create: including all thoughts, behaviors, motives, and emotions coming out of them.

My client was entering into the problem from a poor premise. He was asking the wrong question! Instead of dividing blame between the two marital combatants, I told him that he *gets to* own 100% of ALL the *problem-making* and *problem-perpetuating* that is coming out of him, and his wife gets to own 100% of ALL her problem-making and problem-perpetuating too! Whatever that is: however each person's mess . . . manifests, be it a little or a lot. Whether YOU are the larger or smaller offender, YOUR way out of the tangle is to *own everything that comes out of you.*

Owning "everything" means owning all *offensive-ness,* of course, but it also means owning all *offended-ness,* too! In the Changing Your Stripes paradigm, we learn that Being Offended is just as *offensive* as Being Offensive. Being Offended is simply the *response end* of bad behavior, while Being Offensive is the *constraint end* of bad behavior.

Average thinking on this issue maintains that the bad behavior that happened first is . . . "badder." One can easily get tangled into a dead end debate: The offended person will inevitably argue, *"but if you had not done this, then I never would have done that!"* Getting trapped in this mental conundrum will drive you crazy: it will make . . . your head ache!

Because Life is a Set Up, you could sing the "I'm-offended-by-your-offensiveness" song for the rest of your life. Also, if you are tempted to hang on to the "but-they-did-it-to-me-first" excuse, then you might as well invoke the ultimate alibi: *"but if Mom hadn't given birth to me, then I wouldn't have . . . yada yada yada."* With this lousy line of logic, you could blame your parents for every bad thing you've done since birth. It is indeed a fact that IF your parent had *not* brought you into the world, THEN *you* would *not* have done anything bad—but you would *not* have done anything good, either. You just would *not* have done anything . . . PERIOD.

Nevertheless, the given hard-wired realities of this world ARE that you were born and that Life IS a Set Up, and the quicker you *get used to it*, *get over it*, and *get on with it* . . . the sooner you'll be Changing Your Stripes and responding in the *productive patterns* of the new creature you are becoming!

* * * * *

"Life is a Set Up" means that you live in a world of ever-pressing Constraints. Learning to own and hone your Ability to Respond well is at the apex of Life's purpose. When you fully embrace this aim of excellence, each pressing constraint is viewed as a Test and a Teacher, instead of just a Tormentor.

* * * * *

The difference comes as you see the big picture, realize the way the world works, and accept the realities of "The Zoo You Live In"—rather than fight against it. So here you are living life: You can be *flexible* or you can be *miserable* . . . you can *celebrate it*, or you can *suffer it!*

If you want to celebrate Life, then you *get to* accept that "Life is a Set Up," and you *get to* own all Response-Ability for everything that comes out of you: Always remembering that Bad Behavior in the 1st place (the initiating or constraint end) compared to Bad Behavior in the 2nd place (the receiving or response end) still boils down to . . . *Bad Behavior.*

* * * * *

Owning your "Bad," regardless of unfair set ups and extenuating circumstances, is a "Good" beginning!

* * * * *

The aim of excellence invites us to rise above the level of average and mediocre responses: Anyone can react poorly when mistreated, and most people do; whereas, it takes a person of high character to respond with compassion and patience when mistreated—this kind of excellence is our aim!

The purpose of the first two chapters of this book is to help you understand the given realities of *Self* and *Situation*, where Life offers both *oppression* and *opportunity;* further, *who you are* can be your own *worst enemy* or your own *best friend.* Which of these alternatives you emphasize and embrace will depend upon whether you Change Your Stripes! As you come to know the hard-wired realities of *who you are* and *the world* in which you live, you will absolutely be . . . more free, to live richly. Within the constraints and causes of this world, you *get to* go from here.

Two Types of Suffering

Situational Suffering. When difficult, distressing, or disastrous events erupt in our lives—beyond our control—we may experience what I call "Situational Suffering." This type of suffering is felt in the immediate moments that a tragedy presses directly upon us; it is the *primary* type of suffering that Frankl and his fellow prisoners experienced while incarcerated in Nazi concentration camps.

Situational Suffering happens in those direct moments we are the objects of unkindness or abuse; it occurs because of the untimely movements of Mother Nature, and is also brought about by mechanical failure and other accidents due to human error.

When man-made misfortunes or natural catastrophes *cause* distress and destruction, one of the "things" that can be harmed is the human body. Situational Suffering means that outside physical impacts may *cause effects* to the body, inflicting necessary suffering as opposed to self-inflicted suffering. But even without physical harm to the body . . . unprovoked adversity is *emotionally* hard to bear.

While the effects of physical harm may linger over time, in contrast, emotional anguish need only last as long as the initiating adversity, and can completely disappear . . . as the distressing event disappears. Further, seeing tragic events from the broad perspective of Life's purpose can help us endure and "get over" tough times. C.S. Lewis offers insight:

* * * * *

I suggest to you that it is because God loves us that he gives us the gift of suffering. Pain is God's megaphone to rouse a deaf world. You see, we are like blocks of stone out of which the Sculptor carves the forms of men. The blows of his chisel, which hurt us so much are what make us perfect.

* * * * *

Again, in situations where *no physical damage is done* to a body, the average person will still feel emotional distress when afflicted by verbal or emotional assault—just as distress is physically felt when the body is battered. While much emotional suffering can be attributed directly to a challenging situation, on the other hand, all emotional responses are *amplified* or *diminished* by the individual *disposition* of the impacted. Whether emotional suffering is large or small, when a challenging moment is *in the past* . . . there is literally nothing to directly *cause* further distress, but you! This means, there is a moment of choice—a point of transition—where situational suffering can *morph* into another type of misery that I call . . . Self-Inflicted Suffering.

The transition from *situational suffering* . . . to *self-inflicted suffering* commonly goes undetected. When an aggravating event is over and a reasonable amount of time for emotional adjustment has passed, then from the dawning of a new day further *emotional suffering* is optional, it is chosen. And when the fresh energies of a new day are willfully declined, then further distress beyond this *point of transition*—this junction of choice—becomes self-inflicted suffering.

* * * * *

The bitter truth for those that amplify & extend Situational Suffering beyond the point of impact: After the dust of yesterday's difficulties has long since settled, any pain that you retain . . . is Self-Inflicted.

* * * * *

When faced with situational suffering, the importance of Inner Liberty looms large! For in the face of tragedy beyond your control, you are still *at choice* to *respond* with either compassion or contempt, and by choosing contempt, you intrinsically retain unnecessary pain that is no longer *initiated* by the intrusive event; rather, it is a pain paradoxically *initiated* by you—self-made misery. As if the crushing causes and constraints of a difficulty were not enough, you can actually inflict yourself further by harboring *emotions of contempt.*

Self-Inflicted Suffering. This second category of suffering is termed "self-inflicted," because it is initiated by choice; it is the suffering of soul that comes in consequence of our failure to keep Inner Liberty. When people complain of this inner pain, they are not faking it; the anguish they feel is real, and at the same time, it is unnecessary.

Even if a situation brings horrific suffering—as in the case of Viktor Frankl and his fellow prisoners—keeping Inner Liberty brings inner peace of heart and soul amid outward oppression. Self-inflicted suffering is an inner anguish due . . . to our failure to be true.

* * * * *

There are bad things that happen
and suffering that I experience
because of bad situations;
then, there are bad things that I do
and suffering that I experience
because I have not been True.

* * * * *

A traumatic event will typically *explain* how suffering may have started, but then that same event can become a person's *excuse* for not keeping Inner Liberty. Tough times can be an *excuse* to remain down; yet history is replete with examples of how the human spirit can *rise above* circumstance. Thus, the very same situation that may *trip us up* can be our opportunity to *stand taller.*

Tough times will either be a *stumbling block* or a *building block;* they can be our *oppression* or our *opportunity.* Within the *constraints* of each challenging situation, it is *you* who puts the *cause* of your life into motion; the determining difference is in YOU! Ultimately, your destiny is not determined by how intense or terrible the afflicting fate; rather, the defining factor *resides* . . . with the being who *decides!*

Why We Choose Self-Made Misery ?

Self-inflicted suffering is most often chosen *in connection* with past trauma. While an aggravating event may have "caused" misery back then, after the dust of that difficulty was well settled, we stood at *a junction of choice*, . . . *a point of transition* where the traumatic event that initially "caused" our suffering, now becomes our "reason" to continue misery. From this *junction of choice* the suffering is no longer *caused,* instead, it is willfully *contrived* for a reason—it is chosen . . . be-*cause.*

* * * * *

I experience Situational Suffering due to "Causes."
In contrast,
I experience Self-Inflicted Suffering due to "Be-Causes."
I stir up Self-Made Misery for "Reasons."

* * * * *

Contriving continued suffering may not be a deliberate decision made in the now (like buying a pair of shoes at the store); instead, it's more likely an *un-conscious decision* that subtly flows from our disposition. After all, what reasonable thinking individual would intentionally take hold of a big thick "misery stick" and commence self-flagellation? Thus we bludgeon ourselves with the *cane of pain*, and at the same time, we do not *think* that this is what we are doing—we are deceived.

* * * * *

Choosing self-made misery means that I keep bitter waters
running even after the inflicting faucet has been shut off,
and as the initiating aggravation passes into the past,
Self-Made Misery becomes my ironic alternative of choice;
a choice that is made either consciously or un-consciously,
either way, . . . I am the author of this misery.

* * * * *

When *un-consciously choosing* self-made misery, the actual *deliberate choice* was made in prior days, months, or years; thus, all un-conscious choosing that emerges *today* . . . comes from decision-making energy that was set-in-motion *yesterday*.

One of the *reasons* for contriving self-produced pain is to preserve evidence of victimhood. Those who invest in victimhood need "evidence" to bolster the credibility of their accusing campaign. Preserving evidence IS one of the more conspicuous *reasons* to continue self-made misery.

* * * * *

As pain is self-perpetuated, a paradox appears: Because Continued Misery IS essential evidence in one's accusing case, having Evidence becomes more important . . . than having Peace.

* * * * *

Since the accusing case against yesterday's offenders depends upon maintaining today's personal pain, strangely, some victims find further suffering advantageous. While there may have been real suffering that was "caused" by an aggravating event initially, continued suffering gradually becomes psychosomatically "contrived" by the inertia of an accusing imagination. This means, *present suffering* is neither caused nor constrained by yesterday's adversity; instead, it is solely caused by an unforgiving heart. Thus, today's proof of yesterday's abuse is conjured evidence—tampered evidenced.

Even though self-made misery is initiated by an accusing imagination, again, this does not mean the suffering is imaginary. It is *real* suffering . . . but it is also *really* contrived in its creation. Psychosomatic effects can arise from an agitated, anxious imagination; hence, bad biology is produced by stinkin' thinkin'—the mental machination of a Migraine Mental Block! (see page 176).

Hitting Myself with the Misery Stick!

Why Would Anyone Choose To Make Themselves Miserable?

While some misery is inflicted in the moment by others or by accidents, . . . beyond the "Point of Impact," after the dust of a difficulty has long since settled: All further Misery is Self-Inflicted.

Seeking Support for Victimhood. An additional entanglement unfolds: the more time a victim invests into vengeance toward offenders; the more a victim needs to realize a return on that investment. Yet, as time passes and the aggravating event floats downstream into a vast sea of vague memories, it becomes increasingly hard to maintain accusing momentum; it is more difficult to maintain intensity of misery—a.k.a., evidence.

The longer one hangs on to self-inflicted suffering, the more one's accusing story must parallel the intensity of today's claimed misery; this means, yesterday's purported *offensiveness* must be proportionate to today's *offended-ness.* If yesterday's offensiveness is not sufficiently appalling to *justify* the intensity of continuing offendedness, then those *hanging on* to this version of "victimhood" are tempted to embellish and amplify the nature of the initial offense. In other words, the "victim" needs to make yesterday's abuse *bigger* than it ever was, to justify today's *bigger* claim of emotional pain; hence, a *justifying story* is artificially contrived by a victim to enroll sympathy from an audience of observers.

When I use the word "justify," I'm not suggesting that this type of *justification* is genuine, exactly the opposite. We will learn that *justifying* is a tell-tale sign of inner imbalance (see pages 173, 177). People who wrestle with inner turmoil have a heightened *need* to *appear justified* in the eyes of observers; thus, they concoct a plausible story that is as *big* as the pain they claim. So, this is the paradoxical position we twist our way into: we're whacking ourselves with the *misery stick*, but we contrive a story to explain why we're not really hitting ourselves in the head . . . and why someone else, or something else, is causing this misery.

Attempts to *outwardly* "justify" are only needed by those who feel *inwardly* "un-justified." Said another way: *If you have to try to convince yourself, that means . . . you're not convinced.* Those who feel insecure will seek security through various means of "convincing," . . . first themselves, and then others.

Vote Getting. The saying goes, *"Time heals all wounds,"* but in the case of a person prolonging self-produced pain, the opposite adage applies: *"Time wounds all heels."* Instead of relishing in the relief that *time* brings after the initial source of suffering has ceased . . . instead of letting go of it, getting over it, and getting on with it, some victims use "time" to continue their accusing case, and search for every piece of evidence to embellish, exaggerate, and add to their *justifying story*—a *contrived* production of emotion and manipulation aimed at securing votes.

People who are truly justified in their thoughts, words, and deeds enjoy *inner* peace; therefore, they do not seek *outward* approval or campaign for popular votes, because they have no use for them. In contrast, people who prolong self-produced pain, do so for the benefit of an *outside* audience from whom they wish to get votes and *outward* validation.

* * * * *

People who are inwardly unsettled seek the supportive votes of others, precisely because they don't have the only vote that counts: the Vote of inward validation.

* * * * *

When a person's life is in *harmony*, lobbying for lesser votes is not needed because the only Vote that counts is already secured. Those who anxiously need the popular vote and fretfully seek the popular vote, will also tend to maintain self-made misery because it is useful in gleaning sympathy through the vote-getting process. But just how long might a person *hang on* to this continuing campaign of victimhood and vote getting?

Resentment Retention Time. When a person is offended, approximately how long should that person *continue* to feel hurt or humiliated, thereafter? This is the question of Resentment Retention Time, a question that gives priority to the "politically correct" popular vote . . . over being true to the heart. Consider this scenario: A person says they are upset at being insulted, and observers ask, "what was the insult that brought on this distress?" The offended one answers: *"that ill-mannered ignoramus blurted out in front of everyone that I was having a bad hair day!"*

Now let's locate this insulting event upon the Resentment Retention Time Continuum: how long *should* a person *feel insulted* for being accused of an *unruly hair do*? Just how long should the pain . . . be retained? 2 minutes . . . 2 hours . . . 2 days . . . 2 weeks . . . 2 months . . . 2 years . . . 2 decades?

Sane-thinkers would not deem this insult egregious enough to warrant two weeks worth of resentment, the *trauma* is simply not terrible enough (but you'd be amazed at how some people hang on to oversized resentment, for undersized offenses). In this situation the oppressive insult may warrant being *bent out of shape* for about 2 hours or 2 days tops, but as the silly insult remains stuck in the hypothetical craw and this victim of insult wants to prolong "suffering," then the *offended* person needs a *bigger* story. If Resentment Retention Time is extended, the claim of personal pain needs to be proportionate to the purported oppression, especially in the minds of observers who will be called upon for a "vote" of sympathy and support.

Wanting votes and seeking votes doesn't always mean that you will get votes; now if you can't win the popular vote with an accurate portrayal of an offense, then you might be persuaded, even by a blame-biased society, to *let it go*. The other alternative is to engage in *story stretching*—a tactic used commonly in vote-getting campaigns.

After the *politically correct* Resentment Retention Time has expired, the victim stands at a point of transition: Let it go and move on to bigger and better horizons OR engage in story stretching! To justify a longer "RRT," the offended person necessarily needs to expand the story. Of course, *stretching the story* is a softer way to say . . . lying! But once the *adrenaline of selfishness* has kicked in, what really happened "back then" is secondary to the purposes of today's accusing crusade; thus, the insulted person searches the past for dirty details that can be found, or plausibly invented; even offenses thought to be forgotten are resurrected and added to the expanding story. Thus, *blaming* and *harboring resentment* become more important than *personal peace*, and here's an intriguing twist: The willful act of *harboring resentful emotions* about yesterday's offenses IS today's self-made misery.

Besides maintaining "evidence" that may persuade the popular vote, an additional explanation for why people *choose* the paradoxical pursuit of self-inflicted suffering is this: They don't really think that they are doing it; they don't believe they are "choosing" self-made misery, and they don't see themselves as *trying* to be victims, . . . they simply see themselves *as* victims. The fact is we are all victimized in this life . . . for Life is a Set Up! Everyone falls victim to unfair accidents or abuse; everyone experiences their share of Situational Suffering. But here's the burning question: Who is going to *hang on* to suffering after the *point of transition* . . . when the dust of a difficulty as long since settled?

The person who *hangs on* to resentment far into the future becomes a *self-made victim*—which is an oxymoron! The very definition of "victim" means that *"someone has done it to me,"* therefore, someone else is responsible for my pain.* This is where such reasoning can go wrong, because there are actually two types of *pain* to be claimed, according to the two-fold nature of being human: *body* and *being* (see page 61). While you may be a victim of *body*—physical injury—you can never be a victim of *being*, without your consent.

---

* It is true that perpetrators initiate a chain of subsequent actions and reactions. Like the creep that cried "fire" in a crowded theater, similarly, the enacting of abuse . . . "sets up" the abused to respond as poorly, or as well, as current character is capable. If that character needs growth, the abusive "set up" can be a Test and Teacher, OR if the opposite alternative is invoked, unnecessary Torment will continue over time.

The Division of Response-Ability Principle maintains that a perpetrator is indeed directly responsible for enacting abhorrent behaviors, and if physical contact occurs, the offender is also responsible for intrusions and abrasions to the *body.* Nevertheless, everyone (including victims) get to own *responses* of mind, motive, emotion, and action—all responses of *be-ing.* We get to own every response that comes from us, except effects *caused* to the *body.*

Thus, every *victim* eventually comes to a junction of choice, a point of transition: to continue misery . . . or embrace Inner Liberty. For victims to escape self-inflicted suffering of soul, they must fully accept the reality that *resentment* is an emotion originating from "ME," and *own* that they are the authors of all anguished emotions. Beyond necessary physical pain felt *in the body* due to accident or abuse, the *resentment that a victim harbors* IS that person's primary *suffering of soul.* Resentment is unsettled anguish that is chosen and expressed *in one's be-ing.*

* * * * *

Self-Inflicted Suffering comes from
My failure to honor my own sense of Truth,
My inability to hear and heed the whisperings of my Heart,
My inability . . . to keep Inner Liberty.

* * * * *

When people actively participate in the willful creation of anguished emotions, and then deny that participation, this is a phenomenon I call, "Fooling Yourself." It also goes by other names: Freud referred to it as "in denial," Jesus called it "blinded," C. Terry Warner termed it "self-deceived," and common folks call it "deluded" (see Blindness of Mind, page 192 & Einstein's Mind Bind, page 175).

Since it makes no sense to make yourself miserable, thus, when people actually do this self-defeating dance, they are also "blinded" to a clear picture of their self-flagellation. Here's the truth: When self-inflicted suffering is ironically chosen after the *dust of a difficulty* has settled, inner anguish continues through one's failure to keep "inner liberty," . . . and not due to the aggravating event that as passed into the past. As I speak of the "dust of a difficulty" settling, I am acknowledging that there is little relief for some victims until *after* direct assaults of abuse, oppression, or terror have completely ceased. Yet, a person need not wait for the ending of adversity to invoke Inner Liberty.

* * * * *

***I need not wait for the dust of a difficulty to settle,
I can embrace Inner Liberty immediately,
even amid an aggravating event.***

* * * * *

Keeping Inner Liberty while in the midst of a trauma, doesn't mean that all pain disappears, but it does mean that "self-inflicted suffering" is not added to, and heaped upon, the distress caused by a difficult situation. In other words, one need not feel *suffering of soul* even as physical pain is present.* Experiencing *outward* affliction that may cause physical pain while still feeling *inward* peace is a possibility taught by the Apostle Paul:

> *"For all things are for your sakes, . . . For which cause we faint not; but though our outward man perish, yet the inward man is renewed day by day. For our light affliction, which is but for a moment, worketh for us a far more exceeding and eternal weight of glory; while we look not at the things which are seen, but at the things which are not seen: for the things which are seen are temporal; but the things which are not seen are eternal" (2 Corinthians 4:15-18).*

---

* An example of inward peace amid severe outward affliction is given in the account of Christ's crucifixion: Though wracked with the extreme physical pain of having nails driven through his hands and feet, yet Christ's thoughts were not consumed by a bitter soul. He extended compassion to the very people who had crucified him, and had the loving presence of mind to comfort his mother.

Frankl and his fellow inmates went through a long hellish ordeal that was hard for them to bear. Such is the nature of Situational Suffering, and such is the nature of living in a world where Life is a Set Up!

Understanding the twofold nature of being human (explained in the Self chapter) helps us to see . . . our full response-ability. Again, we are not always responsible for intrusions and abrasions that happen to the *human body*, but at the level of *human being*, the Division of Response-Ability Principle fully applies: *What Comes out of You . . . is Yours!* The condition of your character is revealed by how you respond to tough times—namely, responses of heart, mind, and soul.

EVERYTHING HAPPENS FOR A REASON ?

Situational Suffering means that bad things can happen completely without any bad input from you. Conversely, Self-Inflicted Suffering means you bring suffering upon yourself directly because of your own bad input. This is the given reality of human life: You are capable of making choices that go against yourself—decisions that betray inner harmony, choices that mess up outer relationships, decisions that grind against your best destiny. Human beings are capable of making miserable, dumb decisions.

Because we don't like to *appear* wrong, incompetent, or stupid, thus, when making dumb decisions, most people tend to defend a winning image; they defend a superficial facade I call *The Self as Advertised* (see page 98). Once a person has invested much time and effort into a personal "ad campaign" that sells a certain self-image to others, that person is more prone to protect the advertising investment.

Openly owning *dumb decisions* means going against the purposes of one's published promotions; thus, admitting to mistakes means exposing one's stupidity. Since most people do NOT want to appear as stupid—when really, they have acted stupid—plausible excuses are sought. Instead of *owning* one's error, bungling behaviors are rationalized away through a very common disclaimer:

* * * * *

Everything Happens for a Reason.
In the name of "Destiny" this oft-invoked axiom
provides people with a Rationalizing Release from owning
Response-Ability, when owning one's "bungle"
IS exactly what Destiny had in mind.

* * * * *

Bob came to me in the midst of crisis: His wife had just filed for divorce. He told me that he wanted to remain in the marriage, but his wife was "finished" with trying to salvage an unsatisfying relationship. He mused aloud during one session: *"I wonder why this had to happen?"* I asked, "What do you mean?" Bob continued, "well, since *everything happens for a reason and there are no accidents in life*, I'm wondering about *the reason* my marriage had to end?" Bob was looking for a Reason (with a Capital "R") that resided in divine Destiny; in contrast, I could easily see a reason (with a regular "r") that was far less lofty: Bob was being a bumbling buffoon, and worse, . . . he was oblivious to his buffoonery.

Bob was talking as if his marital demise was "meant to be," that Fate had foreordained this divorce. I asked Bob if I could be blunt, and he consented: I told him, "You got dirt, instead of dessert, and the most compelling reason IS . . . you made some dumb decisions."

Lurking beneath the seemingly innocuous phrase "everything happens for a reason," is a crucial philosophical question: Fate vs. Free Will. Many people are schizophrenic on this issue; on the one hand, they eagerly agree that we humans are "free to choose," while on the other hand, they paradoxically pursue an irresistible itch to have their cards read, palms perused, horoscopes scoped . . . or to have some soothsayer psych-them-out about a future that is falsely assumed to be "set in the stars."

The idea that *everything happens for a reason* implies that life is largely driven by forces of Fate; therefore, things happen "for a Reason" (with a Capital "R") and people are just passive passengers going along for a predestined ride. So when unexpected or unwanted earthly episodes occur, we wonder, "What is the Reason this happened?"

* * * * *

While many things do happen with inspired serendipity, still some decisions are simply uninspired, irrational, or just plain evil, and such decisions can lead to accidental or intentional outcomes that are very un-reason-able.

* * * * *

The direct explanation for so many of life's unwanted twists and turns is NOT necessarily because of some *higher* Reason, but most often because *un-reason-able people* are capable of making *un-reason-able choices* . . . and those *lower* decisions, in turn, set in motion *un-reason-able* results.

The reality of living in a world of "free will" is that *chaos and confusion* can be chosen over *calm and clarity*. Even barring evil intentions, people are still *free* to make inept, awkward, and dopey decisions; accordingly, from *clumsy* or *chaos* comes consequences that can be un-reason-able. In this life, some things really *do* happen "for no good reason at all"—awkward, unintended, and unfortunate "accidents" actually *do* happen, because of human error.

The idea that "there are no accidents" is a contradiction to the realities of God-given *free will* and *self-responsibility*. When people incorrectly conclude that "everything happens for a reason," it logically follows that all undoubtedly dopey decisions are really *meant to be* . . . and *written in the stars*. Reality Check: Many awful outcomes occur by accident or by evil intent, and do not happen for a good reason—in terms of how the misfortune was initiated, or *set up*.

Still, hoards of dopey-decision-makers *assume* that they are *released* from personal responsibility because a Higher Reason *had to* happen: it was set in the stars! The truth is that Higher Reasons unfold directly because people *willingly fulfill* inspired responsibility to be messengers and servants—as opposed to passive puppets. News Release: the *Holocaust* and *9/11* did not *have to* happen, and neither did a million other man-made tragedies.

* * * * *

When things happen for no reasonable reason,
in time . . . . . there can be lessons learned;
much wisdom and growth of character is
gleaned from the rubble of unreasonable
and senseless situations. . . . . Life is a Set Up
precisely because people can express their free will
to choose actions of incompetence or premeditated evil.

* * * * *

Our *freedom to choose* exists by Divine Design. Life's Highest Reasons are realized by learning to *respond* with patience and compassion in the face of *unfair accidents* and *intentional abuses.*

When Life hands you a lemon, the potential of making lemonade is before you! In the face of tough times, you always have the choice to either be a *lemon sucker* or a *lemonade maker*, you are free to be *bitter* or to become *better.* Even amid devastating decisions—that did not have to happen, but did happen—still, *something good* can be salvaged from the rubble of trouble, and that *good* is manifest best in *growth of character.*

In time, Bob quit thinking that his sad situation was "meant to be" and "written in the stars." He eventually accepted his *Response-Ability*, and thoughtfully examined the poor choices he made that set-in-motion his wife's response to *want to* leave the marriage. Bob reflected upon the dumb decisions that ultimately delivered dirt, instead of dessert.

* * * * *

If you want to know what you're
sending out . . . see what's coming back.

* * * * *

Certainly, Bob's wife bears complete *Response-Ability* for all the bad behaviors that "came out of her"—but regardless of the judgments that might be made about his wife's actions and decisions, the fact is Bob could only directly control his own behavior. Since Bob was the only one I was talking to (not his wife), Bob was encouraged to focus upon this principle of self responsibility: *The Goal within Your Control is to Become Loving and True.*

We are beings capable of choosing between alternatives of good and evil; the power is in us to express ourselves both creatively and morally in *response* to *what happens.* Shakespeare alluded to this truth in these words:

* * * * *

"Sometimes men are the masters of fate:
The fault, dear Brutus, is not in our stars, but in ourselves."

* * * * *

Now, if you accept this reality of life, then YAHOO . . . this is great good news! For as you own your response-ability for choices that dragged you down the drain, then you can un-choose your way right back out of the sewer. Nevertheless, there IS a force of Destiny that does supply serendipity, but that sweet *Serendipity* is *constraint* and never *cause.* Amid the interventions and influences of Destiny, human beings remain *at choice* to *flow with* OR *go against* this best Destiny. While winds of Fate are gently blowing, we bear response-ability to set our sails to catch those winds—or not.

In the end, I told Bob to pick himself up, own and admit all the choices he made that helped create his unhappy situation—the dumb decisions that constrained his wife in such a way that divorce became *the cure* she preferred. With the wisdom of that hindsight is willing to teach, Bob saw how he "set up" the downfall of his marriage, and he learned that the destiny of his marriage was not "in the stars," . . . but in his hands.

LIFE IS SELF-CORRECTING

Even though Bob did not get what he personally *wanted*—to remain married to his wife—he did get exactly what he *needed* for his growth of character. Life inherently supplies consequences that teach us precisely what we need to become healthy happy humans, and those self-correcting consequences come in the form of 1) Feedback from others, and 2) Feedback from our feelings.

How others *respond* to us will *reflect* what's going on with us, and therefore, inform how we might adjust and re-order our actions. The other self-correcting clue is found in our feelings, specifically, our *lack of inner contentment.* When we are not being true to *innate intuitions of truth*, we will sense this by a loss of emotional harmony. Through our own conflicted feelings, Life sends a clear clue to correct our course.

* * * * *

Life is Self-Correcting:
Whenever you make a mistake,
Life will make sure you are properly notified.

* * * * *

Life will *bite you in the butt* until you get a clue that you are not doing Life right. Life will consistently let you know when you're off track, and will also prompt appropriate adjustments—the possibility of Serendipity. The phrase

"Life is Self-Correcting" means that when you do bad, . . . you feel bad. Conversely, when you do good, . . . you feel good, and when you feel good, Life is saying, "this works, keep doing what you're doing."

Caring for your heart and soul is much like caring for the health of your body. In taking care of your body you must listen to built-in biological signs *designed* to protect the body and maintain proper functioning.

For example, bodily pain is a signal for us to slow down or stop moving certain muscles. In this way, bodily pain leads us back to healing; similarly, the pain felt in one's soul sends a signal that adjustment is needed. But pain of body and anguish of soul are two very different things: One is felt *beyond* our perceptual participation and choice (bodily pain), and the other occurs directly *because* of our perception and choice (suffering of soul). Even so, both kinds of pain are helpful, as we listen to the self-correcting signals.

* * * * *

After the dust of a difficulty has long since settled,
Further sadness of soul is my clue,
that I have not been True.

* * * * *

When you don't do Life right, . . . Life doesn't do you right either: Uncomfortable consequences are the clue . . . that you have not been true. Through bitter consequences, you get from Life exactly what you need for adjustment and growth. Thus, as afflictions befall you, Life is "doing you" precisely right!

Through the responses coming back from others and the signals of your own anguished emotions, Life reveals all inadequacies that need improvement. The Principle that "Life is Self-Correcting" means that humans inherently know how to fulfill the measure of their creation.

What Goes Around, Comes Around. In life, self-correcting adjustments happen through the Law of the Harvest: When you sow *good seeds*, you reap a harvest of goodness. Like planting good seeds . . . doing good deeds eventually leads to a harvest of good fruit—in some way and in some form, always. On the other hand, sowing the seeds of *dark deeds* eventually leads to uncomfortable fruits of outward contention and inward commotion.

* * * * *

In time, I will receive according to what I send out.
In direct proportion to the goodness I have
given, or the darkness I have done.

* * * * *

Life will bring all things into balance, harmony, and justice. What goes around, eventually comes around. The wise will watch what they send out to others, because it's coming back sooner . . . or later. In eastern philosophy, this reality is called "karma," which basically contends that all negative or positive thought or action maintains its original energy until, that energy is expended upon the originator.

The question arises: "If Life returns to me according to the good seeds I sow, and I'm presently sowing good seeds, then why are bad things happening to me today?" The answer resides in the hard-wired realities of your mortal Situation—the given nature of the Zoo You Live In. Being Human means to live in a world where people have free will to do good or bad: Life is a Set Up! Further, four basic sources supply *Constraint and Cause* to your personal path—impacts that may bring bad, even when you are being good.

- The Inconsiderate or Abusive Acts of Others,
- Accidents that happen due to Human Error,
- The untimely movements of Mother Nature, and
- Consequences of Mechanical Failures.

This is the way the world works. Bad things happen beyond your control, and thus you are "Set Up" for heartache and frustration. Welcome to earth! Get used to it, get over it, and get on with it . . . with gusto! Life is your Test and your Teacher: You *get to* eat the cookies with the crackers—both pleasure and pain have lessons to teach.

Listening to Life's self-correcting lessons, and making the appropriate adjustments will naturally lead to joyful living. Enduring trials and troubles IS the "classroom of character development" designed by an infinitely wise Creator. It is a constraining context within which human beings may fully develop the single possession that *"you can take with you"* after the mortal body returns to dust, and your spirit self lives on. Earth life is designed for the perfecting of your character. The words of Neil Maxwell offer insight:

* * * * *

Endurance involves much more than just putting up with a situation; patient Endurance is more than pacing up and down within the cell of circumstance. True Enduring represents not merely the passage of time, . . . but the Passage of Soul.

* * * * *

In the end, fulfillment of Life's highest purpose is not determined by *what happens to you*, but by *how you respond to . . . what happens to you.* How you handle hardships reveals the very core of your character, and therefore allows you to take *inventory* . . . and *improve.*

FREE TO CHOOSE . . . NOT REALLY

So given the nature of a Self-Correcting World and in light of the Law of the Harvest, . . . let's grab with gusto the good stuff! But here's the problem: You can't grab the good stuff with gusto if that emphatic energy is not in you!

You *can* only choose and you *will* only choose, those options you presently *feel* to choose according to the current condition of your disposition; hence, you will choose *gusto*—or something *less-than-gusto*—because of the *animal you are.* Just like a tiger will always be a tiger, and act like a tiger . . . until that tiger becomes a new kind of creature, you will also be *who you are* until you . . . Change Your Stripes.

The over-simplified idea that there is a world full of thrilling alternatives that await "your choice," is a popular doctrine preached by a glut of self-help gurus. The alluring pitch . . . goes like this: *"YOU can create your own reality, YOU can reinvent yourself according to your wildest whim!"* Of course, the magic that makes it all happen is through the marvels of mind power. Even though the rhetoric is tantalizing, a human being's ability to *choose freely* is greatly exaggerated by purveyors of positive thinking. Sorry to burst your bubble, but let me break it to you gently:

YOU ARE NOT FREE TO CHOOSE!

Of course, you do have some freedom, but in order to have complete freedom of choice, you need to possess two itty-bitty, teeny-weeny things:

* *Knowledge of all alternatives, and*
* *The Power, or Ability, to enact any alternative that you Know.*

Ever heard the words *Omniscient* and *Omnipotent?* These are two words that do not describe YOU! (And they don't describe me, or anyone else on earth either.) So, here are the facts we all *get to* face:

FACT: There IS a world full of alternatives, opportunities, and choices out there, and we possess an awareness of only a small fraction of the whole; as we are not aware of certain alternatives, we are NOT free to choose them.

FACT: Even if we become aware of more alternatives, we may not presently be empowered to enact many of them, let alone, all of them; if we don't have the ability to enact them, then we are NOT free to do them; hence not free to choose them in the fullest sense of freedom.

As to *knowledge*, we can only choose alternatives that are available to our awareness; as to *power*, we can only actuate alternatives that we are capable of doing. Therefore, until we become *more informed* and *more capable*, we remain shackled by our *ignorance* and *inability*. Let me illustrate:

While you may not be free to play the piano today, you are free to begin piano lessons . . . today (unless money to pay a piano teacher restricts your freedom); anyhow, let's hire a hypothetical piano teacher and pay her* with imaginary money. With some practice and in time you may be *free* to play a simple tune like Chop Sticks, but without many months of persistent practice, you may NOT be immediately free to play, for instance, the Minute Waltz by Chopin—one of thousands of intermediate pieces you may not be free to play, today.

The Minute Waltz is more difficult music upon which you'll need to keep working; thus, playing the Minute Waltz (especially within 60 seconds) is something that you are NOT *free to choose* right now.

---

* Only in a few cases have I indulged in gender-biased language. The fact is that the more expensive piano teachers are typically male; thus, in this hypothetical scenario, I'm sincerely trying to budget hypothetical funds. And if you can't laugh at that, . . . you need to loosen your grip . . . on the misery stick! But to balance things out, I believe the other slip of gender-biased wordage involves a male who is a prodigiously dimwitted chowder-head. Since I am a man, I should be free to insult my own gender classification, and if you aren't amused by that, you need to loosen your grip . . . on the "other" misery stick, the one you are clutching in your "other" hand. If you've wondered the meaning of "the Double Whammy," now you know!

Let's summarize the boundaries of your limitations: You are NOT free to play advanced music or perform with the proficiency of a concert pianist; yet, you are free to keep improving your capabilities, line upon line, one step at a time.

By the way, Dr Matt is actually "free" to play the Minute Waltz by Chopin, but he is not free to play it without some *clinkers,* and is only capable of playing it in about one minute and forty-five seconds—therefore, NOT free to play "the Minute Waltz" in a minute. As to piano playing, your freedom and my freedom is likely limited; human beings are likewise limited in a million worldly ways, but especially limited in our *understanding* and *ability* as to things that matter most in life: To *play* the pleasing music of *highly accomplished character*, the joyful melody of *absolute integrity*.

Generally speaking, human beings are often NOT free to be *patient* in all situations, with all people. Like Chop Sticks, you might be able to *play* the simple *music of patience* in the presence of peaceful people in pleasant places, but making the harmonious music of *being gracious and kind* in the midst of a pressing moment? This may be a musical score . . . beyond your current capacity of character.

This more difficult music may be something that you are *not free* to play, today. *Choosing* and *doing* the things that matter most is particularly limiting because *choosing* a change in character IS NOT as simple as picking out a new pair of shoes; you can't just toss *integrity* and *character* into a shopping cart and possess them with the swipe of a credit card.

* * * * *

The simplistic notion that human beings are free to make any choice in any situation is simply false! Everyone is limited in awareness of alternatives and the ability to enact options—even when aware.

* * * * *

The exercise of human choice is ever LIMITED: Limited by situational constraints that come in a myriad of varieties and intensities, but most importantly, human choice is limited by . . . *who we are.* Our freedom is immediately constrained by our present progress of personal character—a character that hasn't yet learned to play, in a most pleasing way, the most magnificent music of Life.

The good news is that you are *free* to commence *character development lessons* today. You are *free* to make a commitment to the process of Changing Your Stripes. In terms of integrity and character, we all have *a long way to go* before we get to where we need to be, but we can begin by facing the right direction . . . NOW; and in a single moment, we are immediately better than before. The trick is to keep facing that good direction, and then keep moving forward one step at a time . . . line upon line.

* * * * *

Ascending lofty mountain tops may be exhilarating and motivating, but it is the faithful and unfaltering trek through gloomy valleys that is expanding and maturing.

* * * * *

Making the beautiful music of proactive patience and love is not a matter of making strategic, calculated decisions; instead, the sweetest music of Life rings out by making simple, sincere decisions. Character is not forged through a determined force of mental will power; rather, character comes forth naturally through a *release of will*—a yielding to the inherent intuitions of the heart. Integrity is not attained through cleverly conjured techniques, or by perfecting outward appearances that "look like" integrity at the surface; instead, pure integrity emerges from the depths of your soul, as you recover the innocence that was *inherently in you* as a child—a returning to the simple ways that *spontaneously flowed* from you, in your youth.

* * * * *

Because Pure Integrity is
Who You Are from your beginnings,
You don't need to learn Integrity, you need to Recover it.
When you are True, . . . Integrity will flow from you.

* * * * *

Making the beautiful music of being consistently loving and patient is a function of *who you are* today, and the only choose-able options available to you *today* . . . are the ones that flow from *your present disposition.* If you are not presently a patient person . . . then patience will not flow from you, today! This means that you and I cannot "choose" to play the most magnificent music of Life until we recapture *who we are* from our beginnings, until we recover our original childlike innocence. But just how far from recovering this innocence are we? The gap between *who we are* now and being purely loving and patient is measured by what I call the "P.Q."—the Provoke-Ability Quotient.

Provoke-Ability Quotient: What's your PQ ?

Just as I.Q. measures intelligence, the P.Q. represents a person's *propensity to be provoked.* On a scale from 0 to 10, higher scores point to the tendency to be quickly and easily inflamed. A score of "10" would describe a maniacal RAGE-aholic, and lower scores would reflect a greater propensity for being patient when faced with provocation. Jesus would have a P.Q. score of "0", and the rest of us would have a score somewhere between 1 and 10.

You've likely heard the terms *"reaching a breaking point"* or *"hitting hot buttons,"* these words describe the threshold at which we literally CEASE to have *character capacity* sufficient to choose a patient reply. Once people pass this "breaking point," choosing rationally doesn't really happen. Instead, *patterns of reaction* are "automatic" due to an entrenched history of previous choices (notice I didn't say "an entrenched history of social influence").

In the pressing moment when the P.Q. threshold is breached, your *exercise of will* ceases to be "free" will; instead, you are chained to emotional and behavioral consequences that are intrinsically tied to choices made . . . in prior days—it's karma calling, to kick your butt.

P.Q. explains the human tendency of *knee-jerk reactions*, a.k.a., going nuts, flipping out, boiling over, blowing up, blowing your top, blowing your cool, acting whack-o, going berserk, in a tiff, in a tizzy, losing it, or raging, etc. Because these *reactions* are not *consciously* chosen in the moment, but flow from us quite *unconsciously*, therefore, it is erroneously assumed that an "unconscious mind" controls "unconscious behaviors."

The only *mind* human beings "have" is the one that they experience consciously.* It is your conscious mind that *puts in motion* the very knee-jerk behaviors that *squirt out* of you—precisely because of prior patterns of *conscious* choosing. This "breaking point" I call the P.Q. threshold can also be visualized as a *squirting point:* If you squeeze a lemon long enough and hard enough, the lemon will spontaneously "squirt" at a particular point of external stress. Changing Your Stripes means becoming the kind of creature that has a low propensity for squirting!

---

* Mind is a noun-word that really represents verb-phenomena. John Dewey maintained that the activity of being consciously aware is better labeled "minding." Thus, the word "mind" represents the "activity" of being aware of one's world. In contrast "brain" IS a mass of material in your head that serves as a "switchboard" to connect the functions of your mortal body to your spirit self—the part of you that lives on when physical flesh returns to dust. Through thousands of well documented "near death" experiences, we learn that "dead" people continue be "aware" in a spirit realm of form and substance. This means that "thinking" isn't actually done directly by the mortal brain . . . for brainless, "dead" people continue conscious awareness beyond the grave! Conscious awareness, or "mind," must necessarily be a function of the spirit self.

The person who has a High P.Q. is unlikely to choose a loving response when confronted with a pressing situation. High P.Q. people tend to retaliate with mean emotions; yet, they like to blame their berserk behaviors upon those who provided the first provocation (page 21).

High P.Q. people like singin' the classic hit, that solid gold excuse: *"I wouldn't have done this . . . if you hadn't have done that!"* When you fully understand the P.Q. Principle, then you will change your tune to: *"If I didn't have such a high P.Q., then I wouldn't have done this . . . even if you did do that."*

The reality of P.Q. explains why most thoughtless crimes of passion are committed; indeed, they are completely "thoughtless" because they flow "unconsciously" from *who we are.* But here's the catch that many don't get: While a person may act "insane" in a particular moment of passion, that person is still responsible for the history of choices that produced the *propensity* to react insanely.

The P.Q. Principle helps us understand that those who commit crimes of passion remain *responsible* and *accountable* for their *disposition of reaction.* While people "acting whack-o" may NOT have consciously chosen an "insane" act in the moment, they DID choose the disposition from which their "insanity" squirts (see Emotion as Energy-in-Motion, p. 131).

One conscious choice at a time we all choose the kind of creature we become; this means, we each choose . . . our PQ's. From the fountain of *who we are* flows our knee-jerk reactions—reactions that we regret, in retrospect. We remain responsible for the "fountain" that we are, and the behavior that "flows" therefrom.

* * * * *

One Conscious Choice at a time,
You choose your Propensity to be Provoked;
You even choose your Propensity to . . . Insanity.
You are Responsible for the Person that You become.
You are Response-able for both your "premeditated" acts,
and the "thoughtless" reactions that flow from You.

* * * * *

The Division of Response-Ability Principle maintains, "What Comes out of You . . . is Yours," therefore, the mean and hateful emotions that come from a perpetrator . . . completely belong to that perpetrator; however some people do not apply this same Response-Ability Principle to those who are victimized. When mean and hateful emotions *squirt out* of victims of tragedy—in efforts to sympathize and support—angry retaliations are often *excused* and *justified.* Yet, if peace and closure would heal an afflicted soul, victims must also cease drinking the same hateful brew that poisons the perpetrator.

Not wanting to own their venomous reactions, victims will also sing the familiar strains of . . . *"I wouldn't have done this, if you hadn't have done that."* Thus, the same principle applies to perpetrators and victims alike: *"If I didn't have such a high P.Q., then I wouldn't have done this . . . even if you did that."* Perpetrators need not remain prisoners of mean, aggressive tendencies; neither should victims be prisoners of poisoned emotions in *response* to accidental or abusive intrusions. Both perpetrators and victims *get to* put their feet upon the path of recovery.

* * * * *

It is overly obvious that Offenders need to Change Their Stripes, but it is less obvious, and much less accepted, that Victims who harbor hateful emotions need to Change Their Stripes, too.

* * * * *

Life is a Set Up: There will be tough times, that's life! Here's the bitter truth: The emotional torment that victims feel, years after an abusive event occurred, is directly explained by the *poisoned emotions* generated by the victim.

* * * * *

After the dust of a difficulty is well settled, there is a junction of choice, a point of transition where further misery becomes self-made. Harboring Hateful Emotions IS the self-inflicting Venom . . . that Poisons Peace.

* * * * *

When hateful emotions flow from a victim, this inner bitterness IS the Response-Ability of the victim; the reason why victims harbor hateful and mean emotion is directly explained by each person's P.Q.—their Provoke-Ability Quotient. Even if the object of hate is "Hitler," emotionally healthy people will not waste precious energy on hating Hitler (or anyone else) because that negative emotional energy is the venom that poisons personal peace.

Time Heals All Wounds ?

As the bright sun rises upon a new day, there is an opportunity for all to recover and renew from the mistakes, offenses, and abuses of yesterday. It is said that "time heals all wounds," yet there is another possibility that can flow from free will . . . which is: "time wounds all heels." (Definition: Heel = A hateful person). With the same passage of "time" there are two alternatives before us:

* *Recover & Renew, or*
* *Rationalize & Resent*

The former bringing fresh feelings and new life, the latter drags along continued misery. We live in a culture that *justifies* and encourages contentious retaliation. Choosing rancor and retaliation simply keeps us mired in poisoned emotions; whereas, the remedy of *recovery* and *renewal* brings peace. The course of recovery means extending forgiveness to those who offend; yet, forgiveness does not mean that offenders escape the consequences of their abusive acts. For the long-term benefit of offenders, the choice to "recover and renew" can also include seeking justice through appropriate channels; such *justice* will be guided by *promptings of heart*, not by *impulses of hate* or a *rationalizing head.*

Choosing the resentful option is like willfully taking hold of a rope tied to the dreary and depressing details of past happenings, and then choosing to drag this heavy load of useless cares behind. REALITY CHECK: Who's holding the rope? A song by *The Eagles* offers some choice words about dragging along emotional baggage:

GET OVER IT

I turn on the tube and what do I see
A whole lotta people crying "Don't blame me"
They point their crooked little fingers at everybody else
Spend all their time feelin' sorry for themselves
A victim of this, a victim of that
Your momma's too thin and your daddy's too fat

Get over it! Get over it!
All this whinin' and cryin' and pitchin' a fit. Get over it!

It's like going to confession every time I hear you speak
You're makin' the most of your losin' streak
Some call it sick, but I call it weak

You drag it around like a ball and chain
You wallow in the guilt; you wallow in the pain
You wave it like a flag, you wear it like a crown
Got your mind in the gutter, bringin' everybody down
Complain about the present and blame it on the past
I'd like to find your inner child and kick its little ____

Get over it! Get over it!
All this blamin' and moanin' and pitchin' a fit. Get over it!
It's gotta stop sometime, so why don't you quit
Get over it! Get over it!

To *Get Over It,* you can start by *Letting Go of It . . .* letting go of the rope that ties you to yesterday's misery. Recalling the Principle of P.Q. and Not-as-Free-as-you-Think Free Will, "getting over it" is not really as simple as *letting go.* It's not as easy as just . . . *choosing it!* Unless *you* become a "let-it-go-able" kind of creature, you will not be capable of applying the get-over-it admonition. You will NOT be free to make the music of more intricate "character" compositions (p. 46); first, you will need to Change Your Stripes and Recover the True You.

To *get over it*, you will need to experience a *recovery* and *renewal* of *who you are* from your beginnings. For now, you may be a "can't-let-go-of-the-rope" kind of creature . . . and literally cannot *choose* the "let-go-of-it" option. You may be a *heel* who needs to be *healed*. Time can be used in service of two opposing options:

* * * * *

I can seek Recovery and Renewal and be Healed . . . OR
I can continue to Rationalize and Resent
and remain . . . a Heel!

* * * * *

Human Doings are Co-Authored

Just as the idea of "free will" is often overstated, I've probably overstated *The Division of Response-Ability Principle* . . . a little bit . . . well, maybe a lot? The truth is that all external behavior IS actually co-authored; in other words, what comes out of you at the level of external *doings* and *sayings* IS absolutely explained by the words, behaviors, and events that occurred before you *responded* to them. This is the mutually responsive "conversation of life" that is considered by some to be a *causal chain*. There is an element of truth to this notion, and there is also one BIG EXCEPTION.

First, the element of truth: Apart from morally-loaded aspects of human be-ing (see Inescapable Impact Always, page 83), the *outward physical choreographies* and *verbal statements* that come from of each of us are a function of dialogical dance with other people primarily, and with all things and beings within our immediate world. In other words, all *human doings* reflect what circumstance and/or people are *asking* of us in the mildest sense, *requiring* of us in a stronger sense, or oppressively *coercing* upon us in the strongest sense. Life is a Set Up: Situations inherently constrain!

Here's an example on the milder end of *constraint:* If a person calls you on the phone and you *respond* with the outward choreography of picking up the receiver, your act of answering the phone is *explained* by the telephone ringing—a ring that was initiated, or *caused*, by the person calling.

Question: Why did you answer the phone? Answer: Be-*cause* it was ringing! Answering phones that ring is what normal, rational people do. The *cause* of you answering the phone is not a mechanical or necessary *hard* cause (as in one thing physically impacting another thing), this kind of *soft cause* is what I call "sufficient cause" or . . . *Be-Cause.*

A *"Be-Cause"* is a *"Reason"* why you respond as you do when confronted by a given *Constraint.* When answering a ringing phone, your behavioral movements are not necessary, they are *voluntary.* You move and respond for a *reason*, . . . you pick up a phone *be-cause* it made sense to do so.

* * * * *

Variable "Be-Causes"
happen within a Communicative and "Meaning-full" realm.
Necessary "Causes"
occur in a Physical and "Mechanical" realm.

* * * * *

Back to the telephone conversation: As you converse with your friend, an appointment is set for next Monday at 2:30 p.m. When Monday rolls around, you are prepared and ready to follow through with that appointment. Your *response of readiness* is explained by the fact that another person constrained and *co-authored* your expectation of meeting together on Monday; your *readiness* is explained by both the *outward constraint* and your *personal character*—you tend to follow through with your word.

Accountability for Be-ing is Individual. As daily interactions unfold back and forth within a dialogical dance, people do things directly *be-cause* others and situations may invite, require, or coerce certain *outward* bodily behaviors and verbal statements from them; hence, these mutually responsive dialogues and deeds ARE directly explained by the constraints that precede them—co-authored responses of *doing* that are not necessarily *morally-loaded.*

Now, for the BIG EXCEPTION to the "causal chain" assumption: What IS NOT a direct "effect" of situational constraints IS the *inward* emotional tone and intention with which you say your words and do your deeds. The emotional tone that flows from you IS always a response explained by your disposition of character; a response for which you are solely accountable, and a response of *be-ing* that is always *morally-loaded.*

* * * * *

Responses of Be-ing are a direct function of
Personal Character—or lack thereof.
Emotional Tone & Intent is always
morally-loaded; meaning, emotions always
carry an inward intent of either Honesty or Deception.

* * * * *

Let's pretend that your "Monday, 2:30 p.m." meeting falls through. The fact that your friend made a commitment to that time *explains* why you turned down other dates in order to keep this prior appointment; further, the fact that your friend promised to show, *explains* why you're waiting at 2:30 p.m. for the rendezvous to happen. Again, people act and respond *Be-Cause* of *Reasons* that make sense to them. So, there you are all dressed up and ready . . . and your friend cancels the "dance." Many people would feel frustrated in such a situation, and some might even *erupt* with anger or *squirt* (as I like to call it)—they've passed their P.Q. threshold.

Given this situation where a friend fails to show and thereby disrupts your effective flow of time and opportunity, any frustrated or angry emotions that well within . . . ARE ALL YOURS. Your emotional response is directly due to your current disposition of character; your way of responding is explained by your pre-disposed tendencies to be *frustrate-able, anger-able,* or possibly . . . *drive-able-up-the-wall-able.*

In your defense, you may logically reason, "but I would not have gotten angry if my friend would have followed through." This is a fact! But it is also true that IF *you* were a more patient person, you would not have gotten angry in the first place! This is why the word "unflappable" exists in our language, to describe people with a character capacity for unruffled patience. Because, *persistent patience* may not be music you can currently compose; this points to the urgent need for Changing Your Stripes!

In the preceding paragraphs, co-authored behavior has been described from the perspective of you being *set up* by others—they coauthor your behavior. Now let's turn the tables and consider co-authored constraints coming from the other direction: You are *setting up* others for the *responses* you see coming back to you, based upon their disposition of character, . . . their P.Q.

All behavior is enacted, experienced, and understood within a co-operative context: You co-author the behavior of others; you help create in others the very behaviors you dislike! If you want to know what you're sending out, see what's coming back; the behavior of others always reflects: what you are *saying*, what you are *doing*, and how you are *being*.

* * * * *

Even though "Outward" Doings are Created Cooperatively,
Moral Responsibility for "Inward" Tone & Intent
is Always Individual; thus, at the Level
of Inner Response-Ability
If It Comes Out of You, It is All Yours,
and If It Comes Out of Them, . . . It is All Theirs.

* * * * *

The Set Up Flows Both Ways. The phrase "Life is a Set Up" applies both *from me to thee, and from thee to me.* Because the world is filled with inconsiderate and self-serving people, you can expect selfishness to inevitably pester your personal path—thus you are impacted and constrained—but please realize that YOU . . . will also dish out an unloving load of selfishness too! Still, there is value gleaned from moments when you are mistreated: *now you know how it feels!* You have the opportunity to *learn empathy* for the feelings and afflictions of others, through the suffering that you endure. Consider the rich meaning in Christ's invitation to empathy: *"whatsoever ye would that men should do to you, do ye even so to them."*

Beyond the value of nurturing an empathic perspective come the lessons of karma: Every ounce of energy you send out—positive or negative, honest or deceptive—will return to you, at some future point in time.

For the moment, think in terms of the view that you have been *set up* and put upon. Recall the situation where your friend failed to show up at "Monday, 2:30 p.m." as promised? Logically speaking, what good does it do for you to get upset or angry when the appointment is broken anyway? Regardless of how you respond, the occasion is canceled: the milk is spilt, water has passed under the bridge, the perfume is out of the bottle, . . . you can't put the stink back in the skunk! Therefore, you are at choice to either: *celebrate it* or *suffer it*, . . . you can be *flexible* or *miserable!*

The ironic twist is this: people literally choose the "suffer it" option, this is what "Hitting Myself with the Misery Stick" means (p. 28). But faced with frustration, you may be asking yourself, "what is there to celebrate?" Consider these possibilities: It's great to be alive. Breathing is definitely good! It's also good to have a friend PERIOD, even one that *stands you up* occasionally. The words from a Broadway song express this same sentiment:

BEING ALIVE

Someone to hold you too close, someone to hurt you too deep,
Someone to sit in your chair, to ruin your sleep,
To make you aware of being alive.

Someone you have to let in, someone whose feelings you spare,
Someone who like it or not, will want you to share
A little, a lot, is being alive.

Make me confused, mock me with praise,
Let me be used, vary my days.
For alone is alone . . . not alive.

Somebody crowd me with love, somebody force me to care.
Somebody let me come through, I'll always be there,
As frightened as you to help us survive,
Being alive, . . . being alive!

When confronted with a vexing situation, you really can *celebrate it.* It's possible! And it's even more probable as your spiritual commitments run deep. Consider this: The Apostle Paul was five times beaten with forty stripes, shipwrecked three times, unjustly jailed, and survived a stoning, and yet he declared, *"but we glory in tribulations also; knowing that tribulation worketh patience; and patience, experience; and experience, hope."*

Return again to the missed-appointment scenario, let's imagine that your spiritual roots are pretty shallow and you choose to "suffer it." You decide to get real angry at your rude, unreliable, so-called "friend," and you cuss and spit and break a few things; then, later you find out that your friend was seriously injured in an automobile accident. Now, how do you view the retarded tantrum that you threw? Every aggravating situation in life will expose . . . your depth of character! Without the mirror of affliction, you cannot clearly see yourself; you will not be aware of your weaknesses, or know how to correct your course.

So the moral to the story is this: when you are *stood up* for an appointment, always double check to see if your *date* has experienced circumstances beyond his/her control. When you know this person is safe and unharmed (and stood you up because of inconsiderate selfishness), THEN and only then, should you throw a childish tantrum, cuss, spit, and break a few things? . . . NOT!

Imagine that someone really was injured in an accident, and if you could conjure up concern for this person's bodily well-being, then *why not* expand your concern to someone's emotional and spiritual well-being? This means, that EVEN IF your friend acted out of inconsiderate selfishness, you still have the opportunity to respond compassionately . . . to the *emotional car wreck* that your friend may be living! Whenever others don't show up for you, there is always an opportunity for you to show up for them! Not because they have been good, but because good is *who you are.*

So when a friend fails to show, the obvious options are *celebrate it* or *suffer it* . . . right? WRONG! *(Now I have your attention: it's really half right, and half wrong.)* Here's the catch: For certain people, the "celebrate it" option only exists in *theory* and is not actually choose-able because of deeply entrenched dispositions incapable of choosing a better way.

You will see long-term value when faced with affliction ONLY IF you are a *glass-half-full-able* kind of creature, else the opposite option will instinctively *squirt* from you. Your dreary disposition will dump you in the *glass-half-empty* ditch, by default. It's as simple as this: When provoked by pressure, the virtue of patience will NOT proceed from impatient people; pure water cannot flow from impure fountains.

If you sincerely desire to respond compassionately to tough constraints, it's NOT merely a matter of choosing *patience* or *compassion* in that stressful moment: It's too late! Under the press of distress . . . you will *squirt* according to your present PQ. You've already *set-in-motion* how you will *respond* or *react* under pressure; this is precisely why emotion is well conceived as E-motion—Energy-in-Motion.

A conscious commitment to Changing Your Stripes will set-in-motion fresh energy that will spontaneously appear in future days; compassion and patience will flow from you *tomorrow*, as you initiate loving energy *today*.

* * * * *

Today is the day to put Patient and Compassionate Energy-in-Motion, that it might freely flow from you in future days, effortlessly & naturally, like pure water from a pure fountain.

* * * * *

In the mean time, you need to get a good grip on *who you are* . . . right now. You need to take inventory of your Self.

~ 2 ~

Self:

The Animal You Are

WHO AM I?

Both Body and Being. Take a moment to think of a person you greatly respect and admire? What attributes does he or she possess? . . . Answers will inevitably come in two categories:

1 - The *Physical* attributes of the *Body*,
2 - The *Expressive* attributes of a body in motion: *Being*.

Unless your admiration goes to a super model, most of the attributes of a greatly respected person will fall in the *Being* category, for example:

Body		***Being***	
Nice-looking	Tan	Dependable	Fair
Olive Skin	Slender	Generous	Kind
In-shape	Blue Eyes	Friendly	Helpful
Blonde	Pretty Smile	Loving	Accepting

You are a human *being.* The word *being* can evoke an image of *"entity,"* . . . a physical thing; this is the "noun" aspect of self, . . . your *body.* The word *being* can also evoke an image of *"activity,"* moving realities of action, expression, and emotion; this is the "verb" aspect of self, . . . your *being.* Human existence, or human *be-ing*, is simultaneously manifest as *noun-and-verb*, inseparably expressed as both *body-and-being.* This is "The Animal You Are." This is your...Self.

Although intimately correlated, Self and Self-Identity are two different things. Self is the total attributes and expressions of *body-and-being*, and how that whole reality occurs primarily within the context of human relationships, but also how the Self is expressed in relation to animals, plants, the land, and material things. In contrast, Self-Identity is how you *imagine* yourself to "be" within this broad relational context. Self-Identity is established and maintained by the *perceived* characteristics of your *body* and *being.*

Further, how you think of your self, and how others think of you . . . are two different things; in the case of a person who is completely clueless as to how he or she *comes across* in the world, there can be a wide disparity between the two perceptions—but there is usually overlap.

* * * * *

Self-Conception of my body and being
is formed in a social mirror:
as I relate with others,
I receive feedback on how I come across.

* * * * *

It is in the mirror of your interactions with other that you come to know *who you are.* In fact, it is other people who have the best access to discerning your *way of being.* Because they have a view . . . from outside of you, they can better sense and see how you occur (see pages 92, 155).

What it means to be human is to be embodied; thus, you live life from a perspective within your body. This means that the "outside" view . . . is not directly available to you. You can only get indirect reflections of yourself in the *mirror of your associations*—feedback on both your physical presence of *body* and your expressive presence of *being*. This feedback is essential in coming to understand *who you are*. Without these looking-glass reflections, what you think of yourself . . . is fantasy (read about the "myth" of self-identity, pages 91, 92).

Of the noun-self, others come to identify you by your shape and size, by the colors and contours of your eyes, ears, arms, and other body features—tangible characteristics that become uniquely associated to . . . you! Because *bodily traits* can be discerned in one single moment in time, they can be captured in a *still photo*—a snap shot. In contrast, attributes of *being* are harder to capture in a single photo. While bodily attributes are instantly apparent, differently, your expressions of *being* are discerned over time and through experience, and are better captured in *motion pictures*.

To visualize and emphasize the active and expressive character of the verb-self, I sometimes spell the word *being* in this way: *be-ing*. This symbol accentuates the *in-motion* quality of the verb-self.

* * * * *

While be-ing is not technically tangible,
the expressions and emotions
of human be-ing are made possible
by the mobilizations of a tangible body;
without the body, ... be-ing could not "be."

* * * * *

But *be-ing* transcends the boundaries of the body, and extends to the communicative context within which *be-ing* is mutually expressed with others. Human be-ing is always manifest in relationship to other beings and other things within specific situations. Expressions of *be-ing* require a social context to make sense and have purpose (see page 95).

Social psychologist Charles Cooley also viewed the Self as inseparable from the context of social relations. His theory called "The Looking Glass Self," maintained: *"There is no self, without the other."*

This socially situated conception of *human be-ing* is what the Philosopher Martin Heidegger was striving to describe with the term "Dasein"—literally translated from German, "being-there." Dasein was Heidegger's word for the Self of body-and-being.

Instead of just focusing on *What-ness* of existence, Heidegger was concerned with . . . the *IS-ness* of existence; he reconceptualized human *beings* from a "noun" orientation of individualized human *bodies* . . . to a "verb" orientation of human *be-ings.* A "verb" emphasis embedded within the sentences, paragraphs and stories of life; an embodied Self inseparably situated within a holistic context: *Being-with-others-in-the-world*, hence . . . "being-there."

VERB-SELF

To this point *being*, or the verb-self, has been described as the expressive and communicative aspect of *who you are.* More specifically, the verb-self is manifest in two types:

* *The outward activities and roles of "doing,"*
* *The inward tone & intention of a "way of being."*

Human Doing: External Choreography. This aspect of the verb-self is manifest through . . . what you "do." Human Doings are the outward performances enacted by the body and are characterized by the descriptions and titles associated to those "doings." *Doings* come in the form of occupational roles like: *nurse*, *doctor*, *lawyer*, or *secretary*. The verb-self is also revealed through the *doings* of recreation and hobbies like: *runner*, *reader*, *board-gamer*, or *skate-boarder*. In contrast to the motives and emotions of human be-ings, "human doings" are just outward activities: from *bowling* to *bird watching*, *weeding* to *walking*, or *reading* to *relaxing*.

These *choreographies* are always and ever *coauthored* with other people, and when *human doings* do not happen with other human beings, coauthoring occurs with other creatures and creations in the world: playing fetch with a dog, shoveling snow off the driveway, or driving a car through rush-hour traffic.

Coauthoring means that *what you do* is a function of a responsive, relational dance that is enacted with others beings and other things. So, as you are *doing* what you *do*, the variation of chosen body behaviors are largely explained by what other beings and things are constraining.

* * * * *

Others actively constrain
your thinking, saying, and doing,
by inviting, requiring, or coercing
specific responses from you.

* * * * *

Passive constraints also impact your responses; the *mere presence* of the *beings* and *things* in your immediate world impact *what you do*, and *how you be.*

The coauthoring of *human doings* occurs reciprocally: You *set up and influence* others as they *set up and influence* you. So on the flip side, others are also *doing* what they *do*, as a direct function of how you are actively *inviting, requiring, or coercing*—as well as passively influencing by your mere presence. Coauthoring occurs creatively and *meaning-fully*, as opposed to caused necessarily and *mechanically.*

The influence of *co-authoring constraint* can also be termed *soft cause*, or *sufficient cause* (pages 254, 255). "Sufficient cause" means that responses occur according to reasons: You do things "be-*cause.*" An example of *sufficient cause* occurred when Lucifer enticed Eve to partake of the forbidden fruit. Eve ate the apple for a reason, . . . "be-*cause.*" She explained, *"the serpent beguiled me!"*

Eve's dialogue with the devil is termed *sufficient cause* in this way: Without the beguiling of the serpent, Eve would never have been beguiled, thus, she would not have partaken of the fruit. While the serpent did not mechanically cause her response, Satan's temptation was *sufficient*, or enough, to entice Eve to *choose* as she did. Because Eve's act was *chosen*, she could not claim "the devil *made* me do it."

Nevertheless, the "doing" Eve *did* was a co-authored action: The serpent's temptation needed to precede and *set up* the option for Eve to choose. Eve did a verbal dance with the devil . . . and as a result she was beguiled by the serpent's *coauthoring constraint.* Similarly, all human doings are *coauthored* by the constraining impact of other beings, and other things. This is precisely why Dr Matt says: *Life is a Set Up!*

Short of incidents of physical impact, Life's *set ups* are always meaning-full, and not mechanical. *Cause and Effect* occurs only and exclusively within the "noun realm" of our world: where two physical things are *mechanically effected* by physical contact. Whereas, the governing principle for the "verb realm" of our world is . . . *Constraint and Choice.*

* * * * *

Cause & Effect occurs in the "noun realm" of our world, whereas the "verb realm" operates by the Principle of Constraint & Choice. Human Do-ings and Human Be-ings are "verb realm" phenomena.

* * * * *

However, similar to a cause-and-effect chain reaction, *constraints* and their associated *chosen responses* will also reflect a chain of *preceding moments of constraint* that largely explain the emergence of the subsequent responses. Again, this is not a *mechanical* chain of necessary effects, but a *meaning-full* chain of *optional responses—a chain of choice*—and it is *you* doing the choosing (see Human Doings are Co-Authored, page 54).

Conceptual confusion on this topic mainly comes from the fact that the human body is one of the physical things in our world, and is thus subject to *cause and effect* intrusions—like the toe contusion you *necessarily get* when you accidentally kick a concrete curb (see Physical Constraints, page 8).

Conceptual confusion continues as people fail to distinguish the difference between the principles governing *things*, as opposed to the principles governing *do-ings* and *be-ings.*

It is common for people to erroneously apply notions of *mechanical* cause and effect to verbal, behavioral, and emotional responses. Because some incorrectly apply the *facts* of physics, to the *acts* of human *be-ings,* it is especially common to see people blame others for *causing* their *emotional reactions.* To avoid this error, it is valuable to get clear on the other aspect of the "verb self"—your *way of being.*

Human Being: Inward Tone & Intent. In addition to outward choreographies of "human doing," the other fundamental aspect of the verb-self is your "*way of being.*" This is the undercurrent of *motive* and *emotion* that flows with and flavors the *doing* . . . while you are *doing.* Simultaneous to doing what you are doing, the emotional tone and intention of a *way of being* infuses physical activities. Your *way of being* communicates much even when words are not spoken, and IS the most important component of nonverbal language. Others can observe and sense *emotional tone and intent* . . . as physical *deeds are done.*

The unique attributes of a *way of being* are illustrated by the contrasting words we use to describe a person. Consider these adjectives: *short*, *fat*, *blonde*, *bowlegged*—these words point to, and describe, a human body. In contrast, human *being* is more than the characteristics of our material mass, consider the words: *kind*, *gentle*, *generous*, and *patient*—such attributes are not found within the individual boundaries of our bodies, rather they are located in specific relational moments as expressed *one-to-another.*

The typical image evoked by the word "self" is that of an individual person, more precisely, a single body; but as we are learning, "human being" is more than body. While human bodies are separate in physical space, . . . the most important aspect of "self" is not separate, but inseparably unified with others.

* * * * *

You are bonded to others
by meaningful, linguistic relations.
Your Way of Being IS the way you are
"Being-With" another person. This Verb aspect of
Self is literally made possible by the presence of others.

* * * * *

For this reason, philosopher Chauncey Riddle asserts, "the self is located in the *space between* two bodies." Riddle's *space between* metaphor represents the *communicative expressions* we convey to others; messages of emotion and intention that always require both sender and receiver to be *meaning-full.* Your *way of being* IS this "space between" and exists through the interactive synergy of *self-and-other.*

There is rhetoric floating around in public discourse that curiously concludes: "you are not what you do." The logic goes: "who you are is an inner self of eternal heritage." This second statement is true on the basis of our beginnings and our potential, . . . but such reasoning ultimately falls flat: It's like an obnoxious pouting *prince* who constantly oppresses the peasants, yet keeps reminding: "I am the son of a *king*."

So who is the prince? He is BOTH *of royal blood* AND *obnoxiously oppressive.* The truth is that the prince is not presently living up to his heritage. While all humanity can rightfully claim the divine heritage of a King, we only *become* royal as we live true . . . by what we *do*, and how we *be*—such is inseparably *who we are.**

---

* In the day of Judgment, God will not separate you, from the unrepented deeds that you do—you are accountable for all dishonest and abusive acts, and they are part of "who you are" until Christ makes you a "new creature" (2 Cor. 5:17). Jesus taught that those who "do the will of my Father" will enter into the kingdom of heaven (Matt. 7:21). The Apostle Paul taught that our ultimate identity is not separated from what we do: "For as many as are led by the Spirit of God, they are the sons of God" (Romans 8:14). It is thru what we *do* (good works), and by how we *be* (heartfelt faithfulness) that we live up to our divine heritage, and become the children of a King—this can be, our ultimate identity.

The Human Self is all the combined characteristics of one's tangible *body*, with all the active choreographies of *doing*, plus all the emotional tone and intention of a *way of being*. The Self is all of these at once and all of these in continuous living motion, hence human be-ing. While the descriptive aspects of *body* and *being* can be talked about and analyzed separately, they do not exist separately. They exist as one undivided whole. This is . . . "The Animal You Are."

Be-ing is Located in the Space Be-tween

Human Beings are more than their Body, and more than their activities of Doing, and more than the Self they Imagine:

The Most Important Aspect of Self Is Located In the Space Between Two Bodies

The Self is manifest most importantly by:

How You are Being with Others

Human Be-ing IS:

How You Be with Others
How You Express to Others
How You Respond to Others

Body	**Way of Being**		**Body**
Five Foot Nine	*Controlling*	*Loving*	*Five Foot Four*
Brown Hair	*Hateful*	*Patient*	*Blonde Hair*
Green Eyes	*Angry*	*Gentle*	*Blue Eyes*
Muscular	*Mean*	*Kind*	*Slender*

To identify and distinguish each of these descriptive aspects is essential because the heights of human fulfillment depend upon directing one's *way of being* toward honest and loving ends. Your *way of being* is the foundation upon which the other aspects of Self (your doings and your body) are supported and made stable. When one's *way of being* is out of harmony, psychosomatic consequences occur that effect both the body's *physical appearance* and the body's ability to competently *do* what needs to be *done.* Giving primary attention to the development of your *way of being* means connecting to Life's primary purpose.

The *tone* and *intention* by which you live determines whether your days are a drudgery or a delight. Emotion and Intention are manifest in two fundamental ways: *Honest* vs. *Dishonest*, or framed another way, *Loving* vs. *Less-than-Loving.* Regardless of the external situations that constrain you, your ability to express a *loving tone* and *honest intentions* is essentially what it means to *embrace Inner Liberty.* Nurturing the inner life of heart and soul naturally leads to *contented living.*

INTENT DEFINES THE ACT

A closer look at the distinction between activities of *doing*, and the tone and intention of a *way of being* is illustrated as follows:

Doing (Action)	**Being (Tone & Intention)**
Attending Church-1	*Glad to be in a place of peace*
Attending Church-2	*Bothered by the hypocrisy of others in attendance*
Cooking a meal-1	*Happy to have enough food for the family*
Cooking a meal-2	*Annoyed that no one is offering to help out*
Bowling-1	*Celebrating the success of all participants*
Bowling-2	*Irritated that fellow competitors are scoring higher*
Vacuuming-1	*Thankful to have a home and a carpet to clean*
Vacuuming-2	*Feeling unappreciated for hours of hard work*

Even though the outward choreographies are essentially the same, when the motive and emotion is different, then the "act-as-a-whole" becomes different. Evaluating an activity without considering intent and emotion . . . can lead to a profound misunderstanding of the act-as-a-whole.

For example, visualize the outward activity of: *forcefully pushing another person.* Without taking into account context and intention, most would conclude such an act to be aggressive and uncivil. Giving someone a hard shove would be very *politically incorrect*, but that same "shove"—when applied within a specific context and colored by a particular intent—can completely change the *act-as-a-whole.* How would the "act" be defined if that *forceful push* moved someone *"out of"* the path of an oncoming car? This particular "push" would be deemed an act of *heroism.* In contrast, pushing someone *"into"* the path of a car would be defined as an act of *attempted murder.* The raw outward choreography of *shoving someone* changes . . . as *context* and *intention* change.

Some institutions within our culture reinforce an orientation of emphasizing outward evidence to the exclusion of understanding inward motives. Because of the elephantine influence of the legal system in our culture, it is becoming more common for people to focus upon outward superficial *Facts* . . . to define an *Act.*

* * * * *

When Motives are not factored into
the Definition of particular Doings, such
interpretations become Acts of Dishonesty
by those who observe and interpret.

* * * * *

Such blatant dishonesty regularly occurs in courts of law, where whatever *story* can be concocted to explain away obvious guilt . . . is the story that is told. The legal system calls it a "defense strategy," but common folk call it . . . "lying." Disregard for the meaning of the "act-as-a-whole" also happens when politicians endeavor to further political agendas; when an outward act can possibly be interpreted to the advantage of political "spin," then the true intent that undergirds that outward act is routinely ignored.

* * * * *

Political and Legal "lying" is business as
usual: taking words and deeds out of context
and judging acts upon their superficial appearance
is what the Politically Correct Police do daily.
And as factual fragments are taken
out of context,
such dishonesty
hides conveniently behind
the legitimized label of . . . "strategy."

* * * * *

Twisting the *facts* to one's favor is so common in our culture that the masses have largely become desensitized to it. As propaganda is peddled to a gullible public, or a fleece-able jury, some accept that intentionally distorting presentations is a clever *strategy* to be applauded. When words and deeds are taken out of context, intention is obscured and the very heart of an act's meaning is negated. Understanding the entire context of an act is critical, because awareness of context reveals intent.

For the purposes of Changing Your Stripes, *the truth, the whole truth, and nothing but the truth* is told by *Intentions* and *Emotional Tone* within the larger *Context* of particular situations. Such is the big picture for understanding the *meaning* of all human doings. When we focus on superficial facts only, *the facts can fool us*—for things are not always as they seem on the surface. Intention must be discerned! As interpreted within each living context, *Intent* defines the *Act-as-a-Whole.*

Two Aspects of the Verb-Self

Can You Distinguish "Doing" from a "Way of Being"?

DOING = Outward Action

What People are Doing: Their Physical Choreographies

What Is Happening In Terms of Objective Content:

How People Communicate & Respond

How People Constrain Each Other

How People Set Up Each Other

WAY OF BEING = Tone & Intention

Honest or Deceptive Motives & Emotions

that Color the Content of Outward Action

SELF AS LANGUAGE

When we think of the verb-self, we visualize a person engaged in expressive interaction with others, within specific situations. *Meaning* is expressed in every human act, and in each human act, a *speaking* or a *saying* of some sort is communicated with or without words. We speak by symbol, word, gesture, and deed, all of which constitute "language" in a broad sense. Every human act is a language act, an act that conveys motive, emotion, meaning, and purpose. Life is manifest in daily interactive dialogue. As to language and life, Jergen Habermas remarked: *"Reality happens in language. Language is not merely an object in our hands, it is the reservoir of tradition and the medium in and through which we exist."*

* * * * *

Human beings do not just use language, we are language; . . . . speaking, expressing, hearing, and understanding is inherently Who We Are. Therefore, enriching Who We Are from our core is a superior approach for improving communication, compared to learning "techniques" of communication, as if language was merely a manipulative tool.

* * * * *

Whether we acknowledge it or not, we always speak from our core, and the *way* we speak and the content we express reveals that core. As Jesus taught, *"From the abundance of the heart, the mouth speaketh."* The motives of the heart manifest *who we are.* The intents of the heart determine the flow and effectiveness of all our communications, and thus, the happiness and harmony of all human relations.

As we grow in strength of character, we naturally become better communicators. The issues and obstacles of good communication are seldom *only* about word selection, "saying it just right"—yet this is a common conclusion within the "technique" paradigm of communication. When it comes to communicating well, the *emotional tone* and *intention* that accompanies our words are of paramount importance. This is why Dr Matt likes to say . . . and so he does:

* * * * *

When the Tone is True,
The Argument Evaporates!

* * * * *

You Can't Say What You Mean. The philosopher Nietzsche said this of language: "Reality is captured in the categorical nets of language only at the expense of fatal distortion." Affirming a similar line of logic, Sir Francis Bacon stated, "words still manifestly force the understanding, throw everything into confusion, and lead mankind into vain and innumerable controversies and fallacies."

A broad definition of "language" includes all ways of communicating: both written and spoken words, vocal inflections, emotional expressions, body gestures, and all doings and deeds that "say" something—which is ALL doings and deeds. For instance, the way we obtain and order material possessions has rich symbolic meaning; likewise, the way we regard plants, animals, and the land "says" something too.

Everything we do, say, and feel . . . expresses "meaning," and reveals the core of the communicator, but all that is "meant"—via a myriad of symbols—requires *interpretation* by those who receive or observe those *meaningful* expressions. Because intended meaning is literally at the mercy of those who translate, it is *hard to say what you mean* when others on the receiving end are not "getting it." In a precise and exact sense, you *can't say what you mean* anyway—at least not through a one-time attempt. Continued dialogue is required to double-check nuances of intended meaning, for it is in the *ongoing conversation* that meaning comes clear.

Language is the medium through which "meaning-makers" make meaning. Indeed language *"is the reservoir of tradition and the medium in and through which we exist."* Because human beings are inherently social and expressive, we don't merely "use" language, . . . we "are" language! Life happens in language. Therefore, understanding the inherent properties of symbolic language can expand our understanding of Self—thus draw us nearer to Self-fulfillment.

THE NATURE OF LANGUAGE

1 - People are meaning makers! Words are symbols that only have meaning as living beings negotiate and assign meaning to them. Words—in and of themselves—do not mean.

2 - During communicative exchanges of *sending* and *receiving*, words provide descriptive, definitional constraints that disallow certain meanings, and open up other *possible* meanings. Most words have more than one meaning or definition.

3 - Because any particular word, or string of words, will inevitably have more than one meaning, the sender of symbols can't simply put *accurate ideas* directly into the mind of the receiver. One cannot convey *accurate ideas* using *approximate symbols.*

4 - Because our world experience is detailed, particular, and specific—and the words we use to describe it are categorical and approximate—a loss of meaning is unavoidable. Reducing the richness of directly-lived experience to a string of sounds or symbols inevitably leads to a loss of meaning; this unavoidable loss of meaning is called communicative *entropy.*

5 - Human beings often do not possess the competency to adequately use linguistic symbols to convey meaning; hence, the oft used phrase is invoked, "you woulda had to been there," as well as the worn cliché, "you know what I mean?"

6 - Even if people are very articulate with their word selection, words themselves cannot fully encapsulate the richness of reality. Words provide only *approximate* description as opposed to *accurate* description.

Nevertheless, there is a degree of *sufficiency* that can be attained as a conversation patiently continues: "I see what you mean" or "I get it now."

7 - After *speakers* have done their best to *send* a series of symbols, *receivers* then try to understand the mind and meaning of the sender by translating that *approximate* set of symbols. The inevitable *loss of meaning* that occurs as translators extract incomplete ideas from a *sound* or *symbol* is called communicative *ellipsis.*

8 - In written communications, readers do not have the benefit of voice inflection, body gestures, or experiential context to more fully understand the intent of the author.

How Words Work. Words provide definitional *constraints* that narrow possible meaning-full translations. Meaning is not directly *in words* per se; rather meaning resides *in human beings.* As the meaning-makers, people "bring" meaning to words, and that act of *bringing* is called *translation* or *interpretation.*

A good illustration of how words *work* is given in the following phrase: *"I had a piano stolen."* Is there a single meaning in this string of words? As words can only provide approximate definitional boundaries, it is clear that our five-word phrase can have more than a single meaning; yet the phrase does *constrain* the translator to a few likely possibilities. Putting vocal inflection upon the underscored words in the following phrases, consider these three possible *meanings:*

1 - I <u>had</u> a piano stolen (from me), in the past;

2 - I had <u>a</u> piano stolen; I had "a" single piano stolen (from me)—whether in the past or present; and

3 - I had a piano <u>stolen</u>; I enlisted the help of another person to pilfer a piano (for me), a piano that was not mine.

The five-word phrase provides interpretive boundaries that narrows meaning to *at least* three feasible options, and there are more, especially as we add various vocal inflections and emotion into the speaking of these words.

When we *expect* words to simply *funnel* meaning from the mind of the sender to the mind of the receiver, we may lose patience with the process, prematurely. Therefore, it is important "to get" that good communication requires *redundancy* and *elaboration.* Notice how 19 more words were used to clarify the third *possible* meaning of "I had a piano stolen." More words and more exchanges are usually needed to achieve understanding—especially when talking about important matters. Sending symbols back and forth numerous times will increase the chances that communications will come clear.

Because *proximal* words—that convey *multiple meanings*—are used to express the *particular* message of this book, will readers misunderstand my words? Probably! But misunderstandings created by words can also be overcome by using *more* words.* Giving an extended explanation is precisely why books are written, so that the *particular* and *full* meaning of the author might be understood. Yet, if there is a message of truth expressed herein, . . . it will only be wholly realized *you . . . live true* (see page 127).

In daily conversation, sufficient understanding can be reached through a continuing and patient dialogue—a dialogue that double-checks assumptions, clarifies concepts, and interprets words relative to context. When communications are not careful, continuous, and composed, it's very easy to misunderstand . . . and to be misunderstood. Here is a case in point:

---

* I acknowledge many repetitions herein, but in order for Key Concepts to become KEY in the mind of a reader, redundancy is done by design. Effective communication and learning is facilitated via patient repetition.

The Bobby. In my garage, I have a small bust of a bobby—the informal name given to policeman in Great Britain. "The Bobby" is a paperweight that a drug company gave my dad, the original Dr. Moody. Because my son had a hard time driving the car into the garage in a consistent manner, I suggested that each time he entered the garage, he simply line up the car to the bust of the bobby; of course, I placed "the bobby" in *just the right spot* to facilitate that goal.

For the next few weeks, as my son drove the car into the garage, I noticed that he was veering substantially to the left of *the bobby*. I'm thinking, "has my son gone bonkers, what could be more simple than driving straight in on the bobby?" About two months later, I happened to be in the Garage—the scene of the crime—to witness the "felony" first hand. My son had parked in an errant fashion for the umpteenth time and was a whopping 2 feet left of the bobby. I reacted zealously, "why didn't you just drive straight in on the bobby?" My son fired back bluntly, "I did, . . . I'm exactly right on the bobby."

Faced with his firm insistence, I carefully calculated what his version of *straight in on the bobby* was by using a measuring tape. He was about half a car width *OFF!* I held the tape measure up, to empirically document his evildoing—a massive 28 inches *OFF* the bobby! He then proceeds to point to the *NOSE* of the car and retorted, "I am exactly and precisely, not even an *INCH* out of alignment, from the bobby."

I sighed as I realized the breakdown in communication. Exasperated, I explained, "No, you're supposed to line up your *EYE BALLS* to the BOBBY . . . JUST look yourself INTO THE BOBBY!!! Alas, he had lined up the *nose* of the car to the Bobby!" This was his *innocent interpretation* . . . of my *vague* parking directive.

As in all communication, none of us were "born" with a pre-knowledge of any assumption, expectation, conclusion, or tradition; they must all be learned—hence, articulated and taught in some way. The saying goes "you teach others how you want to be treated," and when you're not treated in the way you want, you have an opportunity to teach that person how to make adjustments. If you want to know how well you're sending out, . . . see what's coming back!

When others don't understand us, we must teach them how to understand us by explanation, elaboration, and redundancy. One of the worst ways to clarify communication is to GET ANGRY and IMPATIENT. Such an approach may capture attention for a time, but it *will* also "teach" others an unconscious curriculum: It will teach others to "avoid you" instead of "understand" you. Clear communication requires repetition, . . . much minding and re-minding! You will only know what you, or the hearer, have missed IN an ongoing conversation that continues . . . patiently. With that said, let's revisit the words of Friedrich Nietzsche:

* * * * *

Reality is captured in the
categorical nets of Language
only at the expense of fatal distortion.

* * * * *

If this statement by Nietzsche seemed shocking at first, you may now understand what he was *getting at.* You may also better appreciate the insight of Sir Francis Bacon: "Words still manifestly force the understanding, throw everything into confusion, and lead mankind into vain and innumerable controversies and fallacies." Speaking of *fatal distortion* and *fallacies*, here is another example of how *categorical* words cannot accurately point to *particular* things.

The Bag. A friend of mine forgot something and asked me to fetch it. She asked, "Would you go upstairs and get my bag?" Well, I went upstairs as she requested and looked around for something that appeared *bag-ish* . . . and could see no bags. I visualized the meaning of *bag-ness* as possibly the "brown paper" variety, or maybe the "plastic grocery" variety, or even the "book bag" variety—the kind made of canvas. I concluded, "nope . . . no bags in sight."

Frustrated with my search, I returned downstairs and requested more information—being the good communicator that I am. I soon discover that *all along* she simply wanted her purse. I impatiently panted, "why didn't you just say so in the first place, duh!" In her mind, I'm sure she *thought* she did "say so," but the words got in the way! While the word "bag" did inform my search into certain conceptual avenues—at the same time, in my mind—*this very word* actually excluded the very thing I was looking for, . . . the "purse."

The reason why she couldn't say what she meant is because the inherent nature of words wouldn't let her. Words do *constrain* certain facets of meaning that *enlighten*, but at the same time, they also *constrain* meanings that *mislead.* This is what happened when my friend referred to her purse as "a bag." Verbal and written language happens through a categorical set of symbols that are both *generally* and *multiply* defined. This is precisely why language cannot consistently facilitate *accurate* and *specific* description.

* * * * *

Words clarify and obscure in the same communicative stroke; . . . they allow certain meanings and disallow others—and there is always more than one meaning. Redundancy is required to overcome inherent limitations of language.

* * * * *

When you unwisely assume that you can "say what you mean," you set yourself up for frustration. Again, the process of communication is inherently inexact because the language we use to describe our world is general, while the world in which we live is personal and particular. Much meaning is lost in this inexact juxtaposition of *general proximal words* . . . to our *specific detailed world.*

We should NOT *expect* language to do what it *cannot* do: be specific! But we should expect ourselves (the meaning-makers) to do what we *can* do: redundantly double-check, patiently elaborate, and lend a lot of attentive listening!

Having a good understanding of the limits of symbolic language is helpful in becoming a better communicator, but even with this good understanding, human beings are *a mis-understanding waiting to happen* ANYWAY. The *best I can do* thru these explanations on *language*, is to minimize the inevitable *train wreck* of interpretation; and when that translation *train wreck* happens, then the *best you can do* is . . . continue in the conversation and be *patient* in the process.

* * * * *

Being Patient is NOT a function of symbolic language—it is a function of YOU. The question is: How will you ever endure much-needed elaboration, explanation, redundancy, and attentive listening IF you are not a Patient Person?

* * * * *

We return full circle to the most important imperative: Because you don't *just use* language, instead, *you are language*, the need for Changing Your Stripes arises again! Knowing the limitations of language may help you ask better questions of Life, but your ability to communicate well will be directly proportionate to the quality of your character.

Inescapable Impact Always

Self and others are intrinsically tied in communicative bonds that breathe meaning and purpose into Life. Human beings communicate in every waking moment; even if you consciously try otherwise, you cannot NOT communicate. Every act communicates, and every communication carries impact. Because linguistic relations are ever *impact-full*, you are tied to others in bonds of moral obligation. Human life is a constraining context of mutual impact, where *decisions of moral influence* are made continuously.

Even in silence, meaning is conveyed continually through bodily positions, gestures, and doings. Further, inward motives show on our face and in our eyes; others can *sense* our emotional *moods* and *motives.* Every subtle message of a *speaker* . . . and every delicate discernment by a *listener* supplies influence. When no verbal words are spoken and no particular intent or emotion is held, still there is *impact* received and sent solely through physical presence. Just *being there* provides to others an *audience* that alters *performance.*

The Heisenberg Effect. German physicist Werner Heisenberg, founder of quantum mechanics and winner of the 1932 Nobel Prize, maintained that it is impossible for a scientist to observe any living organism without necessarily changing it; observation alone changes the behavior of the observed. "The Heisenberg Effect" means that no one does, or can, enact the same *performance* before an *audience,* compared to unobserved *rehearsals.* Further, people need only imagine they are *under observation,* and the perception of *being observed* will inevitably alter behavior.

* * * * *

Human Beings live together in Bonds of Mutual-Impact.
This is precisely why "Life is a Set Up," . . . because
Living Life means: Inescapable Impact Always.

* * * * *

William James, who wrote the first American psychology text book in 1890, recognized that social relations inherently promote *perpetual impact,* stating that a person *"has as many different social selves as there are distinct groups of persons about whose opinion he cares; he generally shows a different side of himself to each of these different groups."* Contemporary philosopher Chauncey Riddle also acknowledged this human tendency to adjust responsively to each particular life-context; he maintained, "We create ourselves in every relationship."

Again, this *responsive influence* of behavior occurs not only through *passive* physical presence, but also by the *imagined* presence of others, and when relations become *proactive* the impact increases commensurately. In both active and passive scenarios, behavior is *mutually influenced* and altered.

This means that all *communicative* and *physical impact* will necessarily land on either side . . . of a moral divide: Every expressive, meaning-full moment delivers influence felt in two basic ways:

* Impact that *furthers personal fulfillment*, or
* Impact that *impedes personal progress*

These two types of moral impact are sent and received reciprocally. Recognition of this *moral context of inevitable impact* is reflected in marital vows made between man and wife: "For better or for worse."

TWO WAYS OF BEING

Through language, the self is inseparably tied to others through communicative necessity. Life's purpose *comes alive* via the meaning made in everyday dialogue. Human life means being engaged in an *ongoing discourse* that is symbolic, meaningful, and mutually impactful. Philosopher Martin Buber recognized this *inherent connectedness* and maintained that human relations manifest in two fundamental ways, *two ways of being:* "I-Thou" or "I-It." These *ways-of-being-together* are two ways of impacting others "for better, or for worse."

* * * * *

Every human act . . . has an impact.
By virtue of mutually impactful relations,
the human world is inherently a moral context.
We inescapably impact each other to either:
Betterment or Detriment.

* * * * *

Buber writes specifically about the "being" aspect of self. He described a human self as inseparable from others and conveyed that connectedness with hyphenated words: "I-Thou" and "I-It." By connecting two individual words with a hyphen, Buber symbolizes a unifying of *two separate embodied beings* into a *one unity of relational being:* "I-Thou" or "I-It." Buber's notion reinforces the previous explanations of the verb-self—a relational self located in the *expressive space* between two human bodies.

For Buber, "I-Thou" establishes the world of respectful relations. In the "I-Thou" world, the other is real before the I; the other is esteemed like the I; the responsibility of an I for a Thou is the bond of human love. "I-Thou" means that others are always empathically approached as an end, and not a means. In contrast to "I-Thou" relations of respect and regard, human beings can also live and perceive the world as "I-It." In this *way of being* and *way of seeing,* the other is not emotionally real to the I, the other is not esteemed like the I, and the other is a surreal entity to be used as a *means* for I. In relations of "I-It," the bond of human love is broken by self-serving action and intent. "I-It" means that self and others are entangled in bonds of anguish.

"I-It" is a *way of being* that manifests commonly in relations with strangers or infrequent associates, especially in the buzz of big cities; the "I-It" *way of being* can also appear in relations of family, friends, and ironically between those who call themselves "lovers." Within the "I-It" *way of being* there may be compelling physical chemistry and attraction, still the richest bonds of love are only realized . . . in the realm of "I–Thou." In the mutually impactful conversation called "life," *two alternatives* are perpetually possible, and *one choice* will make the difference between the best life you can live, OR something less:

* * * * *

As I face fellow beings, I can impact others to
their growth & betterment, in Bonds of Love, . . . I-Thou,
OR
I can "live" something less, and impact others
to their loss & detriment, in Bonds of Anguish, . . . I-It.
In every moment there is opportunity to Be-Loving,
and as I fail to embrace this Way-of-Being,
by default, I choose something less,
I "am" something less.

* * * * *

Because social relations are mutually influencing, human beings necessarily have *moral impact* upon each other in daily relations, hence the ever-appearing question: *"Will my influence upon others be for their betterment or detriment?"* All Human *influence* will either encourage the relational *Bonds of Love* and enhance the joys of unity, or embolden the *Bonds of Anguish* and further the sorrows of selfishness. By simply omitting acts of love, or by impacting others in a way Less-than-Love, we are relegated to the self-centered realm of "I-It."

In a world of *inescapable impact always,* we cannot choose <u>not</u> to impact others, and that *necessary* influence of *physical and expressive being* will manifest as either "I-Thou" or "I-It." Two fundamental Ways of Being that can also be characterized by the terms: Altruistic or Narcissistic,* and by the words: Empathic or Selfish.

Selfish versus Empathic. Because we experience our world from a perspective located within our individual bodies, it is very common for one's *way of seeing the world* to have a default position that is inherently selfish. Living in a world that is predominantly driven by selfish motivations explains this Old Testament passage:

> *"Although affliction cometh not forth of the dust, neither doth trouble spring out of the ground; yet man is born unto trouble, as the sparks fly upward"* (Job 5:6-7).

Living in the center of your world is to live selfishly. Selfishness IS the fuel that feeds the fires of human trouble; the "sparks fly upward" directly because of *selfish words and deeds* so routine in human relations. Comes the common quip, "how else can I live, but to live for my self?" This is where conceptualizing the verb-self, or the self as "be-ing," becomes centrally important. When we finally *understand* that the most vital and purposive aspect of self is manifest in our *way-of-being-with-others*, then an alternate possibility of looking at Life emerges—seeing the world through empathic eyes.

The importance of an *empathic way of seeing* will habitually *smack you in the face* during a marriage relationship. It is then you finally realize that *you are not the center of the universe*—instead, the universe revolves around your spouse (*wink*). If you *fail to acquire an empathic view* in marriage, a *decrease in relational satisfaction* will consistently correlate to your *near-*

---

* It is sociologically significant to note that as people move from populous cities to rural communities, it becomes increasingly hard to casually pass another person with un-acknowledging numbness. As people become more rare, they also become more valuable; hence acknowledging even a stranger is more common in rural locations—but especially in nature settings. Experiencing the beauties of nature fosters fresh feelings. Showing regard for others seems natural, when our "influencing audience" is . . . Nature.

sighted, self-centered vision. Yet there is another impact that will habitually *poke you in your egocentric eyes* if you don't *get a clue* from your spouse; eventually, you may *open empathic eyes* as children are born into your family and the vulnerable innocence of a child breaks down selfish barriers. This *empathic vision* gains further clarity . . . as children grow up and begin to behave badly. It is THEN that you may remember treating your own parents poorly, and you empathically feel as your parent felt—you are finally able to see as they saw.

What goes around . . . comes around. Because Life is Self-Correcting, if you fail to *be empathic* and *see empathic* early on, then Life will smack you hard in the head till your selfish attention is captured; moreover, Life will keep on smackin' your egocentric head until you get the clue that it's time to Change Your Stripes and become a New Kind of Creature. A new you that is able to "Be" empathic, and thus you will naturally "See" empathically.

* * * * *

You See the World according to Who You Are,
Your Way of Seeing is inseparably tied to Your Way of Being.
A New World unfolds to view through Changing Your Stripes
and Becoming a New Kind of Creature.

* * * * *

One way of mentally dislodging *Self* from the chronic rut of *Me-Centered-Seeing* is to realize that the *Animal You Are* is not only an "I" to numerous "others," but also an "other" to numerous "I's." To remember this "out of body" perspective is to *taste* the sweet fruits of empathy, and *desire* the rich relations of love—and with "desire," . . . a seed is sown.

But more than a *change of mind* is required to become empathic. You cannot change your mind and your connected way of seeing, until you first experience a *Change of Heart*, and that vital change happens EXCLUSIVELY through . . . the redeeming power of the Creator. The metamorphosis of Changing Your Stripes does not happen through *mind power*, but through *His Power*—as we yield our selfish will . . . to His Loving Ways.

Whether you acknowledge it or not, *who you are* IS most fundamentally manifest by the *selfish* or *empathic* intents of your heart. Recalling the words of Jesus, *"From the abundance of the heart, the mouth speaketh."* Just as the mouth speaks according to the conditions of one's heart, it also follows that from the *abundance of the heart, the mind thinketh and the eyes seeth.*

Your intent of heart determines your *way of being with others*, and thus your way of *seeing the world* as well. As Stephen Covey states, "You don't see the world as it is, you see it according to who you are." Thus, you do not perceive your world as raw *facts* only—facts do not speak for themselves, they require interpretation. It is according to your *Acts*—whether empathic or selfish—that you *bring to* the *Facts* of your world . . . a particular *perception* and *interpretation.*

* * * * *

I bring to my world, perceptions of dismay and darkness,
because of the darkness within me. I see and
experience my world with anxiousness,
because of my own inner anguish;
I see falsely, . . . because I am false.
My worldview Changes . . . as I Change.
As I choose Love, I see a World that is only
seen and experienced through the eyes of Love:
A vibrant & exciting World full of Hope & Opportunity.

* * * * *

When you are *being empathic* you are not only *being Loving*, your very *Being IS Love*, . . . and *Being Love* is the highest attainment of existence and purpose. Human *Being* has its richest fulfillment within the relational *Bonds-of-Love*. The *verb* aspect of self—human *be-ing*—transcends the boundaries of an individual body and is expressed in the *space-between-two-bodies. Be-ing* happens at the heart of each and every relationship. Without others to "be-with," human *be-ing* cannot . . . "be." Leonardo De Cresenzo conveyed this inseparable synergy with these words:

* * * * *

"We are each of us angels with one wing,
and can only fly embracing each other."

* * * * *

We literally require each other in order to "be," and because of this *bond*, we face one another in an inherent stance of moral obligation. Mother Teresa taught: "If we have no peace, it is because we have forgotten that we belong to each other." How we are *"being-with"* others—our *way of being*—is the most important facet of *self* and the most essential expression of existence.

THE LOOKING GLASS SELF

In the early 1900's, social psychologist Charles Horton Cooley proffered a theory called "the Looking Glass Self." This view of self is different from the *self* I've previously characterized: The *self* manifest as both *body* and *being,* a *self* that is tangible, touchable, lives in earthly locations, and is expressed within specific human relations. In contrast, Cooley's Looking Glass Self represents the emergence and maintenance of self-identity—or *who you "think" you are.*

Self-identity is not *tangible* or *touchable*, . . . it is *imaginary;* not in the sense that it is pure fantasy—for mental imagery does reflect real life to some extent—but that conceptions of self-identity are the mental machination of . . . *imagination.*

Cooley maintained that self-identity is formed from the reflected images that emanate from social relations. This means that one's individual impression of self develops within and manifests through human interaction: "There is no sense of *I* without its associative aspects of *we, they,* or *us.*" Thus, *who you are* and how you think of yourself is intimately and inseparably bound up in relationships. Human relations entail ongoing conversations, where motive and meaning move *back and forth* in responsive dialogue. Each self-concept is acquired and shaped in a communicative context; it is formed in the *reflected images of an interactive mirror*—in short:

* * * * *

You don't know who you are,
until somebody tells you!

* * * * *

As Chauncey Riddle reasoned, *"the self is a myth to the self."* People develop a *theory* of *who they think they are* based upon feedback from others. In his pithy statement, Riddle used the word "self" two times. His first mention of "self" refers to *self-identity*, and the second mention of "self" refers to the tangible, touchable *self as body and being.* It is who you *imagine* yourself to be—or *self-identity*—that is a *myth* to the self. The word "myth" comes from a Greek word meaning "tale, talk, or speech" and is defined as:

* *A story of such a nature as to explain certain customs, beliefs, or natural phenomena;* &
* *A person or thing existing only in one's imagination.*

People indeed develop a "story" that wraps around and supports *who they think they are;* a story that helps keep one's personal sense of identity and worth in balance. This *story about self* is what forms and *justifies* a person's self-identity—as well as self-worth or self-esteem—which in turn is a product pieced together by *imagination* using *meaning-full* fragments of feedback from others.

* * * * *

Who you "think" you are is really a Myth! You are NOT who you "think" you are, rather, Who You Are IS Your Bodily Characteristics combined with How You Are Be-ing . . . with Others. This Tangible Be-ing is directly discernible to others, but only available to You through secondary reflections in the Social Mirror.

* * * * *

Distinguishing between Self-Identity & Being. The reason why you can only develop a *myth* about yourself is because you cannot directly "experience" *how you occur to others;* instead, you can only "imagine" *how you occur to others,* and *how you occur to others* gets at the heart of *who you are*—your *be-ing*—this is the *verb-self.* This *self* is located at the *heart* of *human relations;* whereas, *self-identity* is inescapably located in your *head!*

It is true that others can only *think* of how you occur to them—meaning, the self they see in YOU . . . is reduced to their *imagination,* too—but their perspective of you, how you occur to them, is still basically different from your perception of yourself:

* * * * *

Others are in a primary position of direct access and discernment: what Others "think" of You is based upon First Hand experience; whereas, what You "think" of You, comes from Second Hand reflections gleaned in the Social Mirror.

* * * * *

Your *self-image* is like leftovers from the feast of directly-lived relations; self-identity is the indirect *second hand* product derived from how others directly view you—this is the Looking Glass Self. The "leftovers" analogy is deliberately given for a purpose: to suggest that concern for self-identity is very secondary.

Concern for "how you come across"—how you *think* others are *thinking* about you—is mostly a selfish endeavor. There is a better reason for gazing in the looking glass, one that is motivated by empathy. Thus, we have two basic motives for looking in the social mirror: One that is selfishly obsesses upon self-image, while the other seeks reflective feedback for growth of character.

It is important to *get in touch* with your *way of being* as seen in the social mirror; paying attention to reflections coming from those who live life with *Integrity*, for they will see you most clearly (see page 127). Reflective feedback coming from those who live with *Less-than-Integrity* (see page 196) can also be helpful, but most often, any feedback filled with anxious emotion says more about the source than it does about you.

* * * * *

If you want to know what you're sending out,
See what's coming back. . . . You will find your Self
in the reflection of relations with others.

* * * * *

The Self that appears in the *social mirror* is the only *self* you will ever know, with one *essential addendum:* If you expand the definition of *social* to its largest boundaries, there is a view of *self* that is also reflected in an *invisible mirror.* Sociality with spirit beings offers reflective feedback of two types:

- *Spirit Feedback of the most reliable sort, &*
- *Spirit feedback of the most deceptive sort.*

Said another way: *The Angel on your Right Shoulder* will always provide reliable reflections, whereas *the devil on your left shoulder* will ever reflect distorted and/or deceptive images.* While you may not *see* these spirit beings, . . . you *feel* their influence and *sense* their invitations.

---

* I say, "distorted" because some reflected images are completely false, and I use the word "deceptive" because other reflected images may be superficially "factual," . . . yet their end intent is evil.

The Search for Self . . . Solved. We are easily persuaded to think of ourselves as *individual entities* because our bodies are physically separate from others; thus, some incorrectly assume that the entire "self" is *completely contained* within the physical shell, as well. Indeed, bodies are separate in physical space, but the expressive mobilization of the body—our *be-ing*—is bound to others by a communicative bond that breathes meaning and purpose into Life; thus, this most essential aspect of *who we are* is best conceived as *Relational Unity*, as opposed to *Individual Entity*—for *Be-ing* requires the existence of others in order to *"Be."*

While the self is most obviously manifest by *physical attributes*, still the most important attributes of self and self-identity are located within *relational-unity*—the space between two bodies. This means that the aim of "self reflection" is not merely about an individual *you*, but about *you-with-others:*

* * * * *

The most important attributes of Self and Self-Identity are located outside your body within Relational-Unity; your Way of Being is the meaningful & expressive space between two bodies. Self-Reflection is best conceived as the examination of how . . . you-are-being-with-others.

* * * * *

The wisdom of seeing the self in this relational context is illustrated by analogy to written text. Trying to understand human beings apart from linguistic, expressive bonds within which they "come alive," is as futile as trying to interpret the meaning of individual *words* without considering the context of a *sentence* within which they are clearly defined; or trying to translate the intent of a sentence without an awareness of the purpose of a *paragraph;* or trying to interpret particular paragraphs apart from the *whole story* that ultimately illuminates a clear comprehension of all contributing elements.

Hence, the meaning and purpose of being human is understood by accounting for the broader context of all relationships—both seen and unseen. Because the most essential aspect of self resides in *relational-unity*, this means that people can neither find self, nor enrich self-worth, with a purely inward look. In this way, self-introspection is literally impossible! Individuals cannot come to know *who they are* by looking within themselves—there is nothing to see, only a couple of kidneys and a lung or two.

* * * * *

Looking within oneself to locate a sense of self is a metaphor and not a directly do-able activity. The so-called search for self is not found somewhere deep within individualistic realms, but is discovered at the heart of each and every directly-lived relationship.

* * * * *

The most important aspect of self—the *Self as Be-ing*—literally transcends the boundaries of the body. While the so-called *inward look* may aptly describe the examination of motives, yet each and every inward intent ultimately applies to—and is manifest in—the expressive "space between."

You will sense your *relational be-ing* in the reflection of the social mirror, as well as the invisible mirror. Gazing in the *looking glass* can occur for two motives: Selfish vs. Empathic. Listening to people tell you *"how you come across"* can be heard with empathic ears, for empathic purposes, OR such feedback can fuel egocentric obsession. The empathic gaze in the looking glass fosters increased character; in contrast, self-centered primping is counterproductive to the aims of self-esteem.

* * * * *

Obsessive thinking
about "how you come across,"
is self-defeating to the aims of self-worth.
A more fruitful focus, and a goal within your control:
Becoming Loving & True, and when you are True,
Self-Worth will naturally flow from You.

* * * * *

Self-Discovery Paradox. It is vital to realize that the so-called quest to "find yourself" is not accomplished by acquiring the flattering accolades of others. Genuine compliments may come as one lives life well, . . . but such are not the foundation of the most productive sense of *self*. The ultimate expression of *self* emerges as one completely ceases concern for self-identity and simply centers upon the quality of relations—focusing on how *you-are-being-with-others*.

The head-heavy exercise of trying to figure out *who you "think" you are* . . . is to begin wrong; it is a quest that fosters a self-absorbed existence. This is the great paradox of Self-Discovery: As one ceases trying to discover *self* and instead puts all energy of heart and soul into loving others, then the You that is True spontaneously appears. By simply *forgetting self*, . . . you *find yourself* and thus connect to *who you are* from your innocent beginnings—you discover your divine identity. Jesus taught *the way* to this supreme self-discovery:

* * * * *

"He that findeth his life shall lose it:
and he that loseth his life for my sake shall find it."

* * * * *

In this admonition the word "life" is used . . . yet the meaning of the word "life" is virtually synonymous with the richest meaning of "self," the tangible, touchable, specifically situated *Self* manifest as both *Body and Be-ing*—this is life! It is interesting to note that in the Japanese language there is no word that cleanly translates to the word "Self," the closest word is "Ji Bun" (Jee Boon) which literally means "life-part." In light of this more expansive conception of Self, consider this interpretation of the words of Jesus:

> *If you seek to find your self through self-attention, you will lose your true self, but if you lose, or forsake, a self-absorbed search for self, and simply "be" and "do" in the compassionate pattern that I have set, then you will find your self.*

The finding and fulfillment of self unfolds naturally as a person faithfully follows inner urgings to *be loving and true.* In contrast, the fruitless goal of "figuring out" in your Head how you "imagine" your *self* to be—in the eyes of others—is an empty, egocentric endeavor that literally blocks the richest expression of *Self.*

Self-identity is shaped substantially by feedback from the *social mirror*, especially in the growing-up years. As we mature, and strive to our highest fulfillment, our primary *looking glass* needs to be the *invisible mirror* that radiates reflections from our Creator; an *immaculate mirror* that provides perfect and reliable reflections for a transcendent purpose: that we might fulfill the measure and meaning of our creation.

* * * * *

In the Immaculate Mirror resides
Reflections to a Transcendent Purpose:
To Know as we are Known, and
To See as we are Seen.

* * * * *

An essential key, to being the best you can be . . . is *found* ironically, in a process of *losing*—losing the self-absorbed self. When we fail to grasp this paradox of self-discovery, we become vulnerable to vain projects of *image management.*

THE SELF AS ADVERTISED

Managing a mythical self-image is like launching a *personal advertising campaign* where the superficial product "sold" is . . . *"The Self as Advertised."* Personal "ad" campaigns can invest countless hours into crafting presentations for the eyes of others, with the intent of being *thought* impressive, or competent, or worthy. In schemes of image management—as in advertising strategies—typically it's the *sizzle* that is sold and not the *bacon*. When selling self-promoting *sizzle*, . . . beauty is only skin deep, definitely.

Those who sell flashy facades are motivated by the fear that *who they are* is not good enough. Insecure people require a *mask* to hide behind, and thus, they promote personal ad campaigns; only people who feel inwardly inadequate have a need to put up a front.

Self-advertisers advance a superficial image of what *they think* will be acceptable to others, and to monitor what other people are thinking, image-managers continually primp in the *social mirror*. Getting praise and approval from others is the gas that fuels egocentric engines; those who sell "the self as advertised" anxiously work to win the popular vote.

Self-advertisers are manipulators. The outward facade is manipulated . . . so that others might be manipulated. Carl Rogers said of false facades, *"In my relationships with persons I have found that it does not help, in the long-run, to act as though I were something that I am not."* And funny girl, Fanny Brice, advised:

* * * * *

"Let the world know you as you are,
not as you think you should be, because
sooner or later, if you are posing,
you will forget the pose, and
then where are you?"

* * * * *

If we fail to commit ourselves to honesty and authenticity . . . by default we put on a *mask of pretense* and primp in the social mirror, and to some degree, we sell *the Self as Advertised.* With vain gazes in the *social mirror,* we regress to a conceited exercise of grooming a self-absorbed self. We invest time, effort, and money into *the myth of self*, instead of investing heart and soul into *the Self that is True*—a self that is seen best in the *invisible mirror.*

You may be asking: *"What's so wrong about paying attention to myself?"* The answer depends upon which "Self" is getting attention: The Body-Self, the Self-Image, or the Verb-Self—the Self as Be-ing.

If complete self-fulfillment is what you want, the best questions need to be identified, and the best answers require our *committed attention.* Jesus asked a central question concerning the Self: *"What manner of men ought ye to be?"* And his answer: *"Even as I am."* The True Self appears as we cease to be preoccupied with self-promotion and self-image, and follow the compassionate pattern of Christ.

* * * * *

Getting mentally enmeshed in the myth of self
means obsessively imagining what others are imagining.
It means living in the ME . . . instead of living for the WE.
Being mired in the mythical self means thinking
about, what others are thinking about,
on the topic of . . . ME!
Narcissistic mental reruns ad nauseam . . . starring ME!
Living in this self-absorbed way, I live a lie
and one false facade at a time,
I feed the Self as Advertised.

* * * * *

Beyond *advertising* impressive images, people can also "sell" a different facade; strangely, a non-flattering facade. People can present themselves as persecuted, misunderstood, mistreated, over-worked, under-appreciated, disadvantaged, discriminated against, being a martyr or a victim. Of course all these variations have a genuine counterpart among people who are indeed disadvantaged, yet some find egocentric advantage in "selling" caricatures of *contrived* victimhood—or embellished and exaggerated caricatures of *real* victimhood.

Self-advertisers that sell "victimhood" are not merely motivated by insecurity or fear, but by an agenda that is accusing and self-excusing. In efforts to appear justified, they contrive a skin-deep facade to get the egocentric goal. When *victimhood* is "sold" for self-serving advantage, one of the "pay offs" is gleaned by getting votes! Seeking votes of sympathy is an *obvious exposing indicator* that *the self as advertised* is being sold. In contrast, true victims—who are also *being true* through their trauma—might *get sympathy* but do not seek it, their heart whispers otherwise.

When people live in *harmony* there is only one vote that counts: The vote that is cast in the core of one's soul. People who enjoy *inner integrity* have no need for manipulative masks or *superficial sizzle*, instead, their motto is *"be the bacon!"* In other words: be real, be genuine, . . . Be True! *Becoming the You that is True* is the richest realization of Self.

Recovering the True You requires a complete mask removal—whether that mask is of *Victim* or *Victor.* Recovery requires you to put your selfish ego upon the sacrificial alter, and burn it to ashes. *The Self as Advertised* must die for the True Self to live! So which Self will survive? Will it be the self of flashy superficiality . . . OR . . . the self of integrity and simplicity?

* * * * *

Agendas to push, reputations to prove
always on the go . . . busy, hurried, harried.
There is another way to live, there can be calm & flowing ease
where layers of complexity peel away, . . . the pace relaxes.
For there is no other place to be but . . . Here
and no other time to live but . . . Now.
There is nothing more important
than savoring the moment
with the ones we love.
Living Simply, . . . Simply Living!

* * * * *

Living Simply means living in the moment with all your Heart, wholly being in the "here and now," and not traveling somewhere else in your Head. Simple Living means not wasting *mental* energy through worry, suspicion, fretting, or fear. Living Simply means *losing* your personal ad campaign—the death of the self as advertised. Simple Living means being honest and straight-forward with others. Living Simply means *losing* the egocentric orientation of ME and acquiring the loving orientation of WE. Simply Living is located in loving relations: *"We are each of us angels with one wing, and can only fly embracing each other."*

False Advertising: The Case of Claude. Claude is a man who is extremely busy. He really doesn't need to be so busy, but he chooses to be busy for a reason, and it's NOT primarily to be a productive person. Claude is absent-minded. He forgets things on a consistent and continual basis. Instead of *owning* his tendency, he puts up a false front. Feeling inwardly inadequate, he has a need to sell *the Self as Advertised.* His personal *ad campaign* projects to others a slick polished image of being competent and intelligent, "a mover and a shaker," a man who possesses a quick and clever wit;

and guess what? He really is all *that* . . . and at the same time, he is absent-minded.

Instead of being *humble about it,* he decides to *hide it;* instead of *owning it,* he feels to *excuse it.* After all, being absent-minded undercuts the exciting image of being *a mover and a shaker,* . . . right? So Claude pushes forward with his personal ad campaign, championing every good cause that comes down the pike; he volunteers himself to worthy causes partly because he does have a *good heart,* but also to be seen as busy—so he can have a plausible excuse for being *forgetful.*

Forgetfulness is his weakness, and for Claude to have inner harmony, he must terminate the *"I'm a Mover and a Shaker"* ad campaign. The superficial self must die, so the True Self might live! Here are Claude's choices:

* *Excuse It & Hide It:*
  "I'm so busy, I have so many things to do, can you blame me if I forget a few things, you would forget a few things too . . . if pressed by so many important tasks to do!" . . . OR

* *Own It & Be Humble about It:*
  "I often do forget to do things; I even fail to follow through with my word, . . . I am sorry."

Own or Excuse: Clarity vs. Confusion. An honest admission, if sincerely offered, could open up the way for Claude to overcome his weakness. Honesty and Integrity naturally foster Clarity, and *lack of clarity* is precisely why Claude forgets. Just as the Light of the Sun enables visual clarity to the physical world before us, likewise, letting the Light of Honesty into the soul illuminates every aspect of daily living—to include increased clarity of mind, emotion, and remembering.

This is the irony of all image-management efforts: The very solution to overcoming the character defect that you hide . . . is realized in "losing" your personal ad campaign and coming clean. You are able to *overcome* and *recover* by losing the *cover* . . . you think gives you *shelter.*

A half century ago, Wang Yang-Ming described this dilemma: "The inferior man attempts a hundred intrigues in order to save himself, but finishes only in creating a greater calamity from which he cannot run." When you lose Life's inherent harmony by betraying your own intuitions of truth, you must face a decision:

* *Own It*, admit it, and be Humble about It, OR
* *Excuse It*, and craft a caricature & cover-up to Hide It.

So what will it be: Maintain *the Self as Advertised* . . . OR live with straight-forward *honesty*—the honesty that brings *clarity.* Because Life is Self-Correcting, correlations between *certain choices* and *resultant consequences* occur consistently. Those who *humbly admit* to their mistakes *live free* . . . and are *happy;* whereas those who *hide behind a rationalizing facade* will *lose inner harmony*, and thus will *not be free or happy.* There is a magical power—a liberating energy—that comes with owning an error. Owning Your Stuff *empowers* the process of *renewal* and *recovery.* When you can *own it*, you can change it!

* * * *

A fundamental choice:
Hide it, or be Humble about it.
Maintain a Superficial Self-Image, or
Preserve your Integrity of Soul.
Continue inner Confusion, or
Live in Peace & Clarity.

* * * *

In world history certain people are notoriously known for perpetrating crimes against humanity of monstrous proportions. While they couldn't "hide" their atrocities, history records how they tried to "justify" what they did; but you really can't "save face" by spinning a rationalizing story, and at the same time, humbly *admit to* and *own* your errors—it's either one . . . or the other. The same is true for harvesting the connected consequences of Clarity or Confusion—it's either one . . . or the other; like the futility of mixing and oil and water, Clarity and Confusion cannot coexist at the same moment in time, thru a single expression of be-ing!

On a daily basis, news media report of tragic mistakes* made by misguided human beings; the kind of mistakes that cannot be completely Un-Done, because restitution of damage is not mortally possible. Happily and hopefully, most mistakes that average folks make (sigh of relief) fall in the category of overcome-able and repair-able.

For most of us, our mistakes will *not* fall in the categories of *spectacularly evil*, or *stupendously stupid*, rather our mistakes will come in the category of *garden-variety goofy*—the dumb mistakes that we all make . . . at one time or another. Whether your mistakes are minor or massive, tossing *the self as advertised* is recommended either way—dropping the facade that hides *who you really are.* By admitting mistakes, you begin to Recover the You . . . that is True.

Maybe you're almost persuaded to come clean, yet . . . you have one final question echoing in your egocentric head: *"but what will people think?"* Answer: In this world everyone makes mistakes, and there are two kinds of people who will

---

* Some atrocities against humanity have generated such hatred that bitterness is deeply entrenched in culture and tradition. On days of commemoration, resentment for perpetrators is sometimes given more energy than empathy for the oppressed and annihilated. No matter how great the evil that was perpetrated yesterday, yielding to hatred and resentment today, pours poison into the soul. Ridding hearts of bitter emotions, and leaving all Judgment to the Highest Court is the way of Integrity and Honor.

appraise your errors. Recalling the teaching of Martin Buber (page 85), people who live "I-Thou" kind of lives, may say of your mistakes, *"there but for the grace of God, go I."* People who live to love, thus love to live, will feel to forego all judgment.

In contrast "I-It" people—the remaining audience to appraise your errors—will likely be so self-consumed with narcissistic agendas, they will have little time to dwell on your mistakes. Yet, they might find enough time to cast a brief barrage of judgmental stones, so strap on your crash helmet and humbly endure the hateful stones for a time; thereafter, enjoy the empathy, forgiveness, and love that comes from the "I-Thou" people in your life.

Long ago Jesus invited an accusing audience to cast a stone at an adulterous woman; however, the prerequisite for throwing stones was to be "without sin." Nobody threw a stone on that day, and centuries later there is still no one worthy—yet the most "worthy" don't feel to cast stones! People who throw stones of *accusation*, *retaliation*, and *bitterness* can expect to find a future day when the same judgmental energy that they send out . . . will return to them again. We honor our Creator as we leave *all* Judgment in his hands.

The Emotional Self

Human beings are emotional beings by virtue of having physical bodies that adapt levels of arousal to meet situational demands; human beings are emotional beings by virtue of having bodily arousal augment and impact *perception* and *action* in the moment.

Because the Self is inherently emotional, . . . you must correctly conceive the meaning of "emotion" to understand the Animal that You Are. This is not an easy task for two reasons: First, emotion is a multi-faceted phenomenon to which people *pick out* and *emphasize* certain aspects to the exclusion of others, and thus fail to perceive the whole. Second, the nature of language obscures clear communication; the very words we use to explain emotion also imply erroneous conceptions of its whole reality. Because emotion is multi-faceted, and because of the inherent weakness of words, there are dozens of diverging definitions of emotion:

* *Explicit* definitions found in the writings of science, encyclopedias, & dictionaries;

* *Implicit* definitions suggested in literature & media;

* *Assumptive* definitions held in the heads of humans, in turn, conveyed & reinforced in everyday dialogue.

Practically speaking, emotion is *understood* by the way people *talk about it.* Common folk come to understand the meaning of emotion by social osmosis: Definitions seep into consciousness one conversation at a time, and most often, emotion is mis-defined and misconceived by the implications of common conversation.

Defining Emotion via the Weakness of Words.

Besides the raw recycling of erroneous ideas through everyday dialogue, the meaning of emotion is distorted due to the limitations of language; paradoxically, the very words we use to *describe* emotion . . . are the same words that *distort* it. As we have learned previously, words are *general* and *categorical,* while the living realities, to which words point, are *particular* and *specific* (see p. 76).

* * * * *

The function of Word-Symbols is to describe or point to the Objects and Activities of Reality; while words do constrain interpretive meaning to fewer possibilities, still words are never Accurate; instead, they are ever Approximate.

* * * * *

This is especially true when it comes to describing behavioral activity that is in perpetual motion; the living fact of e-motion is . . . ever-in-motion, and trying to find just the right words to *precisely define* it is futile. There are no precise and *accurate* definitions . . . only *adequate* descriptions; thus, in shaping realistic descriptions of emotion, we cannot *arrive at accuracy*, . . . we can only approach *adequacy*.

Adequacy is accomplished as words *sufficiently* characterize real-world *actions* or *objects*. An adequate definition of emotion will describe *emotion* as it occurs in directly-lived experience. All adequate definitions eventually "land" on the solid ground of *tangible reality*, as opposed to "hover" in the *abstract air of mental constructs* and *intangible rhetoric*. In defining the word "emotion" we are not simply trying to replace one word . . . for fifteen other words; instead, we are trying to use words to describe a *practical visualizing* of actual *emotional moments*. While the word "emotion" does indeed represent *one category*, . . . it does not represent *one thing* or *one activity;* rather, it is a word that *points to* billions of emotional moments enacted by particular people.

For this reason, speaking of emotion in a *general sense* apart from a *specific human context* tends to mislead; again, it is in the *real world* that all definitions find an adequate end. In defining emotion, we must make sure to shape our words around reality, rather than bending and contorting reality to fit *words* and *definitions*. S. I. Hayakawa speaks to the pervasive problem of letting *rhetoric* used to represent reality, cloud our view of reality:

> *Words, and whatever words may suggest, are not the things they stand for, . . . education that fails to emphasize this fact is more than likely to leave students imprisoned and victimized by their linguistic conditioning, rather than enlightened and liberated by it.*

Expecting that the *reality of emotion* should parallel the implications of a *word*, is to conceive the *world* exactly backwards; whatever the descriptive character we assign to the word *emotion*, we need to allow the activity of *being-emotional* to BE what ever it IS. In every effort to understand the meaning of words, we are trying to describe *tangible, touchable reality* and to wrap our words around reality, rather than vice versa.

Hyperventilating in the abstract air of *ideas*, and being seduced by the erroneous implications of *words*, is precisely the kind of linguistic lovemaking that has given illegitimate birth to the illusory phantasm of *metaphysical essence.** The mirage of metaphysical imaginings is born whenever *noun-words*—that really represent *verb-activity*—are reified into *things* existing independent from the beings that conceive them.

Noun-Words that represent Verb-Activity. Because "emotion" is a noun-word, it is natural to *think of* it as tangible thing like a rock or a chair. In a typical way of talking, notice how language constrains us to think of emotion as an "it," and when we *talk about* "it" as if "it" . . . were an "it," mental conceptions of emotion naturally gravitate to a *thing-ish* state. Our cultural *way of talking* constrains us to misunderstand *emotion* (not to mention many other notions); therefore, to perceive emotional reality for what it IS, we must frequently translate *noun-words* that really represent *action-phenomena* from *entity* . . . to *activity.*

---

* Essence is the counter complement to existence; essence refers to ideas, meanings, perceptions, and possibilities that correlate to the existence of beings and things. Some assume that essence exists in a realm apart from the beings that perceive the ideas and meanings. By reifying "essence" into things, people also tend to endow "power" to ideas—i.e., "The Power of Love," and "The Power of Faith." Such erroneous conceptions lead to relinquishing personal power to a metaphysical "Easter Bunny." Even the noun-word "idea" really represents the verb-activity of thinking or Idea-ing. The so-called "essence" of an idea is simply the consistent conceptual category that organizes and represents particular aspects of "existence."

Consistently making such translations is a subtle mind maneuver that requires a paradigm shift; you literally have to de-construct decades of cultural socialization. Once you've made the "shift" . . . you will begin to notice—like a bride wearing a purple plaid wedding dress—how people routinely *talk about* and *conceive* emotion as if "it" were an "it." This conceptual error explains why many *imagine* that emotion operates independent from personal responsibility, and *assume* that emotional reactions are "caused" by other people's provocations.

It is routine for a *person-being-emotional* to blame others for the emergence of unwanted emotion with an explanation like: "I didn't want to feel angry and I didn't consciously choose to be angry, so it must be your fault, because of your offensiveness." Blaming others, for what comes out of you, is implied by the familiar flare-up: "You made me mad!" This fallacious conclusion is clarified by *the Division of Response-Ability Principle* (see page 17).

Mis-understanding emotion is further reinforced by the way words are traditionally structured within sentences: Generally, *nouns* function as the *subject* of a sentence; hence any *verb* associated with the subject of "emotion" will imply that "it" is doing the action inferred by the verb. By believing the erroneous implications of words, people regularly reify emotion into a "thing" with independent power, as implied in the outbursts: *"I was overwhelmed by emotion!"* and *"My emotions got the best of me!"*

* * * * *

Misconceptions of emotion are spawned and spread whenever the word "emotion" is the subject or direct object of a sentence. The reality to which the word "emotion" points is not an object, or metaphysical entity, it IS living activity. Emotion is a word to represent People-Being-Emotional.

* * * * *

Even though the structure of our language may suggest otherwise, *emotion* is not an *entity* that has power to *do* or *be;* instead, it is people that *do* and *be.* When emotion is correctly conceived, *people* are the subject and substance of an *emotional moment.* The truth is . . . "emotion" is just one of many *noun-words* that really represents *verb-activity*, but so I don't sound like a person from another planet—more than I already do—I am guilty of premeditated use of *noun-words* . . . that really represent *verb-activity.*

Here are some of the words that come in this category: Emotion, mind, concept, idea, integrity, memory, world, faith, freedom, love, and heart (the metaphor not the organ). These words—among many others—represent *verb-activity* * that humans "do" and "be" within a world context, yet we talk about them in the noun-form. While we must necessarily use our given language to effectively function in society, we need not be sucked in by the swirling vortex of *erroneous implications* created by words.

More Distortions due to A Way of Talking. Correctly conceiving emotion (along with many other world realities) is further deterred by the pervasive influence of what I call "science-speak." Common scientific discourse entails a *way of talking* that tends to reify *factors* and *variables* into "things" possessing causal power; for example, consider the seeming innocuous implications of the following science-speak assertion: "Depression is negatively correlated to High Self-Esteem." This correlation statement appears harmless enough, but the eventual implications of this *type of talking* absolutely reinforce an erroneous view of reality.

---

* The active existence of *verb-activity* is always mobilized and manifest through tangible things and beings. Verb-activity should never be conceived as an "essence" existing apart from beings and things. Every-thing IS either a thing, or a thing-in-action, else it is . . . no-thing!

Science-speak *talks as if* there is an actual "relationship" between variables; this *way of talking* implies that an "interaction" is occurring between scientific factors; thus, "Self-Esteem" is granted a thing-like existence, where "it" interacts with "Depression." This so-called *relationship* is no more real than the Easter Bunny doing lunch with Santa Claus—while the *scientific conceptualizing* is real, the literal relationship between variables is not.

The truth is that Self-Esteem, as a scientific variable, has only a general existence in a person's mind as an idea/construct/category.* Imagining that *variables* and *factors* exist as real entities that "interact" is an illusion sired by the implications of *science-speak*. The real referent to which the Self-Esteem variable *points*, is this: A particular person esteeming himself or herself in the moment. The directly-lived reality of "Self-Esteem" IS . . . the specific activity of *evaluating* oneself in the very moment of self-evaluation—to include *positive* or *negative* sentiment held by the self-evaluator. Similarly, the scientific variable of "Depression" points to . . . a particular *person-being-depressed.*

Disappearing the *science-speak* illusion involves continual translation from scientific terms, into specific realities; for instance, the Depression variable represents a category of consistent patterns manifest among multiple *persons-being-*

---

* Again, the word "idea" is a noun-word that represents verb-activity. I hate to put a "run in your panty hose," but here's the snag: Ideas do not exist, above and beyond the existence of human beings thinking them? Though I refer to "ideas" using the pronoun "them," . . . "ideas" are not really "thems," they ARE "the thinking"—the conceptualizing. "Idea" is a word that represents the activity of "thinking-about-something." Just as the word swim-ing better captures the in-motion activity of the word "swim," idea is better conceived by the word: idea-ing. Conceiving "idea" in this active way requires a paradigm shift; because the way of talking that you are accustomed to implies that "idea" should be a "thing," making the shift may be hard to do at first. Shifting to this paradigm means "swim-ing"

depressed, and the Self-Esteem variable represents the consistent patterns among multiple *persons-esteeming-self*. Here's an important point: The reality to which the word "emotion" points is always *specific*, and manifests in *particular* living moments as a *person-being-emotional*.

* * * * *

General Conceptions create a perceptual mirage
that hovers over a specific tangible reality:
there is no-thing that exists generally
Reality always exists specifically.

* * * * *

Undoubtedly influenced by the ingrained traditions of science-speak, our cultural *way of talking* creates and reinforces numerous misconceptions; for example, the way we talk about *love* demonstrates of how reality is distorted by the implications of words. "Love" is commonly conceived and *talked about* as a force or power; people speak of the "power of love" and the obvious implication is that *power* resides directly IN this "crazy little *thing* called love."

The truth is that *love* only comes into existence as people "do" it and "be" it. Yet there IS a power of influence that occurs as *people-are-loving*, but that power manifest through the *activity* of *being-loving*—not IN "love" as an entity or essence existing apart from *people-being-loving*. The same is true of God's Love: Power resides IN God and does not reside directly IN a "Love" that exists apart from God. The metaphor "God is Love" means that the *Being-of-God* is fully and wholly Loving in every expression towards His creations—particularly His children. The poetic phrase, "God is Love" *translates* to the simple reality of . . . *God-Being-Loving*.

Another similar misconception occurs with the word *faith*—a word that is regularly reified into an independent existence where "it" possesses portable power. Due to the implications of a *way of talking* about faith phenomena, the commonly coined phrase "power of faith," leads people to erroneously imagine that there is power directly IN an entity-essence called "faith." Contrastingly, the correct conception is thus: *faith* is a word that points to *people-being-faithful*, and in turn, that *faithfulness* invokes the Creator's Power to bless and empower *faithful-activity* according to His promises. Just as with the instance of a *person-being-loving*, there is also a power of influence that occurs through faithful activity—more specifically a *person-being-faithful.*

While praying in Gethsemane, Jesus spoke these words to his Father, *"Thine is the power."* The phrase "Thine is the power" is a *literal description* of reality,* whereas the phrase *"power of faith"* is a *poetic metaphor.* To correctly conceive living reality, we must perpetually discern between metaphorical descriptions and literal descriptions; we must perpetually rescue reality from the abstract abyss of rhetoric.

The nature of language presents many more obstacles to correctly conceiving emotion than most people realize. The following summarizes impediments to understanding emotion due to the inherent limitations of language:

* Because emotion is a noun-word that really represents verb-activity, clouded conceptions occur by failing to discern between word-ideas that represent *action and being* versus word-ideas that point to *object and thing.*

* Failure to distinguish the difference between *representation* and *referent*, . . . *symbol* and *substance*, leads to reifying the mirage of metaphysical entity/energy/essence, and thus, emotion can become a thing capable of *"doing it to us,"* instead of something *"we are doing and being."*

---

* The ultimate power of faith, love, light, and life are all centered in the substantial Being of the Creator.

* Getting stuck in a general/abstract realm of mental constructs by unwittingly granting *words and rhetoric* greater importance than the *substantial living realities* for which these symbols stand.

* Being fooled by the illusion that *separate words* necessarily represent *separate realities* (an idea to be explained later, page 123).

Making a Mammoth Paradigm Shift. To avoid being fooled by the false implications of words, a paradigm shift in the way we conceive our world is in order; a shift requiring frequent translations from the fallacious inferences of a *way of talking.* If we fail to get completely clear about this "shift," our cultural *way of talking* will continue to blur the distinction between *symbol* and *substance* . . . and confuse the difference between *object* and *activity.*

Our failure to grasp this superior paradigm will lead to the continued tendency of reifying words into *entities:* where ideas, represented by words, take up space in a metaphysical realm and exist apart from the human beings that "think" them.*

This major paradigm shift involves swimming against the constant current of erroneous assumptions that saturate behavioral science generally, and therapeutic approaches specifically: The idea that "thoughts are things" is one such notorious notion; a false assumption likely spawned by the thinking of Plato/Socrates, where consistent and perfect "forms" are *more fundamental* than the so-called "shadows on the cave wall"—or what we see empirically.

This means metaphysical imaginings become more important and *primary* than directly-lived reality, with this logic: mortality is imperfect and corruptible, but ideas are flawless and eternal.**

From the quest to discover the perfection of "the forms" comes the reifying of "factors" and "variables" and "constructs" that are sometimes granted an eternal existence commensurate to the Creator—or worse, in place of the Creator. Thus metaphysics *gone wild* becomes philosophical idol worship, as people are persuaded to put their faith in (for instance) the perfect *essence of freedom*—instead of the power of the Creator to make us free.

To get a firm grip on WHAT IS, we must persistently ask pragmatic questions of every word: What is the *reality* to which this *symbol* is pointing? What does this *Word* "look like" in the *World*? The answers to these practical questions will invariably "land" upon the solid ground of earth within two categories: *Objects* and *Actions.* This particular paradigm is not just a rhetorical re-arranging of words—it is not merely a word game—rather, what I am describing represents an enormous shift. A perspective that stands upon this premise: Reality is manifest by or through *substance* . . . or it is not manifest—it does not exist.

* * * * *

Everything that IS REAL is either
a Thing or a Thing-in-Action, and every
Thing or Thing-in-Action always involves
"the substance of things,"
else it IS no-thing!

* * * * *

---

* Remember, using the word "them" infers the wrong conception of reality, for the idea IS *the thinking*. Idea IS the *verb-activity* of thinking about a particular subject-category of reality.

** Similar confusion occurs with conceiving "truth." Is truth manifest through the perfection of conceptual "forms" that order empirical reality, or is Truth a word that points to the "existence" of He who is perfectly True? To read more about whether "truth" resides in the realm of *essence* versus *existence*, please visit: www.CallDrMatt.com/Truth.

The shift boils down to the constant translation of *essence-talk* to *tangible-talk*—or at least *tangible conceiving!* You may be saying, "I thought you just explained how emotion is NOT like a rock or a chair . . . yet you want me to visualize all reality in terms of the tangible?" Yes, that is what I want you to do! And you may be further protesting, "but emotion is non-tangible energy that I cannot actually touch, for how does one touch jealousy?" This is precisely where the paradigm shift is needed. True, you cannot touch *Jealousy* as long as you imagine and assume that *Jealousy* is *intangible energy*—but you CAN DIRECTLY TOUCH the *tangible substance* of a *Person-Being-Jealous.*

When correctly conceived, Jealousy and all other emotional flavors must be translated from the *subject* of a sentence (noun) . . . to the activity that a living-subject is doing (verb). People ARE the subjects that make the *verb* come alive; they are the "living-substance" or "things-in-action" by which emotion is manifest.

Here is an analogy that can clarify: Visualize the *meaning* of the word "swim." This word refers to an *activity* that is *done;* an *activity* that comes into existence as people or animals *do* it. Even though I use the pronoun "it" to refer to "swim," . . . obviously, the *activity* of a body moving itself through water is not an "it"—not a "thing." When conceiving the *verb-activity* represented by the sometimes-noun-word "swim," it is empirically clear that "swim" does not have an actual existence apart from the animal that is *doing* it.

Since "swim" is an activity that is *done*, . . . the word "swim-ing" more adequately captures the *in-motion* nature of this water *activity*. Different from swim-ing, "emotion" is more than outward physical choreography; it also includes inward motions of body physiology—*motions* that augment *perceiving* and *behaving* in particular emotional moments. Like "swim," the word "anger" is a noun-word that really points to *verb-activity;* this explains why William Glasser suggested that the word "angering" is a better symbol for acts of "anger," because the noun-word "anger" really represents a *person-being-angry* or a *person-doing-angry.* The word *angering* more adequately captures something that is "being done" and thus infers that people are *doing it*—now for the good news:

* * * *

Since Emotion is
an Activity that You Do,
then You are Response-Able,
and because You are Response-Able,
You possess the prerogative to invoke solutions
to Un-Do what you are Doing; otherwise, you empower
an imaginary Anger-Entity to control you!

* * * * *

With a correct conception of emotion, you are better empowered . . . to retain your power, instead of giving it away to an illusory entity/energy/essence that is assumed to exist apart from you—the mendacious mental machination of metaphysical essence.*

To avoid drifting off into the *abstract air* of "symbols" and land on *solid ground* of "substance," it is essential to remember that the *map* is NOT the *territory* . . . and the *word* is NOT the *world.* It is curious to note that one of the ironic outcome of formal education is confusing *rhetoric* with *reality*; to *think* that a word IS its *definition*, rather than a *representation of the real*, is a tendency reinforced by traditions of schooling.

---

* Reifying emotion into a thing possessing power is an outgrowth of the "Thoughts are Things" assumption, where there is an "essence-thing" behind every "thought." Traditional "ways of talking" tend to reinforce this erroneous conception of reality; again, much practical translation is required to rescue our rhetoric from "general" conceptions of *essence*, to "specific" realities of *existence*.

By implication, when a word (or group of words) is the "answer" on a myriad of academic tests, then *answers* can become the conceptual ending point.

By assuming that *answers* are "the pot of Gold at the end of the rainbow," students get stuck in an orientation of *answers* which in turn leads to the conceptual habit of hovering in the *abstract air* of "rhetoric," instead of landing on the *solid ground* of "reality." When multiple-choice-fill-in-the-blank education eventually culminates in graduation, some students are left with *answers* . . . instead of *knowledge*, they are better equipped to succeed on a game show . . . than in life.

Defining Emotion. To overcome distortions due to the limits of language, we must necessarily use more words/explanations to deconstruct false inferences. This is precisely why short definitions of emotion will inevitably impair an adequate conception of emotion. Consider the problems created by this tidy definition from a prominently published dictionary:

* *Emotion = "A strong feeling of any kind."*

This definition is distressingly inadequate because it simply replaces one word . . . for six, and leaves us needing to define the word "feeling." But as definitions go, replacing one word for another—or exchanging *one word* for a *group of words*—IS how definitions are done: synonym swapping. Obviously, exchanging the word "emotion" for the word "feeling" moves us no closer to an adequate visualizing of emotion as it occurs in real life.

Defining "emotion" with the word "feeling" is called a tautology, a circular definition. The tidy tautological practice of synonym swapping is also illustrated by defining the word "salt" with the word "salty," but at least in describing "salt" as "salty" one essential thing is accomplished: the word "salty" refers us to the *experience* of "salt"—which is where all definitions need to *land.* John Dewey, as well as Einstein, maintained that *human experience is the basis of all knowledge.** Better said: human experience is the basis of all *knowing*, for the *noun-word* "knowledge" really represents . . . . the *perceptual activity* of conceiving and comprehending the world.

This means, the best definitions of emotion—and "what is" in general—will take us from the unstable air of *abstract ideas* to the firm ground of *tangible reality.* Moving from symbolic *representations* to empirical *referent*, the "words" we use to communicate need to connect us to the everyday experience** of our "world." Along these lines, an *applied and practical definition* of the word "salt" might be:

> * *Go to the kitchen, find the white stuff in the shaker, sprinkle some on your tongue... that's salt!*

Similarly, to adequately define *emotion*, it is best to focus upon the tangible, touchable *experience of emotion:* Both occurrences of *you-being-emotional* and *others-being-emotional.* With this in mind, consider another definition of emotion from the 1903 edition of Webster's Dictionary:

> * *Excitement of the feelings, whether pleasing or painful; agitation of mind manifested by some sensible effect of the body.*

---

* Knowledge is another noun-word to represent verb-phenomena: "People-knowing" is the "activity" and reality to which the word "knowledge" points. But so I don't sound like some alien from Mars, I am constrained by custom to use the noun-word "knowledge." You see, when we try to more adequately represent the world "as it IS," we end up talking funny; thus, so we can understand each other—and not sound funny—we conform to a common *way of talking*. Yet at the same time, our worldview gets twisted as we assume that reality should "fit" the implications of our words—rather than faithfully "fitting" words to reality.

** Because parables paint a picture and tell a story that allows the listener to conceive a *practical visualizing* of everyday life, this is likely why Jesus used parables to convey the meaning of the principles he taught.

This hundred-year-old definition identifies only two facets of emotion, . . . *Mind* and *Body*. There are actually four facets to what I call *Whole Emotion*—which raises yet another reason why conceptual confusion commonly surrounds the meaning of emotion. Because emotion is a multi-faceted phenomenon, people tend to *pick out* and *emphasize* a single aspect of emotion, to the exclusion of other aspects. Defining emotion can be like the blind men who tried to "define" an elephant: each conceived the elephant in terms of the part he was feeling, i.e., big floppy ears, a snake-like trunk, a whale-like torso, tree-trunk-like legs, or a wiggly thin tail. Similarly, when speaking of emotion, people may talk in terms of just the part to which they are privy.

Emotion: A Multi-Faceted Activity. In addition to the emotional aspects of *Mind* and *Body*, there is a third aspect of emotion identified in most psychology texts. From his book "Psychology," David G. Myers offers the following three facets that combine to make emotion:

* *Conscious Experience: The way we Perceive the emotional moment. (Mind)*
* *Physiological Arousal: The way Bodily Feelings augment Perception & Action. (Body)*
* *Behavioral Expression: The way we Act in the emotional moment. (Behavior)*

By adding the context of *behavior*, we move closer to a more complete conception of emotion. The whole emotional expression of *you-perceiving-and-behaving-in-the-world-while-feeling-inward-bodily-stirrings* always occurs within a particular life context—not in a vacuum. What *you-are-doing* and how *you-are-being*—simultaneous to your *perceiving* and *feeling*—are ever-connected aspects of *Whole Emotion*. The wisdom of including *behavior* to the reality of *whole emotion* is obvious: The emotion of anger, for example, is notoriously known by its outward behavioral outbursts.

Indeed, an *angry* person is most often identified as *angry* directly because of observable behavior. The *whole-emotional-moment* encompasses what is *being-done*—realities of *expressive behavior*—to include outward *doings* and inward *ways of being.* What is *being done* (behavior) occurs in holistic unity with the happenings of *heightened physiology* (body) as well as *conscious awareness* (mind).

Because *conscious experience* is an ever-moving awareness of our world, thus "mind" should not be thought of as a thing, but an ongoing *activity of perceiving.* This explains why John Dewey argued that a better term to represent activities of conscious awareness, thinking, and perceiving are expressed in the verb-form . . . "minding." With a "verb" mindset as to "emotion" in place, consider this definition of emotion and the directly-lived visualizing it invokes:

* * * * *

Simultaneous to your thinking, saying, doing, & being,
the word "emotion" represents those moments
when heightened bodily arousal augments
and impacts particular life experience.

* * * * *

Whole Emotion. To conceive emotions correctly, it is wise to perceive the whole context within which emotion is manifest. Thus far, three (3) aspects of emotion have been identified, but there are really four (4) aspects that comprise what I call *Whole Emotion.* To introduce the fourth facet, and make our *conception of emotion complete*, consider the words of Candace Pert, from her book "Molecules of Emotion."

> *Measurement! It is the very foundation of the modern scientific method, the means by which the material world is admitted into existence. Unless we can measure something, science won't concede it exists, which is why science refuses to deal with such "non-things" as the emotions, the mind, the soul, or the spirit. . . . When I use the term emotion, I am speaking in the broadest of terms, to include not only the familiar human experiences of anger, fear, and sadness, as well as joy, contentment, and courage, but also basic sensations such as pleasure and pain, as well as the "drive states" . . . such as hunger and thirst.*
>
> *In addition to measurable and observable emotions and states, I also refer to an assortment of other intangible, subjective experiences that are probably unique to humans, such as spiritual inspiration, awe, bliss, & other states of consciousness that we all have experienced but that, up until now, have been physiologically explained.*

For those who have never felt the blowing of spiritual wind in this world—manifest as euphoric bliss, inspiration, and awe—they must wonder about the sanity of those who claim regular and sometimes spectacular experiences of spirit.* For the skeptic, my explanation of *Whole Emotion*—to include the aspect of spirit—is presented as a "theory" to be personally proved. The reality of spirit can absolutely be proven to yourself, while this personal proof is not instantly transferable others; others must directly experience the reality of spirit for themselves.

---

* The real existence of the "unseen" social realm is supported by a trainload of evidence: George G. Ritchie's book "Return from Tomorrow," and a thousand accounts like it, give detailed descriptions of the death experience; thereafter, seeing a living realm beyond this mortal one, and then returning back to life as we know it. The serious seeker of Life's meaning and purpose must ask: "Are these accounts merely the product of delusion, . . . are these people crazy?" Secular science concludes: Yes, these individuals claiming "death experiences" and seeing a "life after life" ARE indeed deluded, they are "hallucinating," for human life burst into existence via Big Bang, and "man" really evolved from dolphins; further, when we die . . . that's it! To which I reply: Who's hallucinating?

* * * * *

If the real existence of Spirit Influence could be empirically proven to others easily and instantly, then Faith would not be necessary; by Divine Design, expressing Individual Faith IS an essential part of Life's Purpose and Fulfillment.

* * * * *

For those who hesitate on this view of Whole Emotion, you may be saying, "why can't emotion be defined in terms of physiological energy only, why can't emotion simply be . . . the inner motions of the body?" It can, if that is the way people prefer to negotiate the word's meaning, but the best definitions will always hold up under rational and practical scrutiny. The fact is . . . there is NEVER an inner motion of body physiology associated to an everyday emotion that occurs APART from an *initiating perception* (mind); further, there is NEVER an instance of *physiology* (body) associated to an everyday emotion that occurs APART from a *living context* (behavior); and finally . . . there is NEVER an inner arousal associated to an everyday emotion this manifests apart from one's *way of being* (spirit).

The holistic view of social interaction absolutely includes the interactions and influence of *spirit.* The richest meaning of emotion is embedded within this total context; a narrow conception of emotion as "inner physiology" only tends to tear apart *Whole Emotion* as it occurs in real life.

Separate Words, but not Separated Realities. The distinctiveness of emotion is manifest in *life-moments* when *conscious awareness* (mind) is augmented by *heightened physiological arousal* (body). Because body arousal occurs in concert with the conscious awareness of mind, the aspect of *mind* is inseparable from *body* in occurrences of *emotion.* Mind and body are two aspects that happen together in one unified reality; they are only "separate" as *word-symbols* and as *ideas* that can be talked about separately. The same is true for the inseparable aspects of *behavior* and *spirit*; while they are also separate in word and idea, they occur in concert with activities of *mind* and *body* to make up *Whole Emotion.*

Because we can *talk about* aspects of emotion separately, a misleading implication arises and *Whole Emotion* is regularly ripped apart conceptually. Keeping all descriptive facets of *emotional reality* glued together delivers the best definitions and descriptions of emotion.

The table on page 126 entitled "Understanding Whole Emotion" shows a sequential flow of how emotion manifests: When bodily functions become heightened, that *physiological response* occurs because a prior *perception* has set the physiology in motion; if there were no perception to begin with, there would be no *bodily feeling* to follow, nor *behavioral expression* in connection to the initiating perception. While it is possible to conceptually separate the unity of *Whole Emotion* by a *way of talking*, the reality of emotion remains as it IS . . . undivided and whole.

* * * * *

Aspects of Emotion can be "talked about"
separately, but they do not exist separately.
Emotion is expressed in holistic unity:
Spirit, Mind, Body, & Being.

* * * * *

In every act of symbolic reduction—reducing *realities* to *words*—there is inevitable distortion. Remember, because the words describing *each aspect* of emotion are separate in *symbol* and in *idea*, we can talk about them *as if* they are separate, which in turn fosters the erroneous inference that these descriptive aspects occur separately—they do not! The *living activity* called *emotion* represents a plethora of particular *people-being-emotional*, enacting *emotional-moments* in a unified expression of Spirit, Mind, Body, and Being. Directly-lived emotion is always undivided and whole.

The Fountain from which Emotions Flow

The foundational source from which all emotions flow is not spoken of in psychology texts or in scientific literature generally: That foundational source is "spirit." Spirit is not as mystical as some imagine; it is no more mysterious than the occurrence of "wind." While we don't "see" wind (the *substance* of which is invisible air in motion) we do *empirically experience* the effects of wind all around.

Similarly, phenomena associated to the word "spirit" are as discernible to the senses as "wind." The consequences of *spirit* influence are readily *perceive-able* in the mortal realm, yet the direct *substance of spirit* remains invisible to mortal eyes—notice I said, "substance of spirit." Some conceive spirit to be immaterial, without form or matter, but this is not so! People who have visited the spirit realm consistently convey accounts of "seeing" some-thing . . . as opposed to no-thing; they viewed a world of *substantial things* and *embodied beings.* The spirit realm has been seen and documented by thousands who have *died*—observed and experienced this "spirit" realm—then returned back to mortal life. The spirit realm is real, and emotions flow from fountains of spirit influence.

To understand *why* we respond in emotional ways at particular times, it is best to ask a prerequisite question: "Why do you perceive as you do?" The truth is that *body physiology* follows *perception*, and the foundational source of all *perception* is *spirit*—both the *direct influence* of spirit, and our *way of responding* that is associated to that spirit influence. People perceive the world as a function of their "Spiritual Integrity." Covey submits, "You don't see the world as it is, you see it according to who you are." Because *who you are* is most importantly manifest by your *Way of Being*, you see the world as a function of two opposing responses to Spirit influence:

* *Be True to Spirit Intuitions of Truth* OR . . .
* *Betray those Spirit Intuitions.*

UNDERSTANDING WHOLE EMOTION

Human emotion is experienced and expressed in four aspects:

Four Aspects of: **Whole Emotion**	Positive Impact: **Betterment**	Negative Impact: **Detriment**
* Spirit Two Ways of Being:	Be True *Spiritual Integrity*	Betray *Spiritual Disharmony*
* Mind Two Ways of Seeing: (Perceiving the Stressor)	Compassion *Optimism* *Hopeful*	Contempt *Pessimism* *Hopeless*
* Body Physiological Response: (Morally Neutral)	Release of adrenaline Increase in heart rate Increase in blood pressure Increase in respiration Increase blood to muscles	Decrease blood to skin (pale) Release of glycogen Sweat to cool body Digestive tract slows Dry mouth & dilating pupils
* Being Behavioral Response: (Morally Loaded)	Morally Appropriate: Self-Preservation without malice Peacemaking & Love	Morally Inappropriate: Retaliation, Rage Anger, Hatred, Less-than-Love
Whole Emotion You-Being-Emotional-In-the-Moment:	U-Stress: Anxiously engaged in a Good Cause	Dis-Stress: Anxiously consumed by a Useless Care

You do not see the world as it is, you see it according to who you are - S. Covey

Your way of seeing is inseparable from your way of being - Matt Moody

It is in the darkness of their eyes that men get lost - Black Elk

That which you perceive as real, is real in its consequences - W. I. Thomas

* *Dr Matt Reminder: A Goal Within Your Control . . . Becoming Loving & True*

Spiritual Integrity *means* hearing and heeding your own sense of what is True. Spiritual Disharmony is a term to describe those moments when you go against your own Intuitions of Truth. Because a *way of being* IS a *way of seeing*, Spiritual Integrity and Spiritual Disharmony each come with an inherent *way of seeing* the world. The inseparable connection between your *way of being* and your *way of seeing the world* is taught in the New Testament:

> *"Unto the pure all things are pure: but unto them that are defiled and unbelieving is nothing pure; but even their mind and conscience is defiled."* (Titus 1:15).

The *way you perceive* any particular moment in time is determined by *how you are being* in that moment—whether of integrity or something less. This is why the Indian holy man Black Elk said, "It is in the darkness of their eyes that men get lost," and C. Terry Warner adds, "When we cannot see our way, we think darkness is shrouding our pathway, when really the darkness is in ourselves."

As we live in *spiritual disharmony*, we see a different world, we see our world through darkened eyes; hence, we *bring* to particular situations our dark definitions—not because the situation is dark—but because we are dark. Ironically, we get lost in shadows of our own creation, and it follows that dark emotions flow from our impure perceptions. For this reason "emotions" should NOT be followed.

* * * * *

Because emotions follow you,
you should not follow your emotions.
If you are being untrue in an emotional moment,
then the emotions that flow from you
only amplify your falseness.

* * * * *

Emotion: Life's Exclamation Point. Heightened physiology "kicks in" fundamentally to facilitate functions of fight or flight. When adrenaline flows, we are able to run faster and farther to escape enemies, or we might also be energized to fight more ferociously in defense of family and freedom. If one's *way of being* enjoys the harmony of *spiritual integrity*, then defense is done *without malice.* In contrast, if one's *way of being* is in *spiritual disharmony*, then defense (or offense) is enacted according to *dark motives* and emotions.

The average person living in the 21st Century does not typically confront grave decisions of fight or flight, compared to previous centuries of human history; in peacetime, having *heightened physiology* serves other useful functions. Emotional moments are Life's *exclamation points*—they give emphasis to our experience. Emotional moments *constrain* us to pay greater attention to things that need greater attention; this is true whether emotions flow from *integrity* or *disharmony*. When our *way of being* is in harmony with inner intuitions, bodily arousal will be heightened to prepare our body to meet *productive purposes* at hand; conversely, when our *way of being* is out of harmony, surges of bodily energy occur in support of selfish or *destructive purposes*—falseness is amplified by an emotional *exclamation mark* that signals a need for adjustment.

One of Life's Self-Correcting notifications comes via agitated and anxious emotions; in spiritual disharmony, the discomfort of anguished emotion is instructive, persuading a person NOT to do "something like that again." In this way, *negative* emotional moments *can be* useful "exclamation points" that help us correct our course, but they are only helpful if we *hear and heed* the obvious emotional warning signs; otherwise the experience of negative emotion is just one more needless occurrence of self-inflicted suffering. The saying goes . . . those who do not learn from past history are destined to repeat it: Habitually experiencing the same old anguished emotions over and over again, means we are not making the *right adjustments*, and if adjustments are not made, Life will keep sending *corrective signals*—till you *get it right.*

* * * * *

Life is Self-Correcting, if you are not doing Life right,
Life will make sure you are properly notified.

* * * * *

Learning the Lessons that Emotions Teach. Because emotional experience is generally instructive, it is erroneously assumed that *following your feelings* . . . is a sound principle—it is not! Emotional feelings occur as a function of how *you* perceive your world; therefore, if your perceptions are *incorrect* or *impure*, you will generate body physiology in support of a "false alarm." Clearly, fallacious feelings should not be followed.

Because emotions flow from your prior perceptions and choices, any emotional arousal that arises is actually *following your lead,* hence, it makes no sense to follow something . . . that is following you! YOU are the author of your emotions, and if your perceptions are skewed then the emotions that flow from you will be equally warped; therefore, emotions should not be "followed," but should be "listened to" for what they can teach.

* * * * *

You can trust Physiological Feelings to be a good teacher,
but not always a good leader; as a teacher, Bodily Feelings
are Life's exclamations that point to moments and matters
that need attention, what to reinforce or what to avoid.

* * * * *

You frequently hear people speak of how they *"really felt it,"* and thus, must *"trust their feelings."* This phrase illustrates how a *way of talking* can create an erroneous implication: that "feelings" have an independent sense of what to do . . . apart from you. When emotion is misconceived as an *entity-essence*, this leads to the confused notion that *emotion* is a "thing" that operates with independent *power*, and is strangely *capable of knowing* what to do in certain situations; however, the guiding "power" apart from you . . . that knows what to do IS the Spirit, and not physiological feelings. In the "Understanding Whole Emotion" table (page 126), note that bodily arousal is *morally neutral;* in other words, you will experience the exclamation point of adrenaline, for instance, in both moments of *Integrity* and *Disharmony*.

* * * * *

Bodily Feelings occur
in a morally neutral way. You
should not expect to receive moral guidance
from gorging glands . . . . or hopping hormones.

* * * * *

Emotion—as bodily feelings—are commonly confused with the influence of Spirit; happily, I am here to help you distinguish between the two. The so-called "feeling" that guides is actually a function of *Spirit* and not *physiology*. Bodily feelings may be energized in response to a choice of Spiritual Integrity and therefore emphasize and reinforce that positive moment. But it is your *Spiritual Integrity* that is the fundamental source that *sets in motion* your *Way of Perceiving* and thus, your subsequent *Body Physiology* and *Expressive Behavior*.

You should *listen* to your emotional feeling for what they can *teach*, but you should not necessarily follow those feelings, for they are literally following you; instead, you should *follow* inner impressions of Spirit. Learning to clearly hear the subtle whisperings of Spirit without being deceived is an essential discernment to develop (see page 255-259).

EMOTION AS ENERGY-IN-MOTION

Even though you *author* your emotions, sometimes the experience of emotion feels like something that is being *done to you*, as opposed to something *you are doing*, and therefore *something you are choosing.* You may say within yourself, "I know I am supposed to be the author of my emotions, but often emotions seem to erupt uninvited and unwanted, . . . so what's up with that?" Here's the truth:

* * * * *

E-Motions that are felt today, are not chosen Today;
instead, all emotional responses are set-in-motion
by a pattern of prior choices made Yesterday;
today's decisions set Energy-in-Motion
to be manifest and felt Tomorrow.

* * * * *

You are the author of your emotions; you *determine* the emotional energy you set-in-motion. Once that energy is in motion, it's like an arrow that has left the archer's bow: It's only a matter of time till that arrow makes its mark. *E-Motion* is also like throwing a rock: Once the rock has left your hand it moves in a course determined by the *chosen velocity* and the *decided direction.* Thus, prior decisions determine the course and destiny of the rock. Similarly, once *stones of emotion* are hurled, their ultimate destiny is beyond your control, *you* cannot call them back.* This means that when tomorrow arrives, we are literally an emotional response *waiting to happen.*

* * * * *

As decisions are made Today, your way of reacting
emotionally cannot be controlled Tomorrow:
Energy-in-Motion is already on its way.
You are destined to experience all the consequences
connected to Yesterday's poor choices
at some time in the Future.

* * * * *

Life happens this way because there must necessarily be a *connected consequence* to all of life's choices; otherwise, you would not be able to appraise the *quality* of your decisions. *Emotional consequences* occur as a direct result of your choices because of a governing law of Life: *that which ye do send, shall return unto you again.* While you are *free to make decisions* based upon your own rationale—your personal preferences and values—still, you are *not free from experiencing the consequences* of your choices.* Stephen Covey correctly contends:

* * * * *

Values determine behavior, and
Principles determine
the consequences of behavior.

* * * * *

To make Life Self-Correcting, the Creator intentionally attached clear consequences to every *chosen thought you think*, and every *chosen deed you do.* Consequences are the "fruit" that lets you know that a *chosen* "seed" is good . . . or bad; it is connected consequences that signal whether your chosen values . . . are valuable!

---

* While you may not be able to "call back" the consequences of your choosing, . . the Creator can. Some call this "Divine Intervention." Thru written accounts of "angels" appearing to prophets, we know that these beings can hover—they can defy the law of gravity. Thus, angels possess a power greater than the so-called "laws of physics." The power to hover, comes via our Creator—the Law-Giver. He is the One who empowers the natural occurrences of substance and motion in this earthly sphere. I personally prefer to call the laws of physics, "the descriptions of physics." Newton was merely describing what he "saw" as all physical things tend to gravitate to the core of the earth. By calling them "the laws of physics," some people may get the erroneous idea that there are "natural laws" that are higher than the Creator. Such is big-bang-like logic: Preexisting "forces" in the universe that existed prior to a Creator called Alpha and Omega? The Creator IS the preexisting "force" and "law" of the universe. As Jesus declared, "Thine is the Power."

* * * * *

Whole Emotional Reactions are the natural consequences energized from a Fundamental Choice that underlies all Thinking, Seeing, Saying, and Doing: The choice to Be True or Betray.

* * * * *

Without a whole understanding of what *being-emotional IS* and exactly how emotional responses are set-in-motion, people will be frustrated as they try to *control* today, that which is NOT *controllable* today. Misunderstanding the way emotions occur explains why, when feelings finally flare, the *person-being-emotional* feels like emotions were NOT chosen—it feels that way, because it IS that way! Today's emotions are NOT chosen in the NOW, rather they erupt via *energy-in-motion* sent in prior moments, days, weeks, months, and years.

Due to the disposition of character you've been shaping through a lifetime of choices, you are literally an emotional response waiting-to-happen; your propensity to explode with black and gray emotions is called PQ—*Provoke-Ability Quotient.* Emotional energy previously *set-in-motion* "squirts" out in those moments when the PQ threshold is maxed out. Since the PQ threshold is a function of *who we are*, everyone's emotional *react-ability* will be different; this means, if you happen to have a High PQ, then you can look directly in the mirror and meet the person ultimately Response-Able for your *propensity to pop!*

When people don't understanding the *PQ Principle*—as well as *Energy-in-Motion*—this explains why there is confusion about *who's to blame* . . . or *what's to blame* in the midst of an emotionally energized moment. When pressed with distress sufficient to provoke people beyond their PQ threshold, it is common to *blame* the *constraining situation* for the welling up of unwanted emotions. Curiously, this "cause and effect" conclusion WAS completely the case in childhood when in total innocence, children responded honestly and spontaneously to abrasive approaches.

Young children are like *thermometers:* when people are harsh or abrupt with a child, emotional temperatures climb just like *mercury* and a child may instinctively become upset and begin to cry. Even though the principle of PQ does not apply in the same way for children as it does for those who have matured to an age of accountability, children do have a PQ threshold: ever heard of a *colicky* baby? This kind of child is continually and easily provoke-able.

Nevertheless, because they have not yet matured and been taught principles by which to live, children are not completely *responsible* for what they do. When babies are small, it is the job of parents to do for their children, that which they cannot do for themselves; thus, babies are not able-to-respond (response-able) to their own basic needs of survival. Babies don't feed themselves, or change their own diapers, or keep themselves clean.

Unlike adults, babies are not yet capable of being response-able; oddly, some High PQ people try . . . to invoke the *"I'm-a-Baby-Alibi."* This rationalizing alibi that complains: *"If I had not been provoked as I was . . . then I would not have reacted as I did!"* While this statement may be factually accurate—at the same time—it also fails to acknowledge the pre-existing fact of an "adult" person's PQ; a Provoke-Ability Quotient that has been assembled by every willful choice from the age of accountability.

* * * * *

Prior to entering all situations of pressure or provocation, You are Response-Able for the condition of your Character; this fact of Self Response-Ability supersedes the intervening impact of Constraining Situations for explaining your eventual Responses and Reactions.

* * * * *

This is especially true in terms of accountability to the Creator.* You get to own ALL that comes out of you, one way or the other. You *Respond* as a direct function of your *disposition of character*—a temperament you have personally fashioned—and You *React* as a function of your *PQ*, a propensity for which you are architect.

Responding: *Rationally choosing a reply in the present, according to your condition of character.*

vs.

Reacting: *Irrationally squirting out emotional behaviors that are "landing" today, because of emotional "stones" thrown yesterday.*

Whether you react spontaneously . . . or respond thoughtfully, it is YOU who determines the disposition for which both *responding* and *reacting* flow. Like it or not, You act and react emotionally—for good or evil—as a direct result of *who you are!* If your life were a car . . . then it is YOU who is sitting in the driver's seat, and it is YOU who is driving your direction; thus, you are faced with a decisions at every *junction of constraint:* you can "own" what comes out of you and completely accept your Response-Ability for your *responses* and your *reactions*, . . . OR You can "rationalize" your personal weaknesses away, invoke the *"I'm-a-Baby-Alibi"* and blame *reactions* upon other people and situations.

* * * *

RATIONALIZE:
If this situation had not happened,
I would not have "reacted" as I did.

OWN:
If I were a New Kind of Creature,
a person of greater Integrity and Character,
I would not have "reacted" the way I did.

* * * *

---

* Which brings up another burning question: Would a truly wise Creator simply "create" human life—placing us in a world where there is inescapable impact always, where human choice inevitably impacts others to their betterment or detriment—and then NOT also include an "accounting" for those choices? The Creator IS infinity wise . . . and there will be an accounting.

Putting Positive Energy-in-Motion

Becoming a New Kind of Creature capable of patience and compassion, EVEN IF pressed by accidental or inconsiderate acts of others, is the project of Changing Your Stripes! So *who ever you are* today, you must accept your Self "as is" and work with what you've got. You get to "own" your *way of being* in all its variations, to include your present PQ—this IS the person and place from which you must press forward.

Putting a halt to your predisposition of negative and unwanted emotions is like stopping a train: If you put the brakes on right NOW, . . . the train will not stop immediately; instead, steel wheels *lockup* and the train basically slides via prior momentum, coming to a halt a few miles later.

* * * * *

Emotional Inertia pushes forward into your future:
Inertia energized by your personal pattern
of prior choices, and
if you "lockup the brakes"
on unwanted emotions right now,
anxious emotions will still erupt tomorrow.
All consequences connected to prior choices that
have not yet arrived, will "slide forward" into the future.

* * * * *

You will *squirt out* foul feelings until your "emotional train" comes to a complete halt . . . a few miles later; from that point, all future emotional responses will be governed by *new* decisions that put fresh energy-in-motion—the honest energy of integrity.

In the case of a *real train*, the stopping distance is about 2 miles; as for your *emotional train*, old undesirable emotional patterns may linger for 2 weeks, or 2 months, or even 2 years from the day you *lockup* the brakes. Your emotional stopping distance will be proportionate to:

* *The length of time you've been feeding and reinforcing a negative emotional pattern.*
* *Your commitment to completely cease supplying negative energy to old and unwanted emotions.*
* *Your resolve to put fresh Energy-in-Motion today, and each new day thereafter—honest and loving energy.*
* *The extent to which you yield to your own Inner Guidance, compliments of the Creator.*

Changing the fundamental core of your character requires complete commitment. If it were easy to do . . . then everyone would be doing it, but everyone is NOT doing it and the world is saturated in selfishness and misery. Changing Your Stripes is a goal taken up by the few who would fulfill the measure of their creation, according to the Creator's grand design.

The Challenge of Changing Your Stripes is like climbing a mountain: The pull of gravity and your own weak muscles make this lofty climb more difficult, but with *persistent pushing* against the resistance of steep slopes, muscles grow to meet demands. The gravity that tries to drag you down is like the dogged situational constraints that inevitably and always impact; the steep slopes of adversity place a heavy load on your character, but as you persistently *press forward*—like the muscles in your body—strength of character will increase.

In the mountain-climb of life a peculiar paradox appears: obnoxious and ornery people actually do us a favor by providing a steep challenge. *Life is a Set Up!* Get used to it, get over it, and get on with it! Pick up your pack and start climbing upward, for it is through each pressing and stressing constraint that we come to know the kind of character we presently possess; thus we see more clearly the corrections that are called for. As we make those corrections, we ascend to the mountain summit where clear-headed, whole-hearted euphoria is enjoyed—the heights of happiness! The best life is lived at Higher elevations.

* * * * *

Character increases like the muscles of the body: pressing through heavy moments of hardship and holding up against the weight of opposition, produces an enlarging and building effect.
Integrity is forged in the fires of affliction:
the challenge of Life is to be good, even if things are bad;
Strength of Character is produced & proven at the edge of adversity.

* * * * *

Strength of character does not happen by default, by simply avoiding tough times; avoidance makes one weak, like a lazy, lounging "couch potato" gets weak and fat by *avoiding* exercise and good nutrition. To win the highest prize, Life's many challenges must be met head on.

If you are only *good* when situations are *good*, then when situations become *bad*, your most likely *course* is that of *least resistance*—wherever *bad* waters are drifting! In life, you either navigate faithfully through rough waters . . . or allow your direction and destiny to be determined by wind and waves. You are either at the *helm* of a sturdy *ship* steering straight through the storm or you are a passive passenger in a little boat with no rudder or sail, . . . floating wherever turbulent currents take you.

Turbulent Waters

By Matt Moody

All boats float equally well in still waters,
but when waters are rough,
small boats are vulnerable
and sometimes sink!
It is easy enough to float along in life when waters are still.
But in times of trouble and turbulence, it is then
we see the size of our character
and learn how large or small we are.

The purpose of Life is not to avoid troubled waters,
but to navigate them faithfully,
with patience and compassion.
Life's problems are not solved by running away,
or by going around, but by facing . . . straight on.
To master a difficulty, we must go through it!
A path with no obstacles provides no test of character.
Those who would win the prize must be proven.
It is not how troubled the sea, but how steady the pilot.
It matters not the comparative point in the journey,
but whether we are facing the right direction,
and making unwavering progress.
And the direction we must face, in every case . . . is Love.
Mother Teresa taught:
"We cannot do great things,
only small things with great love."
In easing another's heartache, we forget our own.
Life's richest reward is not paid in silver or gold,
but in fortitude forged
as we faithfully travel through troubled waters.
Gibran wrote: "Our pain carves out a larger space for love to fill."
Without a tear in our eye,
we could not see the beauties of a rainbow.
So be glad, as you sail unsettled seas
knowing that your greatest reward
is your own becoming:
Becoming a more wise and wonderful you!
Recovering the You that is True
Life is a journey wherein we chart a course
toward Light and Love,
or allow wind and waves
to decide a lesser destiny
along the course of least resistance.
Boats of all size float equally well in still waters.
But it is the bigger boats that survive stormy seas,
while small ships sink in the same rough water.
And so we must be Large,
Large in Character,
Large in Love.

The Set of the Sail

By Ella Wheeler Wilcox

One ship sails east and another sails west
With the self-same winds that blow.
'Tis the set of the sail and not the gale
Which determines the way they go.
As the winds of the sea are the ways of fate
As we voyage along through life,
'Tis the set of the soul that determines the goal,
And not the calm or the strife.

~ 3 ~

Solutions:

Recovering the True You

FROM THE HEART, NOT THE HEAD!

The purpose of the first two chapters of this book is to expand your understanding of Self and Situation—replacing erroneous assumptions with reliable realities—and most importantly, make you aware of the principles that facilitate fulfillment. In the search for true principles, it is well to remember G.K. Chesterton's guiding insight: *"An open mind, like an open mouth, has a purpose: to close on something solid."*

If the principles presented herein seem sound and solid, if they ring with a resonant chord within, then prove them against your directly-lived experience. If they hold up, if they work and bear fruit, then it is wise to become *solid-minded* and committed to these principles.

Being open-minded is useful to a point, but if you're too *open-minded* . . . your brains will fall out and that would be bad! So, I invite you to become increasingly LESS *open-minded* and progressively MORE *solid-minded* about principles that bear pragmatic fruit. Being solid-minded means sending your roots deep into the fertile soil of True Principles; it means building your life upon the firm foundation of Integrity, . . . so when the winds and the rains come, you will not be moved. You don't have to take my word for it. The proof is in the pudding: Realistic results will reveal . . . the principles around which you should "close your mind."

The transformation called "Changing Your Stripes" requires a change in your way of thinking—a paradigm shift! But the truth is, you can't change your mind using the *same mind* that needs changing! Strategies and techniques initiated from the *Head* cannot bring about a fundamental change from your core—a genuine change of *Heart*.

You can only change your *way of thinking* when you change your *way of being*, and changing *who you are* is a *metamorphosis of character* that initiates from the *Heart* and not the *Head*. An Old Testament Proverb encourages:

* * * * *

"Keep thy heart with all diligence;
for out of it are the issues of life."

* * * * *

Changing Your Stripes occurs from your *Core* and is not merely *Cosmetic*. Changing Your Stripes is more a matter of *Faith* than of *Figuring*. Nevertheless, you will need to engage your *head* long enough to read the words in this book; thereafter, I invite you to live *unconsciously*, . . . flowing with heart-felt intuitions.

If YOU Can Own It, YOU Can Change It!

A critical key to becoming the best you can be, . . . begins by owning all your *Response-Ability*. This central commitment sets in motion the potentials for Changing Your Stripes and Recovering the True You. Being response-able means that *if* you are excite-able or anger-able or drive-able-up-the-wall-able, you get to "own" all your *abilities* to *respond* and *react.** This is your Response-Ability: All the thoughts, words, and deeds that you are predisposed to thinking, saying, and doing, combined with all the emotional tone and intention that infuse those thoughts, words, and deeds . . . are all yours. Further, the *responses* and *reactions* that come out of you under compelling constraints *reveal the core of your character.*

* * * * *

The willingness to own
Response-Ability for your
thinkings, feelings, and doings
is a Foundation from which
Change can occur

* * * * *

By accepting the explanations of Self and Situation herein, you will be accepting greater Response-Ability than ever before. As the paradigm is understood completely, you will eventually own response-ability for ALL that comes from you—to include every inner movement of mind and emotion (this will be your biggest challenge). You get to own everything except the bodily bumps and bruises, and tangible intrusions caused by outside physical forces. Even then, you get to own the decisions that *may have* put you in the wrong place at the wrong time; the dumb decisions that set up the possibility of physical harm in the first place.

Being in the wrong place at the wrong time sometimes happens randomly and unwittingly; on the other hand, it also occurs as a direct function of a history of bad decisions. Swallow hard and be humble, *YOU* get to *own* your past pathetic patterns of choosing too: the poor choices that put you in a pickle, and continue to keep you pickled—can you say "energy-in-motion?"

---

* The word "react" represents unconscious, knee-jerk behavior. Reactions are NOT chosen in the moment; instead, they "squirt" out . . . as people pass beyond their P.Q. threshold. Provoke-Ability could also be termed React-Ability, Knee-Jerk-Ability, or Emotional-Squirt-Ability.

When bad things happen to your body thru no culpable contribution from you, then you experience the hardships of "Situational Suffering"—a *cross to bear* akin to Viktor Frankl's incarceration in Nazi death camps. But EVEN IF you are crushed by the cruel boot of Situational Suffering (page 22), you still possess the "final freedom" to choose *responses* of heart, mind, and soul—this is Inner Liberty!

As you accept more *response-ability,* you open up yourself to greater personal fulfillment. You are free to grow in strength of character and are free to *set-in-motion* the energy of integrity. So how high, do you want to fly? How wonderful do you want to be? The more *response-ability* you accept today, the more you empower the process of *Changing Your Stripes* tomorrow. Greater freedom always comes with greater *response-ability.*

Response-ability means: "Owning your stuff!" If you can't own it, you can't change it! And if you can't change it—you're stuck! The opposite of being stuck is *living free!* Living free IS living without excuses. "No more excuses" means that YOU are response-able for all the *motives*, *emotions*, and *actions* that come from you. The Division of Response-Ability is drawn:

* * * * *

If It comes out of You, . . . It is Yours!

* * * * *

As you get clear on the difference between *Cause* versus *Constraint*, you realize that responses of heart, mind, and soul are never *caused* by outward abuses to your body. Whatever inner *response* or *reaction** that comes out of you *in reply* to the most terrible torment, is still an *answer* authored by you! Committing to the process of *Changing Your Stripes* means wholeheartedly receiving and wholistically living: *The Division of Response-Ability Principle.*

Because *you* can only directly change *you*, all changes in your life must begin with *you.* You can't directly change another person's behavior, but *you can influence* their actions and decisions by *changing your approach.* You can't directly change undesirable societal or political situations either, but *you can change your attitude* about them; *you can also vote* for leaders and legislation that will effect desired change. Thus, *you* can respond *positively and proactively* to all people in all places, even responding *productively* to situations beyond your direct control.**

We wallow in weakness when we try to blame other people or situations for the *responses* that come out of us. While we may point to a constraining situation to *Explain* the *Set Up* scenario to which we have fallen prey, we cannot lean upon those situations to *Excuse* our bad behavior—we must own our bad!

* * * * *

You can Blame Others for creating Constraints, but you must Blame Yourself for your Responses to them.
Life is a Set Up. Life is Constraining.
If You would live life well
You will Own all your Responses
and eventually Hone those Responses
toward Compassion, and away from Contempt.

* * * * *

---

* A "response" is rationally chosen in the here and now, whereas a "reaction" is what comes out of you today, because of Energy-in-Motion that YOU set-in-motion yesterday, by either a rational choice or a reactive choice. And if today's Emotional Energy "squirts" out because of a prior "reactive choice," thus you can understand how reactive choices are self-perpetuating. This is the very cycle that constitutes habitual behavior and in its extreme manifestations . . . the cycle of addictive behaviors. The term "reactive choice" is an oxymoron, but I use it to emphasize that even your unconscious behaviors belong to YOU. Unconscious behavior flows from Conscious choices made yesterday, thus "reactive choices."

** For more information about three types of problems—direct-control, indirect-control, and non-control—and how you can respond proactively to each type, visit www.CallDrMatt.com/3Problems

You DO your Dis-Eases. Certain psychological paradigms for explaining *why you do what you do* offer enticing *excuses* for bad behavior. Here are a few: "It's not your fault because you're Bi-Polar," or "You're not responsible for acting whack-o because you *have* Obsessive Compulsive Disorder," or "You can't help yourself, because you *have* Attention Deficit Disorder."

In this world, there are millions of people paying *good* money for *bad* psychological service; specifically, people who are paying to be diagnosed and labeled as HAVING a Disorder—when they don't really *have* it, they're *doing* it! Since the Mental Illness Paradigm maintains that you GET *mental* disease, like you GET Malaria, of course you would need a prescription of pills to cure the assumed *biological* cause—it's not your fault, it's just bad biology!

For those diagnosed with disorders, it may be a fact that life is *dis-stressing* and personally *dis-pleasing*, in other words *life is not easy*—it's *Dis-Easing*. Welcome to earth: Life IS a Set Up! The vast majority of people diagnosed as HAVING a mental disorder are being misled by what is called the "medical model" of mental illness: that the *mental* malady has a *physical* cause, a *biological* origin, apart from any choice-making input from you.

The bitter truth for most people behaving badly and feeling foul IS that they themselves have directly contributed to their so-called "mental disease," and without their *direct donation to the cause*, they wouldn't be *dis-eased*—instead, they would HAVE happiness, or at very least . . . Inner Peace. To assume that all *diagnosed mental disorders* initiate and perpetuate like *biological diseases* undercuts a key principle to personal recovery: Owning your Response-Ability.

While behavioral patterns may well fit into categories of disorder descriptions (via Diagnostic Statistical Manuals of Mental Disorders) here's the reality: You don't really HAVE Bi-Polar or Attention Deficit Disorder, as much as you DO Bi-Polar and you DO . . . A.D.D.—just as you DO a plethora of other Dis-Ordered patterns of thinking and actir.g. But here's the good news: Because you DO them, you . thus empowered to UN-DO them; it is counterproductive to the cause of *recovery*, to think otherwise!

If this is not the reality of the world for most people, THEN pill popping IS the only way out. After all, how else would you get rid of a Malaria-like disease? Certainly not by *talking* your way out via interventions of *counseling* or *therapy*. Bottom line: IF you can't fully accept Response-Ability for ALL intents, actions, and emotions that come out of you—plus ALL the Energy-in-Motion that continues to come out of you because of yesterday's pattern of choices—THEN when faced with *disorder-like reactions*,* you must surrender yourself to the second-rate solution of *pill popping*. It's easy and effortless, "why cope, when you can dope!" This largely explains the motivation behind a nation dizzy on drugs.

But Pill Popping presents a problem. As you *temporarily* "escape" from misery through a drug-induced dream, when you eventually "wake up" from altered states, . . . life is patiently waiting for you—right where you *left* it! This means you must inevitably confront the challenge of Changing Your Stripes sooner, or later. Finding *real relief* NOW instead of LATER, by confronting the *root cause*, IS a superior approach.

Those who have taken antidepressants report a common experience: One person described it as *"being dead, with a smile on my face."* Another said: *"all my problems were still there, but I didn't care."* Another called it being *"in a neutral zone with no lows of sadness, but no highs of happiness either."*

---

* Reactions that squirt out of you—in ways described by "DSM" dictionaries—are reactions that erupt because of an entrenched pattern of prior choices that are locked into a self-perpetuating cycle: Each choice sends Mental, Emotional, and Behavioral Energy-in-Motion that, in turn, squirts out even more "reactive choices." This is exactly "why" you act and react whack-o: Your P.Q. threshold has become so easily breached, that it is extremely hard for you to make rational, non-reactive choices to escape the cycle.

In addition to merely delaying real relief to a future day, some antidepressant drugs *may* even constrain reactive side effects that lead to a worse mental condition than before.* Such was the account of a client who remarked, *"taking anti-depressants sent me into an out-of-control mania far more destructive than depression."* Negative side effects like this explain why a certain Law Firm made the following TV offer:

> *"If you've been injured by someone who had a violent outburst while taking any of these drugs: . . . ZOLOFT, PAXIL, EFFEXOR, PROZAC . . . you may be entitled to a monetary settlement."*

While these drugs may temporarily "mask" feelings of anxiety and depression, at the same time, they may *exacerbate* worse consequences than the initial condition. In a highly publicized court case, a "Zoloft Defense" was presented for a teen-age boy charged with the murder of his grandparents. The jury didn't buy the Zoloft Defense and the boy was eventually convicted. The question is to what extent did this drug *constrain* and *mitigate* the boy's behavior? To what extent did the antidepressant provide a Set Up? Hence, what kind of "cure" are we consuming as we gulp down such drugs?

Still, antidepressants may *temporarily* be helpful to people who are suicidal. In such situations the effects of a pill may keep people alive long enough to "talk" them out of *ending life* and persuade them into *embracing Life*. Studies show that "talk-therapy" is more effective in helping people out of a suicidal phase compared to "drug-therapy." This fact undercuts the *disorder-as-malaria* paradigm, for why should *talking* ease or eliminate a *biologically-caused* mental illness?

There is a very good reason why "talk-therapy" should be more effective than "drug-therapy." Talk-therapy gives people a *reason* to Live! Human beings live Lives of meaning

---

* It's been suggested that antidepressants are most useful for "coping" with a therapist (*hah*).

and purpose for Reasons, . . . for Causes. When people are given a *reason* to Live, they live for . . . Be-Causes! An informing dialogue that provides "reasons" IS the only way out of dis-order dilemmas. The best therapy looks like learning empowering principles, and the most effective inoculation from *doing dis-orders* and *doing dis-eases* is through Changing Your Stripes. This means tapping into the Higher Reasons supplied by the Creator.

There are no short cuts to character building. Integrity is not developed by *default* or *denial.* Becoming more wise and wonderful does not happen by taking a pill.** Taking drugs for dis-orders is often motivated by *escape* and *avoidance:* escape from reality, and avoidance of response-ability. Such tactics of *escape* and *avoidance* simply delay solid solutions; time passes with no real personal progress, and people are still left with the need to *cure the cause!*

* * * * *

If you pop a pill to chase away emotional pain,
when you awake from your drug-induced stupor,
Life will be waiting for you, . . . right where you left it.

* * * * *

Logically, *if* you actually could GET Bi-Polar or A.D.D. like you GET Malaria, *then* why do those diagnosing such dis-orders proceed to invest hours in trying to *talk* you out of your condition? In contrast, a medical doctor diagnosing Malaria simply supplies the anti-Malaria potion, and the *pill alone* does the job. Medical doctors don't require further interventions to make Malaria go away, least of all, trying to *talk* the disease out of you!

** With one possible exception: The pill called "The White Rabbit" makes you "ten feet tall!" Now that's growing your stature in a hurry . . . not to mention improved flying abilities. And if you believe that . . . say hello to Dorothy and the Tin Man next time you're in the Land of OZ. (*hah*)

Some who hold to a Disorder Paradigm play both sides of the issue: On one hand, they say you HAVE a disease and "it's not your fault," thus a pill is prescribed, YET they YACK at you for months thereafter *as if* talk-therapy would do you any good; *as if* YOU and YOUR THINKING and YOUR CHOOSING had any correlation to YOUR CONDITION—which was whole truth and nothing but the truth to begin with! Because of the power in you to *cause* the course of your life, it is you who initiates the creation and perpetuation of so-called *mental disorders.* YOU . . . DO your Dis-Eases!

That you actually DO Dis-Ease is evidenced by the fact that virtually all Depression—to cite one kind of dis-ease—begins with a person perceiving a distressing life event. I have yet to find a single example of someone claiming depression that was not embroiled within real or perceived misfortune. This means being depressed is really a *response* people produce . . . in answer to a *situational constraint.* A depressed mental state is directly attributed to one's *Ability to Respond*, to include the whole genealogy of prior choices that set-in-motion today's *Response-Ability* or in this specific case: *Depress-Ability.* When it comes to so-called psychological "disease," there is no germ, no virus, no bacteria to *Cause* the mental malady—there is only your stinkin' thinkin'. Depression is not *Caused* by outside forces, or even biological sources; instead, you choose depression . . . *Be-Cause.*

People get depressed via *perceptions* and *reasons.* More specifically, you *do depression* as an inevitable consequence of decision-making energy set-in-motion in previous days; thus, while you may have the brakes *locked up* on your emotional train, emotions are still going to slide into the future because of bad momentum you previously put-in-motion (page 136).

Comes the retort, "but I can't help it because my brain chemistry is out of whack!" Can you say . . . psychosomatic? I knew you could. In most cases, bad brain chemistry follows the "lead" of a person's stinkin' thinkin'. This means your thinkin' doesn't stink *because* of brain chemistry, . . . rather your brain chemistry stinks *because* of your thinkin'. So once you've created bad chemistry, . . . you've placed yourself in a self-defeating cycle that perpetuates more of the same—more bad thinkin' and more bad biology.

If people really could "come down" with *brain-chemistry-depressions* like they "come down" with *mumps* or *measles*, shouldn't there be a findable instance? If the *mental disease paradigm* has any validity, we should be able to document an *organically grown depression* somewhere; a depression actually caused by bad biology only; a *brain-chemistry-depression* that occurs in a person who enjoys all the benefits of life, and in the midst of a hunky-dory history of bliss—as rotten luck would have it—this person "comes down" with depression.

We know where bad brain chemistry comes from, but where does your stinkin' thinkin' originate? Answer: It flows from the fountain of your Spiritual Integrity—or lack thereof. Integrity determines a person's well-being of mind and emotion. It is impossible for bitter water to flow from a pure fountain; hence, bad biology can't flow from a sound mind—at least the bad biology associated with *mental dis-eases.*

However, it is possible to be afflicted with bad biology that is NOT psychosomatically produced; you can be constrained in compelling ways by real deficiencies of body or brain that organically grew, with no willful contribution from you. In this case, the discomforts of physiological dysfunction may be your personal "cross to bear," while others may experience their dire trials thru adverse situations. Regardless of either of these adversities, Inner Liberty remains available and alive!

EVEN IF painfully pressed by *constraints of bad biology*, by Divine Design you possess the *final freedom* to choose peace of heart and soul. The Creator has faithfully provided a way to escape any and all adversity; thus, *bad brain chemistry* can never overwhelm this freedom, or else it wouldn't be a *final freedom*, . . . would it?

Still the vast majority of Psychological Depressions only happen thru a person's willful *cooperation* and *participation* at the level of Spiritual Disharmony—the failure to keep Inner Liberty. Show me a person who is Living True, and I'll show you a person who is not Depressed—or BiPolar, or O.C.D., or A.D.D., or P.T.S.D., or even X.Y.Z.*

Why is this so? Because the fruits of Living True are the exact antithesis of dis-order symptoms; it is impossible for Light and darkness to occupy the same space. The Light of Inner Liberty will necessarily dispel the darkness of all emotional dis-order and dis-ease.

Consistent empirical evidence will correlate virtually all Depressions to the way people *perceive* and *respond to* what is happening in their world! It is *you* doing the *perceiving* and *responding* to all situations of accident or abuse, and why do you *perceive* and *respond* as you do? The answer is crystal clear: Because of *the Animal that You Are* today! The vital need for *Changing Your Stripes* is confirmed!

Energy-in-Motion Explains Dis-Ease. When you understand the Principle of Energy-in-Motion then you will know why the metamorphosis of Changing Your Stripes may take months and even years to accomplish: Each choice you make in life is like tossing a rock—once it leaves your hand it has a destiny *independent of your continued control.* You cannot call it back. Once a choice is *set-in-motion*, it pushes through to the future with inertia-like energy.

Making choices, like tossing rocks, will inevitably result in a *landing* of some sort; a future *landing* that will make its

---

* Postpartum Depression is a real biological malady that some mothers feel after giving birth. But the physiological "tug" that invites depressed feelings is absolutely a Constraint, and not a Cause. Postpartum physiology invites women to Do Depression; hence each mother either accepts or declines this "invitation" according to her personal P.Q.—which was previously put in place by a history of prior choices). Thus, every woman possesses a potential Veto Vote via "Inner Liberty" to override the Postpartum Invitation to Depression.

mark in the way you behave or feel, even if you don't desire such *reactions* to come from you and even if you exert great mental will power to create consequences otherwise! So, if you have made a series of dumb decisions, . . . brace yourself, because *energy-in-motion* is already "set" to erupt.

Once Energy-is-set-in-Motion, a *landing* IS inevitable and beyond your control *in the moment* it emerges; those "landings" will often look like the *dis-orders* that you do . . . and the *dis-eases* that you feel. For instance, they may manifest as a *Depression-Reaction* to a *Constraining Event.* Because of the momentum and disposition of your personal *Depress-Ability* formed by your *historical habits* of choosing, YOU may be a *Depression-Waiting-to-Happen.* ** Through patterns of prior choosing YOU launch *Depress-Able-Energy-in-Motion* and are thus vulnerable to the inevitable *landing* of Depression. Your history of choices . . . combined with Energy-in-Motion explain how you are able to Do Depression, and Do other Dis-Ordered *thoughts*, *behaviors*, and *emotions.*

As for the possibility of organically grown depressions, EVEN IF people are genuinely constrained with such bad biology—by no fault of their own—if those people embrace Inner Liberty then whatever ailments they endure will absolutely NOT be the same *ailment-experience* compared to what psychology calls a "major depressive episode."

If one truly keeps Inner Liberty with all heart and soul, the experience of enduring any constraint—whether *biological* or *situational*—will *feel* different. When keeping Inner Liberty

---

** Question: What if people had an awful upbringing where their parents failed to teach them true principles, and worse, fed and reinforced many dysfunctional tendencies? Thus, some people may be a "depression-waiting-to-happen" by no fault of their own; they may have a High P.Q. because of situations beyond their control, especially from childhood! Answer: The Creator will not hold anyone accountable for a slow start "inherited" from parents or peers. In the end, *"It matters not the comparative point in the journey, but whether you are facing the right direction, and making unwavering progress"* (see Turbulent Waters, page 138).

there is always a *brightness of hope* shining at the end of a momentary tunnel of tribulation; in contrast, people who experience a "major depressive episode" are overwhelmed by darkness and despair.

Whatever diagnosis you've been given: Generalized Anxiety Disorder, Panic Disorder, Social Phobia Disorder, Bi-Polar Disorder, Television Intoxication Disorder, Obsessive-Compulsive Disorder, Attention-Deficit Disorder, Postpartum Depression Disorder, or Post-Traumatic Stress Disorder, etc.—regardless of the label—the *experience* and *manifestation* of any ailment will feel different depending upon the Light you let into your Heart—depending upon your choice to Be True or Betray. When choosing the harmony of Spiritual Integrity, the *gestalt* of an adverse experience will "mean" something more than the sum of its painful parts. Spiritual Integrity will lift a person up to the synergy of which Gibran speaks: *"The deeper that sorrow carves into your being, the more joy you can contain."*

Given what we've learned about Cause and Constraint, it is completely clear that *Changing Your Stripes* IS the ultimate antidepressant; it is the *root* cure for all mental and emotional dis-orders and dis-eases. As you become a New Kind of Creature then you are capable of responding differently *even under* the press of bad biology or distressing events; hence, you will no longer *Do Depression* or *Do Bi-Polar* or *Do A.D.D.* or *Do Obsessive-Compulsive!* Instead, you are free to *DO Patience, Compassion,* and *Peace: Ways of Being* that naturally flow from a New Kind of Creature—pure water that freely flows from a pure fountain!

Changing Your Stripes begins by Owning Your Stuff. So what is your stuff? Answer: Everything that comes out of YOU! But of ALL the stuff you are owning, specifically *which stuff* is unproductive and needs changing? Of course, you don't need to change the good stuff, only the bad stuff! Here is where a conundrum can catch you: When you don't realize that your "bad stuff" is actually bad and thus you don't *think* it needs changing. In other words, you may NOT be *aware* that some of your stuff . . . IS stuff! You may be slightly blind to seeing *who you are* and the totality of bad stuff that is coming out of you. I call this: Fooling Yourself!

Fooling Yourself: Slightly Blind Or Oblivious?

The "Fooling Yourself" phenomenon is manifest in varying degrees of distortion, ranging from Slightly Blind to Completely Oblivious. The Slightly Blind kind . . . have an inkling in the back of their mind, that they need to be honest with themselves—but haven't yet. The inner imbalance, to which they are slightly aware, keeps gnawing away. Though they may not openly admit it, they inwardly feel that they are "off track." In moments of *utter honesty*, they know that they need to *change.*

In Contrast, people who are Completely Oblivious live life with an almost impenetrable blockage of blindness, a dense denial about every aspect of their personal problems. Usually they are the last to be aware of what's going on. Completely Oblivious people have a problem, but they don't "see" it—and you can't fix nothin' till you "know" it's broke.

When blind and in betrayal, seeing a clear picture of your own bad behavior is difficult; this is because you're viewing life from a perspective located within your body. Conversely, from an outside perspective, it's actually easier to see others doing dumb things because their *way of being* and *doing* is openly apparent. In a similar way, this is why armchair quarterbacks can clearly "see" real quarterback blunders—in retrospect: *"what's the matter with you, your tight end was wide open, are you blind!"* Just as real quarterbacks are actually IN the game, you are living life IN your body; thus, everyone can see your blunders better than you. When the *play* is already *run*, everyone can see a "better play"—in retrospect. This is where *being* Completely Oblivious comes in; this kind of blindness prevents a person from seeing the "better play" to run, even in retrospect.

Because YOU cannot see yourself directly, it is wise to listen to the secondary reflections coming back from the social mirror, so that you . . . can get a clue. But people who are *completely oblivious* also tend to be *completely defensive* about "letting in" reflective feedback; they tend to "tune out" any feedback that is not compatible to their current course—such is the nature of the beast. This is why the "beast" needs to become a *New Kind of Creature*, . . . a kinder, gentler creature.

Humble receptiveness is required to "see" and "receive" reflections coming from the social mirror. For the *completely oblivious beast,* constructive feedback is shunned like the plague. Fittingly, oblivious beasts live in a trap: They are the creatures that need feedback the most, but are the beasts least likely to "let it in." They are perpetually STUCK: The very reflections that would help them see how *they are being* and thus facilitate change . . . are the very reflections that they *defensively block out.*

* * * * *

When you don't know that
you've got a problem, . . . that's a problem!
You can't solve a problem that you don't "think" you have.
Blind, Oblivious, and in Betrayal . . . you're Stuck!

* * * * *

The condition of being blind, oblivious, and in betrayal is self-perpetuating because the very *mind* that chose the *betrayal bind* in the first place, is the same corrupted mind that is TRYING to *figure* a way out (see Mind Bind, page 175). Thus people who are slightly blind or completely oblivious quite naturally seek the wrong solutions, and this because:

- They are asking the wrong questions,
  and this because
- Their eyes are "seeing" the wrong issues,
  and this because
- They're facing the wrong direction, and pursuing the wrong path.

In light of the possibility of blindness, *owning your stuff* is not as simple as you might think. While you may want to *own* everything that's coming out of you, the problem IS that you don't "think" that certain things coming out of you need fixing! This is the problem that you don't *think* you have a problem—when you really do! "Fooling Yourself" means that even though your eyes are fully functional, your *mind is blind;* thus, your perceptions and interpretations of the world around you are off (see Blindness of Mind, page 192).

Worse, the same *blindness* that keeps you from clearly seeing your world also keeps you from clearly seeing . . . YOU! Obliterating this blindness naturally happens as you Change Your Stripes. Another foundational facet for making this vital change is . . . Beginning Right—entering into an issue with solid assumptions and asking the best questions.

Beginning Right: Asking The Best Questions. To arrive at good answers, we must first ask good questions! When we start with bad questions, we begin wrong and thus we will most likely end wrong. Asking unsound questions leads to second-class solutions. When our premise is poor, it's hard to acquire the prize. But the truth is . . . we would not be asking a wrong question, if we knew it was wrong to begin with, . . . right? Mark Twain's insight applies:

* * * * *

It's not what you don't know that makes you a fool,
but what you "think" you know . . . that ain't so!

* * * * *

In pursuit of the best solutions to Life's constraining conundrums, it is of paramount importance to pose the *best questions* from the *get go:* If the issues you entertain are not right and relevant, then the connected answers are as chaff in the wind. In contrast, if you find the right starting point and ask the right questions, the issues framed therefrom will be important and purposeful; asking the best questions will be like a *beacon of light* illuminating a productive pathway.

* * * * *

Beginning with a bad assumption is like climbing a ladder leaning against the wrong wall, it leads to "progress" . . . that ain't progress at all.

* * * * *

So to begin right, it is wise to question the question, thoroughly double-checking assumptions before launching into an avenue of inquiry. But how do you know when you've got a good question? Good questions have these essential characteristics:

* *They concur with the given realities of the world,*
* *They complement the purpose & meaning of existence.*
* *They are more concerned with Truth, than with facts.*

Basic assumptions about the world must be sound and solid, if they will form the foundation from which life's inquiries are appraised and pursued. Because we interpret the happenings of our surrounding world according to a set of assumptions about the world, if our assumptions are OFF, then the way we interpret our world will be OFF as well.

When a train is off track, it will never arrive at the best destinations; similarly, when assumptions are "off track" the search for superlative solutions is inevitably derailed, and the best questions of Life cannot be raised. To weigh the validity of our questions, we must come to know the realities of our world in an honest and undistorted way—especially the meaning and purpose of human existence.*

---

* When one assumes that life began with BIG BANG, then, from this bad assumption is spawned a myriad of bad questions and conclusions about Life's purpose and meaning. In fact, from BIG BANG beginnings, life can only be ridiculous and absurd. Hence, hedonism is hatched . . . and one's contrived purpose for living centers on satiating a selfish lust for profit, pleasure, and promotion—to ignite egocentric fires until that flame is forever extinguished by breathless black oblivion; human existence is snuffed into nothingness. In short, when one "believes" human beings evolved from dolphins, then that person cannot access the best questions raised by the Creator; one cannot tap into a meaning and purpose of Divine Design.

In an effort to help you begin right, the fundamental realities of Self and Situation have been explained herein; it is against an understanding of these solid assumptions that you can then ask the best questions of Life, and thus arrive at sound solutions. Once you clearly realize a question is good, then you can completely commit yourself to an exploration of adjoining answers! But if you fail to fully *double-check your assumptions* and *question your questions*, by default, you become a prisoner of what you take for granted—what you "think" you know . . . that ain't so!

Here's an example of a bad starting point, a wrong question: "How far can I travel across the ocean, before I fall off the edge of the earth?" The asking of this bad question is embedded in a very bad assumption. Curiously, this bad assumption was taken seriously centuries ago; eventually, human beings learned more about this ball of dirt called "earth" and corrected bad questions based upon bad assumptions.

Within human hearts and minds reside certain unquestioned assumptions that may be false: I call them "flat-earth assumptions." Some of these flat-earth assumptions are openly articulated, while others remain unexpressed. Now for the really bad news: These flat-earth assumptions form the basis of our fundamental belief system, and as we harbor false assumptions about our world, from this faulty framework comes defective questions and flawed conclusions about Life. Again, "It's not what you don't know that makes you a fool, but what you think you know . . . that ain't so!"

When you *jump to assumptions*, you may ASSUME to "know" a notion that is wholly erroneous! And as you further fail to question your questions, and neglect to double check assumptions, you inevitably fall into the proverbial pit of: *ASSUME-ing = Making an ASS*** *out of U and ME.*

** ass, noun. *1. A four-footed, hoofed mammal; a donkey.*
2. (Figurative) A stupid, silly, or stubborn person; a fool.

In the process of Changing Your Stripes, it is essential to begin with solid assumptions about Self and Situation; to find the most satisfying Solutions to Life's most perplexing problems, one assumption forms a foundation:

* * * * *

Within the Heart of all Humanity is an Innate Intuition:
To Know what is Good, and to Do what is Good.
All Human Beings Naturally Know how to
Fulfill the Measure of their Creation.

* * * * *

Getting in touch with your own Intuitions of Truth is foundational—it represents a good beginning point, and a sound assumption. The fruits that flourish from following Heart-felt Intuitions are evidence of the solidarity of this foundation. When fruits thrive from a consistent, sincere experiment of honestly-perceived Intuition, then one can conclude: It is real and it is good! The reliability and reality of God-given Intuition is "known" through the fruits of experience and application.

IF what you are doing works, THEN pragmatic proof for an idea's validity is before you: If it looks like a duck and walks like a duck and quacks like a duck, . . . then it's a duck! This is called *face validity.* Evidence that something is good can be observed and perceived "at its face."

When fruitful results are consistent and abundant month after month, and year after year, then this pattern attests to the truth of a principle—a governing guide that universally applies to all, and works for all. Further, one can measure the truth of an idea by the *feeling of Heart* that stirs within, as an idea is contemplated; when an idea *rings true* with calm and comfortable harmony, this also gives credence to a principle of Life. Heartfelt feelings are a reliable guide in recovering the You . . . that is True.

* * * * *

When you feel that something is good,
and you are purely honest in the experience
of that impression, . . . no further evidence is needed.
The Truthful Feeling IS the Evidence. There is no greater
guide to Self-Refinement than the crystal clarity that speaks
as a whisper to your soul . . . and you
know that something is good.

* * * * *

This Inner Authority that confirms the goodness of all things can be counted on completely—as you are honest in the experience of it. Following the whisperings of your Heart is a sound foundation for Recovering the True You.

LETTING ME EMERGE

We begin our lives in innocence. Beings of goodness, love, and light. Observe a young child: pure innocence! No prejudice, no grudges, and no anxiety, . . . just joyful, playful, uninhibited happiness. From birth, not even a shadow of darkness exists in these clean and clear creatures called . . . "bundles of joy." In a new-born babe, there is only love and light. That's a child! And we all began that way.

As we grow older, we gradually lose our connection to pure innocence, yet it is there . . . waiting to be rekindled and recovered. Recapturing our Inner Innocence is the key to becoming a new kind of creature, but not just a new creature different from your former self, rather a *Re-Newed Creature;* for you are returning to *who you are* from your beginnings—recovering your original, innocent self.

Changing Your Stripes means recovering the *you* that is *true* from your core. And as you are renewed, you begin to see the world through new eyes. You see a new view that *comes alive* to Life's highest meaning!

Regardless of where you are in Life's journey, whether personal progress is great or small, still, in one moment of choice . . . you can face the right direction and put your feet on the path of recovery . . . now! Your own *inner innocence* will provide the Light to lead you through trials and troubles to a place of peace—a place of healing and happiness. So move forward towards this guiding Light, and soon your brightest hopes will be *realized* and *recovered.*

The Light of Innocence. When I am physically cold, if I move from the shadows of darkness into the rays of the sun, I become warm again, naturally and consistently. When cold, *the Sun* warms me as I walk into *the Light.* When my soul is cold, . . . chilled with the bitterness of resentment and blame, I can move from the shadows of dark emotions into the Light of Inner Innocence, and there I find a gentle contentment that melts my cold emotions. Like the shining rays of the Sun, the Light within illuminates the way. The *Light of Innocence* guides me to the warmth of *Inner Peace.*

The way to healing and happiness requires the development of discernment—a quiet sensitivity. Only when I hear and heed the gentle whisperings of *the Light within* can I find the path of recovery. But darkness makes me deaf: Walk in the shadows of darkness and the chill of agitated emotions grow colder, and worse, I cannot clearly hear the whisperings of Light; they are muffled by the confusion of my own mind—drowned out by a *relentless inner dialogue* of figuring, reasoning, and rationalizing.

* * * * *

The Voice of Light is heard in the Light.
I must move from the shadows and find
a place where warmth and peace caress me.
Walk in the Light and I am warmed by peaceful radiance.
Walk in the Light and I can clearly hear
the Whisperings of Light.

* * * * *

As I align myself to my own sense of what is good—my Intuitions of Innocence—I restore harmony and balance with Life, I return to the way I began. Being True means I am aligned to the Light of Innocence. Coming into that warm and peaceful Light naturally relieves me from the chill of darkness: cold emotions depart, . . . clarity enters in.

Losing Inner Innocence. As we mature from childhood, our parents and peers either help or hinder our desire to follow impressions of childlike goodness. For some, *doing good* is fostered and reinforced from early ages, and for others, to some degree, they learn from parents *or* peers how to go against their own spontaneous sense of goodness; they learn how to be unkind and unloving, and they learn ways different from the ways which easily flowed as a child.

When you are in harmony with your natural childlike inclinations, you are happy. How does one recover inner innocence? As Pierre De Chardin affirms: *"You are not a human being having a spiritual experience, . . . but a spiritual being having a human experience."* Thus, to attain the highest purpose of existence, you must recover your *spiritual identity*—your eternal birthright. How do you return to your spiritual beginnings? How do you let innocent "me" emerge?

* * * * *

The Recovery I desire requires no special skill,
No complex knowledge or esoteric ideas,
The Way of Recovery is uncomplicated.
I have a plain and simple Intuition:
To know good, and to do good,
It is a Gift from the Creator.

* * * * *

A Gift that is given by Divine Design: a Gift to guide you to the highest heights of happiness. Asking good questions leads us to good conclusions: Would a truly wise Creator simply create, and then leave his creations clueless as to direction, purpose, and meaning? The Creator IS infinitely wise, and thus has given all humanity a Gift of Guidance. What it means to be human . . . is to inherently know the way to fulfillment—your Divine Destiny.

For this reason, finding the best solutions to personal problems IS NOT a matter of mental machination—as if one's best life could be conjured up through *vivid visualizing* and *willful tenacity* (see page 286). That's not the way the world works: The power to change and recover—to be completely fulfilled—does not reside in efforts of *mental will;* instead, change, recovery, and fulfillment reside in a *release of will*, an act of yielding (see p. 288) to the *inner guide* that is your Gift.

But why will you yield? For what reason? Here are two possibilities: You will release yourself from the *frantic figurings* of your Head to the peaceful invitations of the Heart—you will release your *mental will*, and yield to a *moral will*—be-*cause* taking up those inner invitations bears fruit, you observe and experience good consequences; further, you will *release* and *yield* be-*cause* you feel in the core of your soul that it is good!

But if you don't embrace the Light of Innocence by *invitation*, you may be persuaded to return to this Light thru *tribulation*—additional and optional suffering that signals to you . . . your failure to Be True. In other words, Life will teach you thru *self-correcting karma* that following *Inner Light* leads to a most pleasing end.

* * * * *

I can travel the High-way or I can traverse the Hard-way, but either way, Life will teach me . . . "The Way" to go.

* * * * *

In this life, you can walk either path: Traveling the *High-way by Invitation* or the *Hard-way thru Tribulation.* On the High-way, personal progress is much faster, and much smoother—relatively speaking—but on the back roads of the Hard-way there are numerous *stop signs* to slow you down, each sign saying, *"Turn around!"* At each junction of choice, the invitation echoes: *"Get on the High-way."*

Yet, how can you yield to this Intuition and Invitation, today? How can you even hear or heed the whisperings of the Light, if being *hear-able* and *head-able* is NOT IN YOU—it's not *who you are* today? The solution to becoming the kind of *creature* who can hear and heed, resides in the Power of the Creator to *make you new.* You see, Changing Your Stripes is a *miracle* that occurs as you release the *mental will* in your Head, and yield to the *moral will* written in your Heart.

The magic of recovery and renewal unfolds as the Creator *makes* you the kind of creature who feels to *hear* the whisperings of the Heart and *heed* them.* When this choice of Light is embraced whole-heartedly, then the consequences of Light unfold: Light expands to more Light, and a euphoric upward ascent endows you with a clarity of soul that lifts you above the desires of your former disposition.

So, which do you want? The Hard-way of additional and optional *tribulation*, or the High-way of contentment and clarity by *invitation?* Regardless of the one you feel to choose, the final ballot is cast by what you do, and here's the self-defeating bind, of a double mind: *Desiring* one thing, but *Doing* another.

If it were easy to simply "choose" to *hear and heed* the whisperings of the Heart, then everyone would be choosing it. But everyone is NOT choosing it *be-cause* it is NOT IN THEM TO CHOOSE IT—this good choice does not naturally flow from them. Here's the truth: In order to hear and heed the invitations of Light, you must first become a *hear-able* and *heed-able* kind of creature, and how can you "be" someone you are not? You can't! Thus, you must "be" *who you are . . .* until *you* "be-come" someone different.

---

* Recall the earlier explanations that distinguish between Cause and Constraint. It is important to note that the whisperings of Inner Intuitions constitute a "Communicative Constraint" expressed by the Creator, and by consistently hearing and heeding these Inner Impressions, a Mighty Change of Heart is "Caused" by the Creator. You are literally *made* "a new creature" through His Power (2 Corinthians 5:17).

The necessity of Changing Your Stripes is before you, and once you ARE a different kind of animal—a new kind of creature—the simplicity of hearing and heeding impressions of the Heart flows freely. With a new *way of being* comes a renewed *way of seeing*—a new world reveals to view!

Two Possible Worlds: Simple vs. Complex

Without changing my physical surrounding, without changing any geographical facts, there are *Two Possible Worlds* in which I may live: Simple or Complex! In the Complex World there is hurried urgency, layers upon layers of things to do, appointments to keep, and people to see. In a world of Complexity, other people exist as *props* and *problems.*

As Problems, other people are competitors that block progress to my self-serving goals. As Props, others are *used* as a means for effecting my egocentric ends; people are *objects* to be *used* for my personal profit, pleasure, and promotion. When living in complex world, I am constantly consumed with this question: "How can other people be used by me, to get more for me?"

Living in a Complex World, other people orbit around ME. I am *a mover and a shaker:* I busily *move* my Props, I efficiently *shake* loose my Problems. When people are use-able as *props*, . . . I use them, and when they cease to serve my needy narcissism, they are viewed as *problems* to be pushed aside—people as impediments to MY purposes. This is the complex world that Socrates saw when he warned: *"Beware the barrenness of a busy life."*

In a Simple World there are the same errands to run, the same appointments to keep, and the same people to see, . . . but the *experience* of errands, appointments, and people occurs differently. When I am busy with a *heart of harmony*, then being busy is not a bother or a burden, but a blessing! In a World of Simplicity, experiences of daily doings open up as *adventures* and *opportunities:* The mundane routine of tedious assignments and pressing projects no longer *look like* bothersome burdens, nor *feel like* burdensome bothers.

The same people live in both worlds, but my *experience* of others is different in the Simple World—others appear as people like myself. I feel for them, I empathize with them, I hope for their success, . . . their existence is real to me. I see all people as members of a common family—I love them.

In a World of Simplicity, I realize that fulfillment of Self is not about *using others* but about *Loving Others*. When living in simplicity I see that *Being Loving* IS the highest expression of Self-fulfillment. Even though the tangible details of a Simple World appear complex—when viewed in the vastness of billions of happenings—yet, I am only in one place and can do only one thing, in time's immediate moment, . . . Simplicity invites me:

* * * * *

Agendas to push, reputations to prove
always on the go . . . busy, hurried, harried.
There is another way to live, there can be calm
and flowing ease, where layers of complexity peel away,
the pace relaxes: For there is no other place to be but Here
and no other time to live but Now.
There is nothing more important than
savoring the moment with ones we love.

* * * * *

Without changing the physical facts of association or location, two types of people will *see* two different worlds; which world is perceived and experienced flows from the "good treasures of the heart." Jesus taught this truth: *"From the abundance of the heart, the mouth speaketh."* And just as the mouth speaks according to the conditions of one's heart, it also follows that from the *abundance of the heart, the mind thinks, and the eyes see.*

From a heart of selfishness, people perceive a world of competition and contention; a complex, competitive world where egocentric concern is fixed upon the personal profit, pleasure, and promotion of ME. Other people represent competition that needs to be defeated: *"I need to get mine before someone gets it first, . . . I must watch my back."* Such complex concerns breed a downward spiral of suspicion and cynicism. With a hard heart, complex people lust for *promotion* over others, instead of *compassion* upon others. In the midst of selfish and complex entanglements, daily life is stressful.

Life looks different through the eyes of simplicity: Profit, Pleasure, and Promotion take on a new appearance; abundance is *enjoyed cooperatively* and not just *hoarded selfishly*—fruits pursued for the good of all:

* * * * *

My Profit can be shared for the Blessing of Others,
My Pleasure can be the celebration of Loving Relations, and
My Promotion can be in personal Growth of Character,
expanding the Energy of Integrity
in the Service of Humanity.

* * * * *

Living in a Simple World requires a simple heart, a single heart—single to the purposes of compassion. Making a transition from the tangle and contention of complexity to the flowing peace of simplicity . . . happens by simple means.

A Simple Solution: Un-Doing. You've heard the phrase "this will be their undoing." Typically, an undoing is a bad thing: unraveling, falling apart, or breaking up—all these are bad. But consider a type of *undoing* that is good. The truth is that *recovering early innocence* is actually more a matter of undoing, than of doing. In the process of Changing Your Stripes, you don't do it: You Un-Do It!

Solutions *could be* pursued with the *complexity* of what we "think" we need to accomplish: Investing mental energies into a myriad of things to "do" in an arduous effort to become prominent or magnificent—"a mover and a shaker." But this is to begin wrong and enter into the issue incorrectly! Instead, our focus need only be on the things that need . . .

Un-Doing. One step at a time, line upon line, we simply need to Un-Do the NEXT thing.

* * * * *

Letting the Real Me Emerge is not something
I "make" happen, but something I "let" happen,
Recovery flows as I Un-Do darkness and deception.
The Whisperings of Light will lead the way.
I must yield my will . . . to the Light.

* * * * *

The process of Changing Your Stripes is very simple: You need only focus on Un-Doing ONE thing at a time, the NEXT thing, and as you deal-with and Un-Do each NEXT thing—one simple step at a time—then another NEXT thing appears. Line upon line, . . . you climb out of the dark ditch of *deception* and *betrayal*, and begin to climb the mountain of *clarity* and *integrity*. The *clear curriculum* of your personal series of NEXT things to deal-with and Un-Do is written in your Heart. Living life from the heart is simple, yet completely inclusive of Life's central purpose. An Old Testament proverb invites: *"Keep thy Heart with all diligence, for out of it are the issues of life."*

Because you are fundamentally good by nature, you don't really need to *try* to be good, or *learn* to be good; instead, your task is simply to recapture the goodness that is IN YOU. At birth you began as a being of love: You were naturally generous and sharing, naturally bright and cheerful. But as you matured in worldly ways, through bad examples and unloving influences, you learned to NOT *be* who you are naturally. You learned to be different from who you would *be* if only you had not strayed from your spontaneous spark of goodness.

When we fail to follow the intuitions of innocence that flow freely from the Heart, we betray the truth within us—we go against ourselves! Each self-betrayal creates an obstruction to the flow of life-giving goodness that wells within. As we betray our own intuitions, the natural flow of loving tendencies is blocked, and as that stream is stifled, we begin to behave badly. Unblocking that flow IS the focus of Un-Doing.

The Do will Flow from You. The most essential quest in life is to let yourself be *who you are*, . . . to allow the naturally loving "me" to emerge. As you keep your eye focused upon the NEXT thing you need to "Un-Do," then the loving "Do" . . . will flow from you! All your Doings will instinctively arise as you Un-Do that which obstructs the stream of inner goodness. Doing good, being kind, and loving others will inherently happen as you Recover the Innocence within.

* * * * *

I must focus on Un-Doing the NEXT thing, as the Light leads,
Un-Doing all that impedes . . . The Light of Innocence.
I am already fundamentally wonderful,
I must let the True Me emerge!
Because I was born purely innocent,
I need only Recover . . . my natural capacity.

* * * * *

This loving "Do" that flows from you—your inherent capacity for kindness—is not really just a "Do" as previously defined (p. 64); instead, it is actually a unified "Do" and "Be" simultaneously, manifest in one undivided living expression. I have been using the word "Do" because it conveniently rhymes with You. For poetic expediency, I've been using a less precise word. Yet the phrase, "The Do will flow from You" is now *branded in your brain* because of this compelling poetry—the method to my madness!

The word "Do" implies Action; the word "Be" suggests Emotional Tone and Intention. You cannot *do* anything without a concurrent and inseparable *intent of heart*, nor can you *do* anything without some degree of felt *emotion.*

Because the "Do" will naturally flow from you—as you Un-Do the NEXT thing to which the Light leads—there is absolutely no need for your HEAD to "figure out" anything, except the type, size, price, and color of consumer products. In other words, using your HEAD is useful to "figure out" the things that don't matter much. Yet, even these more minor details of daily doing can be choices that flow from the heart, if that is your desire (see pages 70, 71).

Recovering the True You involves no premeditated scripts, techniques, strategies, or choreographies. *Figuring* is NOT required for *Recovery*—only *Faith*. The amazing miracle of becoming a new kind of creature does not occur through mental will power, but through the Creator's Power. Mental machinations can only manipulate cosmetic change, and never fundamental change.* Without the intervening power of the Creator, the positive attitude axiom of *"act as if, and you will become"* can only transform you into one big fat faker! Without connecting to the Light, even the most enthusiastic and determined attempts to "fake-it-till-you-make-it" have no power to *make* much of enduring value.

Mental will power can craft more competent choreographies: Becoming a better bowler or a more dazzling dancer—superficial doings. In contrast, attributes of character are not enacted through premeditated strategies, willful techniques, or as a matter of positive goal setting. Character attributes like Love naturally flow from you like pure water from a fountain, as you recover pure innocence. "Being Loving" spontaneously appears as you faithfully follow Intuitions of Heart. Being Loving means embracing Life's inherent harmony. Being Loving IS Being True.

This is why Dr Matt likes to say: *The Goal within Your Control is Becoming Loving & True.* Simple to say, but not so simple to do. If it were easy to simply "choose" to hear and

* With the exception of Faithful Figuring: Creative cogitation of a Head that is steadfastly fixed to the Heart.

heed the whisperings of the Heart, then everyone would be doing it—but everyone is NOT doing it! Again, in order to hear and heed, you must first become a *hear-able* and *heed-able* kind of creature, and how can you be someone you are not? You can't! Thus, the invitation calls: To Change Your Stripes and Become a New Kind of Creature.

Why Being True is not so easy to Do. Just as whisperings come from the Light, there are also opposing voices of come from darkness. The voice of the Light is as an *Angel on your Right shoulder* whispering the simple Intuitions of Innocence. In contrast, at particular times, there may be a *devil on your left shoulder* selling the enticements of an egocentric agenda—the pursuit of profit, pleasure, and promotion for ME.* This is precisely why Being True . . . is not so easy to Do. *The devil on your left shoulder* is not just a clever analogy; rather, it's a reality of our *social context* expressed in broadest terms—a real context that includes all relationships between *beings of flesh* and *beings of spirit.***

The *voice of Light* leads to *clarity* and *harmony* and the voices of darkness and deception ultimately lead to *confusion* and *contention.* Discerning the difference between these voices is vital to Recovering the You that is True. Having an awareness of Tell-Tale Signs of Betrayal will enable you to distinguish between the *voice of Light* and the *voices of darkness doing an imitation of the voice of light.*

---

* This is Hedonism: A perspective that naturally springs from atheist assumptions. A paradigm which hold that humans are the evolutionary babies of Big Bang, and that people are not creations of a Creator. Thus, there is no absolute source of Truth and moral conduct is "relative"—a mere product of social negotiation within cultures thru history. From this perspective, there is no ultimate Authority to which humanity might be accountable . . . for choices made that absolutely impact others to their betterment or detriment. There is only accountability to the laws of the land—and even then—the Hedonistic goal is to NOT . . . get caught. Instead of living life with honor and integrity, this secular creed often contends "anything one can get away with is game!"

TELL-TALE SIGNS OF BETRAYAL

All Your Troubles are in The JAR. Betrayal is a word to describe moments when a human being is out of harmony with his or her own sense of truth. As Shakespeare expressed, *"To thine own self be true, therefore thou canst not be false to any man."* Betrayal means being false to yourself, as well as to others. When you go against your own sense of goodness, you lose Life's inherent harmony; inner conflict is created, and outward signs seep to the surface. Jesus taught, *"every tree is known by its fruit."* Corrupt fruit reveals a corrupt tree; the fruit that grows on the tree of betrayal is readily identified.

* * * * *

Three Tell-Tale signs that YOU
are betraying your own sense of what is TRUE:
"All your troubles are in the J.A.R."

* * * * *

A thorough understanding of the tell-tale signs of betrayal can provide awareness sufficient to *catch yourself* and correct your course. The patterns are predictable and observable; they are signs central to the aim of Un-Doing! Seeing these signs in yourself will provide a huge clue . . . to what you need to Un-Do:

* * *

J = Justifying
A = Accusing
R = Resenting

* * *

** With the mention of "spirit" comes a chorus of skeptical voices: "Oh, that's just Religion." To which I reply: "No, that just Reality! The firm fact that many thousands of people have ventured into a realm of spirit and then returned to mortal life . . . has Big-Bangers hyperventilating for an explanation. Some secular scientists assert that near-death experiences are a product of "hallucinations" due to "lack of oxygen to the brain." But why do people who "hallucinate" visits to a spirit realm . . . independently report a consistent set of descriptions of their near-death experience? Such is the finding in Raymond Moody's book, "Life After Life."

Instead of *owning* response-ability, the person in betrayal typically tries to *explain away* the troubles at hand: Justifying self while Accusing others is the tell-tale pattern of those trapped in betrayal. Further, betrayers become embroiled in Resenting emotions and rationalize, "because others have made me miserable, begrudging my abusers is what anyone would do in the same situation." Indeed, *most would* begrudge their abusers, but being *average* is not our aim: Changing Your Stripes is about *excellence!*

Whenever *accusing* and *self-excusing* words emerge, words laced with a *resentful* agitated edge, THEN you may know with certainty that a betrayal is in progress! The *outward* behaviors of the J.A.R. expose the *inner* imbalance of the heart—inner conflict called "betrayal."

It's hard to See in the Dark. As the sun sets beyond the horizon, its light grows gradually dimmer. With the onset of darkness, the ability to see become increasingly impaired. Like physical vision, our spiritual vision is also obscured as we leave the Light of Innocence—out of the abundance of the heart, the eyes see.

When the heart is out of harmony, . . . we cease to see clearly; diminished vision is an unavoidable result of walking in the shadows of betrayal. Because we no longer see through innocent eyes, we perceive a different world before us. We see differently, not because the world around us has changed, but because we have changed.

* * * * *

When I go against my own sense of Truth,
I go against myself, . . . I am false.
Being false, the way I experience the world is colored
by my falseness: I see darkness in my world,
because of the darkness in me. My thinking, my emotions,
and how I behave are all tainted by betrayal.
My search for solutions is skewed;
It is wrong, ... because I am wrong.

* * * * *

When caught in the trap of betrayal, we encounter the connected consequence of diminished vision; betrayal and blindness always occur together. People will not even attempt to correct a problem *if* they don't think they have a problem—yet they do . . . and are blind to it! Thus having an *intellectual awareness* of the tell-tale signs of betrayal is a good start in seeing beyond the blindness. But in the end, intellectual acknowledgment is not enough; unless we can *humbly own* and *frankly admit* our betrayals, blindness will persist. Clear vision only comes with whole harmony of heart.

Einstein's Mind Bind. Impaired perceptions inevitably lead to flawed solutions. With clouded vision and confused thinking, betrayers cannot "figure" their way out of their problem. The reason why people do not—and sometimes cannot—find their way out of a problem is explained by a conundrum I call, "Einstein's Mind Bind." In short, you can't *change* your mind . . . using the same mind that needs *changing;* neither can you *fix* a situation, using a mind that needs *fixing.* Here's how this bind of the mind . . . was stated by Einstein:

* * * * *

"We cannot solve our problems at the same level of thinking which existed when the problem was created."

* * * * *

This means, in order to solve any problem, a paradigm shift is required! A shift from the way of thinking that was capable of creating a problem in the first place, . . . to a way of thinking that can perceive a new perspective. Further, thinking that you can solve Life's most important problems with your "thinking," is itself a problem. When confronted with a crucial issue, some will say, "I need to figure things out, I need a strategy."

Using your *head* is a good approach for solving problems of *algebra*, but not for solving problems of *anguish.* The mental mindset used to create an interpersonal problem cannot be used to solve it. As long as the *head* remains disconnected from the *heart*, betrayers will proceed to solve their problems in precisely the wrong way; they will be beset with a blinding mental block that breeds more perplexity.

Being *blind in the mind* is a condition I also like to call, and so I do: the Migraine Mental Block—an ailment of a Head that pays no heed to the Heart. Again, being Blind in the Mind means: the *head* that *thunk* its way into a tangle cannot be used to *think* its way out of a tangle. But from whence comes a mindset capable of creating chaos? It could be a function of shear *ignorance*—that's one possibility—and the other source is *betrayal.*

While Einstein's statement primarily applies to *intellectual* blockage, there is usually a *spiritual bind* that lies at the base of a *mixed-up mind*—especially pertaining to problems of high importance. In other words, while a betrayer's mind may be able to solve *mathematical* problems, it will be incapable of clear thinking about Life's most *meaningful* problems. People afflicted with a Migraine Mental Block are more prone to problem-making, than problem-solving.

In the experience of betrayal, inner conflict is characterized by repetitive thoughts that grind round and round in one's head: *figuring, conniving, strategizing,* these are ways that solutions are sought while in betrayal.

Being inwardly unsettled, an urgent need to bring things back into balance is felt. Constant mental reruns represent a betrayer's attempt to bring things back into balance, but all such attempts are futile while trying to use the *defective mind* that hatched the perplexity in the first place. Such repetitive mental dredging is also called "obsession." While some may suggest such obsession is a function of *having* a psychological sickness, a mental disease, the truth is that most people are really *doing dis-ease* and *feeling dis-ease* due to spiritual dis-order; they have lost Life's inherent harmony.

When we go against ourselves—betray our own sense of what is good—we can't enjoy the clarity and contentment that comes with being true; instead, confusion of mind and emotion is our unavoidable lot. We experience conflict, both *within* ourselves and in *outward* relations. Nevertheless, lousy relationships, foulable feelings, and a *migraine mental block* do serve a purpose: they let us know we're not doing life right!

* * * * *

Life is Self-Correcting: When you are not doing Life right,
Life will make sure you are properly notified.
Inner and Outer Conflict is a clear clue,
that You . . . have not been True.

* * * * *

By choosing to resist the spark of inner goodness that guides, Life's inherent harmony is lost. Through our own conflicted thoughts and feelings, Life spontaneously lets us know that we walk in darkness. When in darkness, we lack the clarity of vision that is amply enjoyed in the Light. Through darkened eyes we misperceive our world; every solution contrived by our *head* ends up wrong, and continues to be wrong as long as the *head* is out of *harmony* with the *heart*. When you're *blind* and in *betrayal*, the tell-tale signs of the JAR provide you . . . a corrective clue.

JUSTIFYING

Self-justification has been a tell-tale sign of betrayal for a few millennia: *"If I justify myself, mine own mouth shall condemn me"* (Job 9:20). People who fall in the trap of betrayal feel an itching need to rationalize their contribution to a quagmire. Betrayers invest much time and energy into telling anyone who will listen, why they are justified in their attitudes, actions, and emotions; they assemble a self-justifying facade so they won't look bad, when really, . . . they have been bad. They offer excuses directly inspired by a self-serving motive: to protect the image of "the Self as Advertised."

Betrayers tell a self-excusing story to convince themselves and others that they are OK and that blame lies elsewhere; they spin a tale that tries to make the wrong they are doing *appear right*, or at least *not their fault.* The very act of rationalizing reveals the imbalance of betrayal. It is precisely because of *inner imbalance* that people get involved in Justifying patterns; in other words, Justifying is only useful to those who are inwardly *out of balance.* Rationalizing has always been easier than admitting mistakes; it is the road of least resistance and least effort. Self-Justifying is the crowded course traversed by a mediocre majority.

Telling Stories: Anxious vs. Honest. People who betray their intuitions of innocence have a story to tell, but not all who "tell a story" are betraying themselves. Some stories are just . . . stories. With no inflamed emotion, some stories explain events and occurrences with straightforward frankness; no blame, no irritation, no resentment exists in the telling of an *Honest Story*—it is a story that explains and may even entertain. This type of story will mostly go away the following day . . . for it has no reason to stay; that is unless you really like it, then you might file it away . . . and enjoy it on another day.

The *Anxious Story,* in contrast, is more than a simple explanation of things and happenings: It's an unsettled story that arises from the mire of internal conflict. It tends to be told over and over, because the teller of the anxious story finds no emotional closure in it; thus, neither the story nor the flustered feelings go away in coming days. Instead, *reruns* and *sequels* continue; such repetitive "broadcasts" reveal the inner conflict of the producer/storyteller.

There are two fundamental kinds of Stories that people tell: One *Honestly and Simply Explains* and the other *Anxiously Excuses and Accuses.*

* * * * *

Two types of Stories:
One indicates Truth, the other Betrayal.
The Anxious Story is self-excusing and accusing;
It harbors Resentment and oozes with Unsettled Emotions.
Because the story hides a lie, . . . there is no peace or closure in it. Many sequels arise from an Anxious Story; It can become complex and sprawling. It continues in a new day . . . and does not go away.
Reruns to be told tomorrow.
The Honest Story, in contrast, Accuses no one,
Resents no one, is not Edgy or Irritated
and goes away . . . the next day,
It has no reason to stay.

* * * * *

Because the anxious story yearns to *appear* convincing, it seeks to be backed by facts—it needs to be lined with logic. The anxious story clings to factual evidence to compensate for the inner insecurity of the storyteller.* The anxious story requires airtight logic to make secure, that which is inherently insecure.

* * * * *

Because the Anxious Story
is inherently insecure . . . from its core,
it desperately clings to superficial facts and alluring logic.

* * * * *

Conversely, the *honest story* is more or less succinct and needs no long, involved logic. Because they have no inner turmoil to resolve, people who tell an *honest story* speak with

---

* A pattern evidenced in courts of law. It is abundantly clear that strategies and "P.R. Campaigns" aimed at getting guilty people a verdict of "innocent," require much more talking than simply telling "the truth, the whole truth, and nothing but the truth." Getting the guilty off often means concocting a convincing story. This is called a "defense strategy" to those who have become morally numb to "business as usual" within the legal system, but to the rest of us common folk, it's simply called . . . "lying."

candid ease—no agitated edge of emotion. The honest story does not try to manipulate or pretend, and it may even be a little awkward or goofy; it is not premeditated or polished, because honest storytellers have no inner motive to appear impressive. The Honest Story will BE, whatever it IS, because *"that's the way things happened."*

* * * * *

People who have Nothing to Hide, . . . Hide Nothing!

* * * * *

Those who speak honestly from the heart do not premeditate impressive presentations, nor do they calculate strategies. But not all *anxious stories* are created in a calculated way; sometimes the story streams out spontaneously . . . with no forethought to finagle—it flows naturally like venom from a snake. And when "snakes" *live a lie* for a long period of time, they can get good . . . at doing bad!

Even though superficial performances are imperfect at heart, impressive appearances can be *perfected* with practice—practice makes perfect *appearance!* A wolf's deceitful motives can be disguised by sheep's clothing, tailored to skin-deep perfection; thus, *anxious stories* will not always *appear* anxious, but will still be defective at heart.

Impressively polished stories can still expose unethical inner motives through another tell-tale sign: the tendency to tell the story over and over again. Because the *anxious story* is told primarily to protect the image of "the self as advertised," by being *stuck in the story*, people not only *reveal* their betrayal of truth, but they also *spill* their selfishness.

Stuck in the Story. With each re-telling of an *anxious story,* the betrayer hopes that the next telling will dispel inner conflict; predictably, stressful emotions remain. Running a story over and again in your head and/or constantly telling that story to others, is a *repetitive rut* I call "Stuck in the Story." It's very easy to recognize people who are stuck in this rut:

* *Anxious emotions are displayed in the storytellers,*
* *The elements of the J.A.R. emerge,*
* *They can't quit telling the story,*
in each new day, . . . it doesn't go away.

The truth is that anxious emotions never go away by endless rationalizing and irritable rambling, instead inner conflict is only cured through *recovery*—a return to innocence. As Stephen Covey concludes, "*you can't talk your way out of a problem that you behaved your way into.*" This means betrayers must *back out* of the very behaviors that initiated the inner imbalance; betrayers must *un-do* their dark deeds!

Thinking that *rationalizing* might bring *relief* is indicative of a betrayers distorted mentality. Calculating and conniving cannot solve the problems of a defective heart.* While deceptive weaseling will not work, neither will well-meaning efforts of positive will power; mental machinations can only prune the outer *appearance* of problems; mind power cannot cure a corrupted root. Solid solutions that *root out* problems from their foundation require more than superficial pruning; sound solutions require a change in whole behavior—motives, emotions, words, and deeds. That fundamental and wholistic change begins with *owning response-ability* for the chosen behaviors that caused the inner imbalance—and then *un-doing* those dark deeds. Tell-tale signs provide a corrective clue . . . to what you need to Un-Do.

Vote-Getting: Another Tell-Tale Sign. Yet another "red flag" that signals betrayal is *vote-getting.* Being inwardly unsettled, the betrayer seeks solace by securing *votes* from others; hoping to make *secure*, a story that is *insecure* . . .

---

* Problems with a physical heart can be corrected through open-heart surgery; but problems with the core of one's character, this "heart" requires "open-soul surgery." And in both cases, "heart" patients need to cure the cause of their ailments at the roots.

from its core. If the justifying story is superficially plausible, then support and sympathy may be gleaned, still betrayers find no inward relief—they may *win the popular vote*, but fail to *win inner harmony.*

* * * * *

In matters of Personal Peace,
the only Vote that counts is the one registered
in the Ballot Box of the Heart.

* * * * *

People who are Being True are not fretfully engaged in vote-getting campaigns; they do not solicit votes in support of an anxious story. When people have *harmony of heart*, they offer no excuses and have no story to tell—at least not one that is laced with justification, accusation, and resentment. The absence of a need to *tell a story of excuse* points to people who are most likely Being True; they have no itching need to *justify* because there is no *inner imbalance* to resolve.

When people are Being True there is *no* case to prove, *no* ax to grind, *no* evidence to offer, and *no* votes of support to seek. Because there *is* no case, no ax, and no argument, . . . no campaign to seek the popular vote—but there *is* personal peace. In contrast, when a person betrays the truth within, there IS a case to prove, there IS an ax to grind, there IS evidence to offer, and there IS active lobbying for votes.

Even though a *justifying story* may be airtight and firmly supported by solid facts and convincing logic; even though a large volume of votes may be cast in support of that story; and even though a betrayer may be sincerely convinced that the story is true, if the elements of the JAR are present, one can confidently conclude: *the story* and *the feelings* are *false* and somebody's being *fooled!* People who are fretfully in need of winning "the popular vote" reveal their inner imbalance. Seeking *the popular vote* is an attempt to convince yourself that *the anxious story* you tell is *the truth* . . . when it's really *contrived.*

* * * * *

If you have to try to convince yourself,
that means . . . you're not convinced!

* * * * *

An Invitation to a Justification: Asking Why?

When someone does something wrong, it is common for people to inquire as to "why" the dark deed was done? This is a particular tendency when watching children make mistakes; observers often ask youngsters, *"why did you do that?"* Through experience, youthful *mistake-makers* learn from an *excuse-making society*, that if they can conjure up a good story, they might "get off." But in truth, there are no excuses, no justifications, that can make bad behavior . . . into good behavior! So when asking the doer of a deviant deed "why," you can expect a justifying "lie."

* * * * *

Ask people Why . . . and you invite them to Lie!
When people are in betrayal, asking "Why"
simply leads to a Self-Justifying Lie.

* * * * *

In the question of "why" . . . there lives a "lie," or at least the potential to a lie—a temptation to a lie. Saving the "face" of *the self as advertised* is usually the reason we tell self-justifying lies; excuses are given to preserve and defend the claims of an egocentric "ad" campaign. But what is the alternative? To *Be True* and resist the superficial facts that fool, the alluring logical facts that make our story *sound* right, when it's *not* right. The alternative to "justifying" is to move from the shadows of betrayal and return to the Light—the Light that warms us, and assures contentment and peace. Personal calm and clarity come from the *Recovery* of inner harmony, not by *Rationalizing;* satisfying solutions flow from the gentle whisperings of the *Heart.*

ACCUSING

A False Solution: Blame as Balm. In spinning self-justifying stories, we portray *someone* or *something* else as being at fault—but what good does this do? To think that *Blaming Others* might bring relief is the accuser's misleading illusion! Even if others are completely blameworthy, motives of revenge, resentment, and rationalization only serve to poison the heart of those who harbor inflamed feelings. In the name of *justice* and *closure*, betrayers embark upon a *crusade of accusation* against offenders. When such a crusade is cankered with accusing emotions, blame brings no healing balm to a wounded soul; fretful feelings make the wound wider! The *comforts of closure* cannot happen while harboring accusing emotions.

Blaming Situations is equally fruitless! It may be tempting to think, "if only I could escape my sad situation, then I could be happy." But a "change in circumstance" is rarely a favorable fix when one is in betrayal, for EVEN IF you move to *some enchanted island*—and you haven't yet recovered—you will end up bringing your old *unenchanted self* with you; thus, you bring to a *new* location . . . your *old* bag full of problems. *Old habits* die hard even in *new locations.* Like a mouse trap set to spring, your personal propensities are ready to snap, and when others bite the bate, snapping *reactions*—just *waiting-to-happen*—will erupt out of you, even on *some enchanted island.*

Because Life is a Set Up, you can expect *selfish people* and *distressing events* to impact your personal path. Life is filled with frustrating twists and turns that unexpectedly arise: *get used to it, get over it, and get on with it*—that's life! While such stressful constraints will *explain* the *Set Up* to which you are exposed, if you would Be True from this day forward, you won't point to those constraints for *excuse.* You will *own* what comes out of you and live without *accusation.*

Playing the *blame game* is a major obstacle to *recovery.* Living life to the heights of happiness means focusing upon the "responses" that come out of you, especially when the going get tough. Character is tested at the edge of adversity.

* * * * *

There are bad things that happen to me,
and there are bad things that I do.
The bad that I do . . . IS my failure to Be True.
By Accusing others I Betray the Truth.

* * * * *

You might as well give up *blaming*, and quit *complaining* too! Unless all *accusation* ends—in both word and emotion—you will never consummate the comforts of closure. In contrast, there is comfortable closure in embracing Inner Liberty, and there is much closure in having compassion—even for offenders. The person with an *accusing heart* cannot access the pleasing possibilities that come with compassion.

Resenting

Because other people have wronged us—or we imagine they've wronged us—our plight *must be* their fault. This conclusion may be true in terms of outer afflictions, but it is false in terms of inner emotions. Confused by this subtle distinction, some conclude that they are *justified* in harboring hatred towards offenders. While perpetrators may be directly responsible for *causing* outward abrasions and intrusions, and though victimized by this misfortune, we remain Response-Able: We are *able* to freely *respond** in terms of word, deed, mind, and emotion, to include the response called *resentment*.

---

* Victims of tragic situations still get to own everything except the physical *effects caused* to person and property. Because "Life is a Set Up," we all feel the "victimizing" constraints of an unfair world—at one time or another. As unloving people cross our path, we become victims of their selfish pursuits of profit, pleasure, power, promotion, or property. The key to living joyfully in a world that treats you unfairly, is in "becoming" the kind of creature that can respond with patience and compassion; not because offenders deserve such treatment, but because we need to "be" that kind of person. What else is there . . . but our becoming?

* * * * *

When I am False, I feel tension, agitation, disharmony.
My Resentful Emotions signal falseness.
When I am True, I am at Peace.
The Peace that flows freely signifies Harmony.

* * * * *

Re-Sending Negative Energy. Resenting other people, or situations, is a *re-occurring* activity: After yesterday's mistreatment has already happened and the opportunities of a new day arise; instead of permitting fresh feelings to lift and invigorate, the *resenting* person engages in *re-sending* negative energy. Choosing to *re-send* the negative energy of *resentment* is today's decision that squashes tomorrow's hope.

Those who *re-send* hateful energy may hold in their *head* an erroneous idea, that harboring hateful feelings somehow sends psychic arrows back to abusers; they may imagine that arrows of anger will somehow pierce and punish offenders. The *re-sending of resentment* does not send *psychic arrows* out, but hurls hateful *boomerangs* . . . that come back—returning to the sender all the bitterness *sent* and *re-sent*, hence re-sent-ment.

Every resentful seed sown returns a bitter harvest; this is a consistent law of Life. When resenting, you ironically sentence yourself to the hard labor of dragging a heavy load of bitterness behind; the act of re-sent-ment tethers you to *yesterday's misery*, and keeps you from *today's opportunity*.

Re-senting is a re-occurring waste of time and energy. The consistent law of Life called *karma* guarantees that offenders will eventually receive wages proportionate to their hurtful works, but those wages should never be paid via resentful retaliation. Whether oppressed or abused, victims who try to exact "pay back," execute a self-inflicting irony:

* * * * *

Resentment is the Poison that You Drink,
while expecting your offenders to die
from the Poison that You Drink.

* * * * *

Resentment Retention Time Revisited. Even though harboring resentment is like shooting yourself in the foot, people have a penchant for "hanging on" to yesterday's offenses anyway. The *Resentment Retention Continuum* is a way of locating the "politically correct" length of time that a person should feel hurt or humiliated, after being offended; just how long should resentment be retained? 2 minutes . . . 2 hours . . . 2 days . . . 2 weeks . . . 2 months . . . 2 years . . . or possibly 2 decades? Remember, *Resentment Retention Time* needs to parallel the nefarious nature of the alleged offense.

Keeping resentment within the "politically approved" time frame may be challenging for people possessing a High PQ; they will naturally want to keep resentment ruminating in their sour bellies for a longer period of time than even the "popular vote" will support.

One particular client, named Gladys, was a Gold Metal Resenter. She accomplished a stunning feat of Resentment Retention that reached back four decades, and bridged the bearing of five children. Forty years later, unbelievably, she was still squawking, fussing, and yammering about offenses from in her teenage years. If she had *reached back* any farther into her resentful memory, she might have resented her mother for *bearing down* too hard in the delivery room!

Her record-setting resentment was a function of a *migraine mental block:* she wasn't seeing or thinking straight because of betrayal. This client's mind bind was further fed by a famous, fallacious Freudian doctrine: *"You're weird today because of something that happened yesterday."* Because she bought into this erroneous conclusion of *cause & effect psychology*, she assumed that she needed to go back to the start of the causal chain—the beginning moments when she met her husband and the *alleged* torment began.

The truth is the only "chain" that encumbered Gladys was the one that she'd been actively *knitting* for forty years—the heavy chain of resentment. With each dawning of a bright "new" day, she willfully shackled herself to yesterday's dark and dreary memories; for an incredible 14,600 days, she chose misery, over "opportunity" (see Frankl's quote, p. 12).

Yet, yesterday's offenses were not as horrendous as she portrayed them to be . . . in reality; she had stretched her story to *justify* her present-day pain—her self-produced pain. Since today's pain was enormous by claim, she needed a large explanation for *her story* to appear plausible! Our Gold Medal Resenter was so invested in maintaining today's suffering—as evidence of past abuse—she had spun an *anxious story* of encyclopedic proportions. To say she was *story-stretching* is putting it mildly. But whether her story was *loaded* or *limited* is actually irrelevant: she HAD a "story" . . . PERIOD. The tell-tale sign of *justifying* was more than conspicuous.

Week after week, I watched this client go through her justifying gyrations to lobby for longer *resentment retention time.* A task that became increasingly difficult because her husband was not being offensive in the present, so the only *fodder* she had to blast from her *accusing cannons* came from the distant past—whether real of imagined. This is what happens when *maintaining a self-justifying story* becomes more important than having *personal peace!* From his book, "Bonds that Make us Free," C. Terry Warner describes this paradoxic position:

> *We devise and hang on to our emotional problems for a purpose, a purpose more important to us than our happiness. And we deceive ourselves about the fact that this is what we're doing. We participate in the creation of our emotional troubles and deny we've had any part in it.*

When confronted with her conspicuous resentment hoarding, Gladys explained, "you don't understand, when those airliners hit the twin towers in New York, a huge pile of rubble was created that takes years to clean up, and build back." Her 9/11 analogy was a masterful piece of persuasion and justification; a story that would have garnered sympathy from the average observer. But I knew that her need to invoke this slick logic revealed her own inner conflict.

Further, she defended the image of *the self as advertised* with ferocity. And what was that *image* you ask? The image of a victim: "I could be happy if it weren't for my husband." The Self as Advertised is not just a *glossy* facade of success (that's only one version), it's *any* facade that that is sold for a self-serving purpose, as opposed to a truth-serving purpose. When one is guided by truthful intent, there is no facade to sell—just authenticity, straight-forward and real.

After literally investing a lifetime into blaming and resenting her husband, the only *way out* for Gladys was to admit that she had been wrong for forty years—she was in a prideful bind. Four decades later, admitting her error and coming clean was a behemoth hunk of humble pie too humungous to swallow. So she stuck TO her story, for she was stuck IN her story!

Like most who claim victimhood, Gladys didn't think she was *choosing* the self-made misery of resentment. Such self-made victims do not see their emotional distress as a *choice*, for the very definition of "victim" means "someone has done it to me," hence, the resentful response is seen as a natural occurrence. Betrayers rationalize: "This is how most people would respond if mistreated, it's a normal response"—indeed, normal as in *average*. *Most people* do respond with resentment when mistreated, and "most people" ARE members of the mediocre majority—people who are not aiming for *excellence*, but aiming for *excuse.*

A real victim experiences suffering and loss beyond any perceptual participation that he or she might *bring* to a tragedy. This is precisely why this book begins by detailing the distinctions between *cause* and *constraint.* Thus, you may be a victim of physical harm to person or property, but you can never be a "victim" of spiritual harm.* Suffering of soul only happens with your *permission* and *participation* (see 1st Corinthians 10:13).

Resentment IS Today's Trauma. For victims of tragedy to escape suffering of soul, they must fully accept the fact that *resentment* is an emotional *response* originating from the "resenter." Each human being is the author of his or her resentful emotions. This means, beside the physical pain that may be felt in the body due to intrusive, tangible impacts, any *continued emotional suffering* that victim's blame upon yesterday's abuse IS REALLY *resentment harbored by an accusing heart.*

The character of one's heart is key! For it is from the "good treasures" of the heart that the mouth speaks, the mind thinks, and the eyes see (see page 89). When one sees darkness in days gone by, . . . it is due to the darkness *in* the perceiving person, because of *bad treasures* of the heart—a heart that harbors resentment.

Curiously, people actively participate in the creation of their own unsettled emotions, then deny this participation—a denial that manifests in the form of blame, a denial that comes from a mind that is blind. Because of a *migraine mental block* that obscures clear vision, betrayers cannot "see" that today's emotional pain IS the self-made misery of *harboring resentment.*

---

* It is true that an abuser can initiate a sequence of responses and reactions; indeed, the enacting of abuse "sets up" the abused to respond as poorly, or as well, as current character can express. Ironically, if character needs growth, the abusive "set up" can be the Test and the Teacher that facilitates needed growth—the very afflictions that perfect the soul. How one *responds* to those afflictions forges the defining difference in life. But if the opposite alternative is invoked—bitter instead of better—an abusive "set up" can also constrain a response of unnecessary Torment. The final cause for either consequence is IN the chooser.

From the impact of Situational Suffering comes *necessary* heartache that real victims endure in direct moments of affliction; thereafter, *optional* misery emerges as the dust of a difficulty settles, and a person stands at a point of transition: to either *keep* or *discard* Inner Liberty. With the decision to "discard" Inner Liberty, people paradoxically put themselves in the bondage of a self-imposed emotional prison.

When I speak of the "dust of a difficulty" settling, I am acknowledging that it takes time to work through a tragedy. But that *working through process* can be done with the Light of Innocence leading the way—a Light of Hope that dispels all darkness and despair. Working through a tragedy with the unfailing anchor of Inner Light *means* that drinking the poison of resentment can be skipped, entirely. Further, a person need not wait for the ending of a trauma to invoke Inner Liberty: this Light and Liberty can be received while directly IN affliction.

* * * * *

Waiting for the dust of a difficulty to settle is unnecessary,
I can fully embrace Inner Liberty immediately,
even amid an aggravating event.

* * * * *

Keeping Inner Liberty when directly in a difficulty does not mean that all pain disappears, but it does mean that Self-Inflicted Suffering is not added to, and heaped upon, any physical distress felt due a difficult situation. In other words, one will not experience *suffering of soul* even if physical pain is present.** Enduring outward affliction, while still *feeling inner peace*, is a principle taught by the Apostle Paul:

** An example of feeling inward peace while being outwardly abused is given in the Book of Mormon: The faithful followers of Christ had their burdens lifted in the very moment a heavy weight of bondage was upon their backs (Mosiah 24:10-14). In this particular case, extreme oppression that should have "caused" physical pain was miraculously not felt. Hence, it is possible for the Creator's Power to override even physical pain.

> *"For all things are for your sakes, . . . For which cause we faint not; but though our outward man perish, yet the inward man is renewed day by day. For our light affliction, which is but for a moment, worketh for us a far more exceeding and eternal weight of glory; while we look not at the things which are seen, but at the things which are not seen: for the things which are seen are temporal; but the things which are not seen are eternal" (2 Corinthians 4:15-18).*

The Division of Response-Ability Principle continues to apply even amid extreme affliction: What Comes out of You . . . is Yours! The condition of your character is revealed by how you *respond* through tough times!

* * * * *

Harboring Resentment is one form of Self-Inflicted Suffering. This Misery arises from my inability to keep Inner Liberty. I inflict myself with discomforting consequences as I fail to hear and heed the whisperings of the Heart.

* * * * *

Being consumed with agitated emotions of resentment, anger, or accusation is a natural consequence of losing Life's inherent harmony. Because perceptions are distorted due to dis-harmony, betrayers erroneously imagine that they can *rationalize* their way out of inner anguish. As we have learned, telling *justifying stories* is only useful to those who feel inner conflict; people who live in harmony with Inner Innocence have no story to tell, for they have no inner imbalance to resolve. When people are Being True: there is *no* case to prove, *no* ax to grind, *no* evidence to offer, and *no* votes of support to seek—because there is no case, no ax, and no argument, but there is . . . inner peace.

BLINDNESS OF MIND

As the *sun* sets beyond the horizon, its *light* grows gradually dimmer and one's ability to see becomes increasingly diminished. Darkness, in all of its forms, is not conducive to both *sight* and *insight.* Like physical vision, our perceptual vision is also obscured by darkness; as we betray the Light of Innocence, our vision is impaired automatically. Betrayal and blindness always occur together; diminished vision is a spontaneous consequence of walking in the shadows of betrayal. And because we no longer see with *eyes of innocence,* we thus *perceive* a different world before us; we see differently, not because the world around us has changed, but because we have changed.

* * * * *

When I go against my own sense of Truth,
I go against myself, ... I am false. Being false,
the way I experience the world is colored by my falseness:
I see darkness in my world, because of the darkness in me.
My thinking, my emotions, and how I behave are all
tainted by betrayal. My search for solutions is
skewed; it is wrong, because I am wrong.

* * * * *

In betrayal, life is disfigured by dark emotions; life is marred by nagging doubts about what a new day might bring. Instead of moving forward with a brightness of hope, betrayers keep their backs to the *sun*, and fix their focus on yesterday's darkness. People who habitually harbor anxious stories, justifying stories, reveal their location: in disquieting shadows, away from the Light of the Sun.

By choosing to resist the spark of inner goodness that guides, Life's inherent harmony is lost. Through our own conflicted feelings, Life naturally lets us know that we walk in darkness.

When in the darkness of betrayal, we lack the clarity of vision enjoyed in the Light of the Sun; we perceive our world through the distorted filter of a *migraine mental block*, thus, we may passionately believe the *anxious story* that we tell, but such blind passion is indicative of those who betray the Light and walk in darkness.

* * * * *

When I am True, I tell an Honest Story:
I blame no one, I harbor no resentment, I am
at peace, and I see the world through Innocence Eyes.
When I am False, I tell an Anxious Story:
A Justifying tale that tries to Accuse others & excuse myself.
I harbor Resentment, I am unsettled and agitated,
and I see the world through Darkened Eyes.

* * * * *

People will not even attempt to correct a problem when they don't *think* they have a problem—yet they do, and are blinded to it! This is why it is essential to become aware of the tell-tale signs: Whenever *accusing* and *self-excusing* words emerge, words laced with a *resentful* agitated edge, THEN you may know with certainty that a betrayal is in progress! The *outward* behaviors of the J.A.R. expose the *inner* imbalance of betrayal; further, with each and every betrayal comes some degree of blindness.

Typically, the *absence of story telling* indicates that people are mostly at peace with the world, and with themselves; however, the mere absence of a story is not always a reliable indicator of betrayal. Some *introverted* and *nonverbal* types may not openly tell a self-justifying tale, yet their *anxious story* is repetitiously hammering within their head; in such cases, the *inner imbalance of betrayal* is exposed by "red flag" emotions that I call . . . BRIAR Emotions.

False Feelings: BRIAR Emotions. When people are not embroiled in betrayal, they display peaceful emotions in their bodies and upon their faces. Integrity of character is evidenced by a calm and contented countenance—an absence of agitated emotions. In betrayal, the tell-tale signs of Justifying, Accusing, & Resenting are typically expressed outwardly, but what brews beneath all accusing, self-excusing words and deeds are anxious and unsettled emotions:

* * * * *

You can lie with your MOUTH or EMOTION:
"When you're in the BRIAR, . . . You're a LIAR."

* * * * *

While the *lies from our lips* are more obvious, lies can also be "told" without words. Resentful and accusing emotions are nonverbal lies that we live; wordless emotional lies that are more subtle and insidious. As we harbor irritated and tense emotions, we are entangled in the thorns of the BRIAR.

The BRIAR represents Lies that we "tell" via Emotion.
The BRIAR represents Lies that we Live!

B = *Bothered Blaming Bitter*
R = *Resentful Raging*
I = *Irritated Impatient Irate*
A = *Angry Agitated Annoyed Anxious Accusing*
R = *Rationalizing*

These unsettled emotions openly show in our very countenance; they reveal our betrayal of Truth. Because these feelings are false, . . . we are Being False as we harbor them. BRIAR Emotions are yet another set of tell-tale signs that signal the loss of Life's inherent harmony.

* * * * *

When I am False . . . I feel
tension, agitation . . . disharmony.
My Unsettled Emotions signal falseness.
When I am True, I am at Peace;
the Peace that flows freely
signifies Harmony.

* * * * *

In Contrast to Pure White. Visualize a canvas of pure white, the kind of canvas that an artist uses to paint a portrait. Think of your life as a collection of colors being painted upon this clean, clear canvas. With every word you think and every deed you do, the portrait of your life is painted, and in contrast to pure white, any tint or shade *less than white* is obvious and conspicuous. Against an immaculate backdrop, you are able to see . . . with perfect clarity, how some motives and emotions fall short of pure white.

In your mind's eye, imagine that all loving words and deeds possess the unsullied shine of bright white. The purity of love would have no hint of darkness, not even the slightest shade of gray. Every word, deed, thought, or emotion that is "less-than" pure white, is a shade of betrayal:

Pure Love		***Less-than-Love***	
Emotions of Bright White		*Black & Gray Emotions*	
calm	approachable	impetuous	edgy
lovely	enthusiastic	suspicious	angry
amiable	nurturing	defensive	cranky
engaging	friendly	arrogant	forlorn
fascinating	happy	jealous	resentful
welcoming	sweet	galled	annoying
cherishing	giving	mean	impatient
animated	genuine	bitter	malicious
gracious	generous	bored	apathetic
cheery	passionate	listless	worried
lively	comfortable	irritated	fearful
real	warmhearted	conceited	tense

Shades of Betrayal: Less-than-Love. When we are being less-than-loving, the portrait we paint upon the white canvas is clouded by confusion; instead of vivid hues of red, blue, and green, a quarreling collision of colors makes the muddied shades of black and gray. Thus the portrait of our Life loses clarity . . . and beauty. Against the backdrop of bright white, even the subtlest shades of gray are easily exposed.

* * * * *

The Light of Innocence shines in the Heart of all Humanity;
It carries the Clarity and Purity of Bright White.
When I betray the Light of Innocence,
tense and agitated shades of black and gray
stand in stark contrast: Emotions Less-than-Love,
these Emotions signal my departure from Pure Light.

* * * * *

Look back on your life: Remember a time when you were crystal clear that something was wrong to do, . . . but you did it anyway. With your very first act that betrayed the Light of Innocence within, you were completely clear that a lesser way was being chosen. With each subsequent betrayal, this crystal sense of honesty became increasingly clouded; you became accustomed to the muddied shades of a dreary portrait. You became desensitized *to* the darkness, deadened *by* the darkness.

* * * * *

Pure White . . . portrays Pure Love.
Anything less than Pure White is Less-than-Love.
All acts that are Less-than-Loving are acts of Betrayal.

* * * * *

The Light of Innocence will naturally lead you *back* to the complete purity you possessed as a child. Followed consistently over time, the Light of Innocence will lead you to recover and renew . . . the You that is True. Returning to pure white is how you began and is *who you are* from your core. When you *recover* and *renew*, euphoric feelings of Love fill you, and flow from you. As you choose Love, you also choose the *peace* that comes with Love. To follow these impressions of Inner Innocence is to experience *rebirth*.

* * * * *

The Light always leads to Love.
Pure Love is an absence of Anxious Emotions.
Acts of Love I feel to do . . . bring Healing and Contentment.
As I choose Acts that are Less-than-Love,
I choose chaos and contention.
They come together just as certain seeds
bring forth specific fruits: confusion, clamor, and
complexity comes with every act that is Less-than Love.
The Motives and Emotions of My Heart, define the Acts I do.

* * * * *

The Fallibility of Following Feelings. The words "feeling" and "emotion" are essentially synonymous. Emotional moments, feeling moments, are the *exclamation points* of life; they give emphasis to a particular experience. Through our "feelings" we are *constrained* to pay greater attention to things that likely need more attention—this is true whether the feelings are white, black, or gray. When emotions flow from darkness, the discomfort of unsettled feelings is *educational*—it can *teach* us NOT to do "something like that again." The rule of thumb, "*follow your feelings*" became a common guide precisely because *all* emotional experience is *instructive.*

However "follow your feelings" *per se* is an unreliable rule—because some feelings are fallible. The fact is that emotions flow from prior perceptions and choices; thus, any physiological feeling that arises in you, is actually following your lead. It makes no sense to follow something . . . that is following you! Because YOU author of your emotions, if your perceptions are skewed then the feelings that flow from you will be equally warped. Bottom Line: Emotions should not always be *followed*, but should always be *listened to* for what they might teach.

* * * * *

You can trust your emotional feelings to be a good teacher, but not always a good leader. You are the author of your emotions; you should not follow, that which is following you, . . . for if you are false, then foulable feelings—which should not be followed— will flow from your falseness.

* * * * *

Feelings are fundamentally of two types: feelings of Light and feelings of darkness; emotions of Bright White and emotions of black and gray. Again, emotions are Life's *exclamations* . . . that *point* to moments and matters that need *attention*—what to *reinforce* in Bright White moments and what to *avoid* when black and gray emotions arise. Emotional feelings "kick in" as a function of how *you* perceive your world; thus, if your perceptions are *incorrect* or *impure*, you will generate body physiology in support of a "false alarm."

* * * * *

Fallacious Feelings should not be followed, but should be "listened to" and "learned from."

* * * * *

The most important function that foulable feelings serve . . . is to let us know we have left the Light. Negative emotions *can be* useful *exclamation points* that help us correct our course; however, they are only *helpful* if we *hear* and *heed* their warning, otherwise the experience of feeling negative emotions is just one more useless, needless occurrence of Self-Inflicted Suffering. Listening to what anxious emotions are willing to teach is one way that Life is Self-Correcting.

Emotion and Spirit are commonly confused. When people use the word "emotion," they are typically referring to the "physiological arousal"—bodily stirrings only. Because *physiological feelings* per se . . . occur in a morally-neutral way, one should never derive *moral guidance* . . . from glandular "inspiration." The so-called "feelings" that guide are a direct function of *Spiritual Integrity* . . . and not *Body Physiology.*

* * * * *

Because bodily feelings occur in a morally-neutral way, you should not derive moral guidance from hopping hormones.

* * * * *

While physiological arousal may be heightened in response to choices of Spiritual Integrity—thus giving emphasis to truthful moments—it is your *Spiritual Integrity* that is the primal source that *sets-in-motion* your *Way of Perceiving*, your subsequent *Body Physiology* and *Expressive Behaviors* (see Understanding Whole Emotion, page 126).

Learning to hear the subtle whisperings of your *Heart* without confusing those moments with a *hormonal surge* is important to the transformation of Changing Your Stripes. Learning to discern the difference between *bodily indigestion* and *spiritual intuition* is a sensitivity that is increases as you yield consistently to the Light of Innocence. Identifying the difference between emotions of *pure white* and deceptive shades of *gray* becomes clear as you move from the shadows of betrayal and into the Light—for it is *in the Light* and *by the Light* that clear vision illuminates:

* * * * *

Emotions of Bright White flow from the Light. There is no more Reliable Guide than the Heart-felt Whisper that speak with Crystal Clarity, and you know that something is Good.

* * * * *

Feelings of Light are felt in *complete correlation* with Being True. Each time you choose to *be true*, you set-in-motion emotions that invigorate that truthful choice. Feelings of Light are reinforcing: bright white emotions perpetuate a positive cycle! In contrast, when you defer to dark feelings, inner peace departs and a *self-defeating cycle* of negative synergy inevitably drags you down to despair.

Because foulable feelings let us know that we have strayed from the Light, the way to discern is clear: Feelings of Light lead to do good, . . . and when you do good, you feel good. In the very same way you recognize a good tree by its good fruit, you may also know that you are *being true* by the joyful feelings that fill you, and shine from you.

Seeing the Signs in Ourselves. To this point, the word "betrayal" has been used a few hundred times and it should be crystal clear that *betrayers* are the guys wearing the *black hats.* By now you may be saying to yourself: "Betrayers, those disgusting bunch of selfish scoundrels!" But now you must also realize that YOU are one of the "disgusting bunch." Betrayal is not the exclusive property of *inmates on death row* or *despicable sinners roasting in hell.* Betrayal is as common as breathing—examples are abundant. In any direction you look, a betrayal is in progress! We all betray the Light of Innocence at one time or another, and this diversion occurs much more than we imagine.

Because blindness accompanies betrayal, we're mostly oblivious to our own deviations from *pure white* to *shades of gray.* You begin to notice deviations more and more as you educate your eyes to seeing them. But you can only *see* as well as you *know* . . . and you will only *know* to the extent that the *good treasures of your heart* open up and illuminate clear vision.

Once made aware of JAR and BRIAR warning signs, it's fairly easy to see these *red flag* indicators in others, but much harder to see the signs in ourselves. Learning to observe these tell-tale signs in others can eventually translate to an increased awareness of seeing the signs in ourselves, but there is a danger in dwelling upon the behavior of others: we may fall prey to the mote-beam syndrome.* When there's a *big honking log* in your own eye, but only a *speck of dust* in the eye of your neighbor, it's a tad hypocritical to be pointing out the failings of a neighbor.

---

* One of many analogies advanced by Jesus; he taught that we cannot "see clearly" to judge others, until we have taken care of our own failings first (Matthew 7:1-5).

But go ahead and NOTICE the *specks* and *logs* in the eyes of others for a time, . . . with a nonjudgmental, open mind; then once you've better learned to recognize the tell-tale signs in others, then swiftly apply this newfound knowledge to yourself! Remember, you can only CHANGE YOU, and unless you change yourself even so–called "objective" observations will be blurred by a *migraine mental block*.

Besides being blind in the mind, it's also hard to see the tell-tale signs of betrayal in ourselves because we perceive life from *within* our bodies; thus from this physical location, we have a built-in bias for favoring ourselves over others. We have an inherent conflict of interest for choosing our own agenda, and turning our back on the best interests of all involved. Because living in harmony with humanity IS the *inner imperative* that naturally resounds in the heart, we lose inner harmony as we live selfishly. Having compassionate regard for humanity requires the "clear vision" only available to those who *live true*. To see the world through empathic eyes, means acquiring a perspective *outside* the selfish one we naturally see . . . from our body.

The view coming from your body is the worst perspective from which to see yourself; it is a one-sided view that intrinsically fosters egocentric acts. To see clearly, you need the Light to *lift you up* . . . to an *out of body* view. This empathic perspective—knowing as we are known—can be roughly simulated by video taping ourselves and watching the play back. In so doing, we might exclaim: "Is that how I am, . . . is that how I come across?"

Have you noticed that people feel uncomfortable watching themselves on video, or just looking at themselves in photos: "I don't look very good in that one," comes the familiar lament. Embarrassment is fairly common when "looking at" yourself, and possibly more frightening . . . when "seeing" yourself. But what is there to be embarrassed about, if all is well in the world? Should there be any embarrassment if you . . . are living true?

This *hesitancy* to see yourselves from the *out of body* view is similar to the moments when you don't want to lift your eyes up to see yourself in the mirror, because you feel guilty about something you've done. This same *hesitancy* happens when it comes to seeing yourself in the social mirror; unless you are "comfortable in our own skin"—you're living true to your own sense of truth—you may *hesitate* to see the reflections in the relational looking glass too.

* * * * *

If I want to "know" what I'm sending out
I must "see" what's coming back.
To know as I am known
and see as I am seen,
I must learn from
the reflections in the looking glass.

* * * * *

The truth is that others have a better vantage point from which to discern *what's going on* with us! They have the best access to all the subtle body gestures and positions that communicate *what we're up to.* They can see the expressions that we wear on our face; they can notice the glow we radiate from our countenance or not; they can sense the emotions that exude from our being (see pages 92, 155). To "know as we are known," feedback from the social mirror is essential, and feedback from the immaculate mirror is vital.

To "know as we are known" will only happen as we drop self-centered defenses and "let in" the reflections from the Looking Glass—reflections that become crystal clear as we Un-Do the darkness we have done. Thus, an empathic view is nurtured and expanded; we begin to "see" with eyes of innocence and are energized by bright white emotions.

* * * * *

Looking in the Social Mirror
can be done for reasons of Self-Improvement,
and for reasons that "see" beyond yourself: Love of Others.
To lose your Self in the service of Others
is the highest expression
of Self-Refinement.

* * * * *

In your mind's eye, try lifting your soul outside of your *body-self* for a moment and observe what you're about: Can you see yourself telling the same sad "victim" story to others, over and over again? And when you're not *telling* others this *anxious tale*, do you notice how that story *grinds away* in your head, hour after hour? Do you find yourself editing *mental reruns*, looking for logical flaws to perfect plausibility, so your next *performance* will be improved and polished "as if" your *anxious story* were true? *

Can you see your own fretful efforts to convince yourself? Do you sense your own insecurity? Can you see yourself in search of supportive votes from others to soothe your insecurity? Do you find yourself managing an image of the Self as Advertised—a false facade to hide behind? Can you feel unsettled emotions within, and realize that they are tainted with shades of black and gray?

If you see the tell-tale signs in yourself, and take action to Un-Do the darkness, you will *naturally recover your childlike nature;* in contrast, if you fail to see the signs of betrayal in yourself, you will *naturally embrace the opposite nature.*

---

* This pattern is pervasive among politicians and pundits who refine their rhetoric to sell half-truths, or even untruths, to the public. While politicians call it strategy, common folk call it, "lying." A basic premise for peddling political propaganda is: "the masses are asses" and a gullible public will buy a lie if the external packaging "looks" impressive and important. Such manipulation is the motive of self-serving political "spin,"—as well as ego-centric personal "spin."

Not One, . . . but Two Basic Natures. There is a philosophical debate about the basic nature of humanity. Built-in to the *average* question that generates this debate—"what is man's basic nature?"—is an expectation that the answer will land upon *one* basic nature. But to assume and expect a single answer, is to begin wrong. An intelligent person can give good answers, but it takes a wise person to ask the best questions from the start. A better question to begin with is this: "What does it mean to be human?"

To be human is to live in a world where *two fundamental natures* are available, two possible natures to which people may yield: One of *Light* and another of *darkness;* one of *Spirit* and another of *flesh.* As we walk in Light and yield to the guiding voice of Spirit, it is natural for us to have empathy for humanity, it is natural to live altruistically. Conversely, when walking in darkness—yielding to the allure of the flesh—it is natural for people to be consumed with self-serving agendas, it is natural to live hedonistically.

Hedonism is sometimes viewed as humanity's natural default position: to selfishly scratch the itch of furthering one's profit, pleasure, promotion, property, prestige, and power—basic motives assumed to *drive* all mortal decision-making. Indeed, human history is replete with examples of the *hedonistic nature* in action. When "seeing" the world from this *darkened perspective*, the *nature of Light* and the possibilities of altruistic living are often dismissed as real possibilities.** In the mind of a hedonist, all human action is motivated by a self-serving "pay off."

** Those who hold this view argue: "People are inevitably motivated by self-serving payoffs, . . . human life operates upon the principle of exchange: Quid Pro Quo." But this is to say that genuine Gift Giving is impossible and that so-called expressions of "love" are always "given" for what one is selfishly hoping to "get" in return. Such is not love . . . but manipulation. The highest expression of love is to impact others to their long-term betterment; a Love that altruistically considers the blessings and benefits of others; a Love that acts in the best interests of others. The life of Jesus is an example of pure altruism.

The hedonist nature is expressed in Freud's notion of "ID"—Instinctual Drives. According to Freud, the ID *instinctively drives* a person to motives of pleasure, power, and reproduction. And Freud was right! Well, . . . half right, the other half is the real possibility of the "nature of Light." It is evident and obvious that the nature we began with from mortal birth *is* the nature of Light—the proof is in the purity of a newborn child.

Because we all began with the *nature of Light*, some argue that *this* is the basic nature of humanity. But, practically speaking, it doesn't matter which nature is more *basic* than the other, because both natures are available to our choosing and thus, both natures can *become* basic! People can choose between these two natures, sometimes switching from one to the other. In other words, either nature can become the *basis* or *foundation* from which we live life; further, both natures have a spiritual power to perpetuate and support it.

Frankl forwarded principles termed "final freedom" and "inner liberty." Final Freedom refers to mankind's** most *basic ability* to choose between two basic natures; Inner Liberty represents the specific choice to embrace the *nature of Light*—and thus enjoy the connected *liberty* that come from the Light.

When we yield to the *nature of darkness*, we are naturally drawn to self-serving ways; being *self-absorbed* is instinctive when wallowing in betrayal. Thus we *see* more clearly *why* betrayers engage in *self-justifying* behavior—it's natural. Conversely, when yielding to the *nature of Light*, it is natural to

---

** I realize the word "mankind" is politically incorrect, but the word "humankind" didn't lend itself to alliteration; so, poetry wins over political correctness. Yet, my personal "meaning and motive" behind the poetry was "correct" from the start: "Intent Defines the Act." This is precisely why *general* campaigns calling for gender-inclusive language are often incorrect, because the "motive and meaning" behind the *individual* use of words is often overlooked.

have genuine concern for others; it is natural to live with compassion; it is natural to live . . . to give. But only when you actually live in the world of Light and simplicity, can you "see" that living altruistically . . . is a real possibility.

SEEING AND KNOWING

Seeing is a function of experience and knowledge. You don't simply *see* because you have eyes. With eyes only, you can *look* . . . but you may not *see.* If you're like me, you've been *looking* at small dark-brown birds and thinking of them *all* as sparrows. But as you educate your eyes thru experience, you begin to *see* finches, dunnocks, snow birds, or maybe a western tanager. With the greater knowledge that comes with experience, you will no longer think that any bird with a red breast must be a robin; instead, with *educated eyes*, you are free to *see* . . . a varied thrush, or a spotted towhee.

In Ecuador there are over one-hundred known varieties of hummingbirds, and the *average uneducated eye* may distinguish a half dozen. Similarly, betrayals come in hundreds of different shapes and sizes, but to the *average uneducated eye*, only a few . . . come to view. *Seeing* betrayals more readily comes with greater knowledge, and greater knowledge requires experience, and "experience" will always be of two types according to two basic natures: The nature of Light or the nature of darkness. Our *way of seeing* is inseparably tied to our *way of being*—we *see* our world according to *who we are.*

But between the different *world views* and *world experiences* that naturally come with *being true* or *being-less-than-true*, there are "intellectual" understandings that people in both worlds can understand according to *book learning*—as opposed to *heart learning*. Thus, there are two types of knowing: one of the *head*, and another of the *heart.* To "know as we are known," cannot be realized by intellectual means, it cannot be *figured out* by the *head*, but can only be known by the *heart* as one lives *faithfully* in the world of *simplicity*.

In terms of "intellectual" knowing, both Albert Einstein and John Dewey maintained that "experience is the basis of knowledge." All knowledge that is applicable and pertinent is not gleaned by just reading books. While books do generate ideas, still every idea must be tied to experience, else it will evaporate like a mirage in the desert—if you don't use it . . . you lose it!

Ideas and experience are two mutually-informing facets of knowledge, with both facets being essential to the claim of knowing. *Ideas* inform one's ability to *see*. Thus when equipped with a few *new ideas*, tomorrow's *experience* of Life opens up differently; in turn, *expanded experience* generates new questions and further stimulates . . . *new ideas*. This interplay between *ideas* and *experience* is one view of the hermeneutic circle: A mutually-informing circle of *ideas* and *experience* that cycle round and round, back and forth, to an ever expanding understanding of the world.*

Thus, as you read about "tell-tale signs of betrayal," you are better sensitized to *seeing* the ideas to which you've been informed; however, you must eventually *observe* and *experience* what I'm describing "in action" for only then will you really "see" what I am saying, and only then can you "know" what I'm talking about. Further, you can't even begin to arrange and remember your *ideas*—your *knowledge*—without *words*. *Linguistic labels* are required "to organize" experience and ultimately "hold on" to it.

* * * * *

Words are the "handles" by which we grasp our World.

* * * * *

---

* The word "hermeneutic" derives from the name "Hermes," the mythical messenger of Zeus and other Greek gods. Hermes was portrayed wearing winged cap and shoes and carrying a "caduceus"—a staff with two snakes twined around it and a pair of wings on top; it is used as an emblem of the medical profession. Hermes was the god of science and invention, of eloquence, luck, and cunning. The Romans called him "Mercury." Having the term "hermeneutic circle" provides a word-handle by which to "grasp" and "talk about" your world.

Whenever the question is asked, "what do you know?" An intelligent reply will be given in words. However, there are some things that we *think* we know, but cannot express them well into words; this vague and dreamy breed of "knowing" is the pre-condition essential to having words make sense—when you hear them.

This vague version of knowing IS the fuzzy residue of experience; unarticulated experience that is key to unlocking a conundrum called the Learning Paradox: *"You can't learn something unless you already know it."* In other words, if you haven't had certain prior *experiences* that pertain to particular *word-ideas*, then the "light bulb" of *knowing* will not "turn on"—you will not relate to the words that describe certain things and happenings, the *word-ideas* will *blow* over your head because you don't have the *anchor of experience* to hold them.

For this reason you cannot "learn" an *idea* unless you have a foundation upon which that *idea* can stand. Knowing happens within a mutually-informing cycle—a reinforcing round of words, ideas, and experience. This is one way of seeing the hermeneutic circle.

Understanding the Hermeneutic Circle is essential to solving the Learning Paradox puzzle: you must already "know" an idea at the level of *experience* in order to "learn" that idea at the level of *words*.* Again, there is an *unarticulated* "knowing" that comes with *experience* only, which is waiting to be articulated and ordered by *words* and *ideas* via dialogue.

---

* This is one the obstacles of classroom education: It is idea-heavy! Because it is typically tethered to a text book and a desk, schooling often does not supply a sufficient foundation of experience. Thus, students think they are "learning lots," but as a giant wave of inspiring ideas come crashing upon the shore of learning, students that hold up "a thimble" of experience can only retain "a thimble" of knowledge. Many insightful ideas melt from the mind, unless they are anchored in experience. This is also a problem with weekend workshops that "pump you up" with exciting ideas in a short period of time; the momentary high of "thrilling ideas" quickly deflates, because inspiring ideas are not reinforced thru experience.

* * * * *

A gallon of insightful ideas cannot be contained by a teaspoon of experience; neither can a barrel-full of experience be ordered and articulated by a teaspoon vocabulary.

* * * * *

This is where schooling comes in: "book learning" gives you "the words" to *grab hold* of ideas and to *express* those ideas—ideas that in turn *describe* the world that *arises from* experience. When direct world-experience is overlooked, some conversations can get caught up in a flurry of rhetoric that completely loses connection to reality; of this kind of ungrounded esoteric blather, Jacques Derrida said:

> *"Where we thought there was knowledge there is only literature.... all our writings—all the texts that we write to represent texts, referring to other texts which represent texts and arguing with their representation of texts—that all these texts are suspended over an abyss of fundamental ignorance about the origin, truth, presence, reality and nature of the things which we are representing.... all our rhetoric lead us only to an awareness of the limits of our knowledge."*

Claims of "knowing" are empty unless they are *grounded* on the firm foundation of directly-lived experience, yet knowledge also requires *ideas* and *words* to be complete. *Ideas* will not "turn on" without *experience*, neither can *ideas* and *experience* be ordered and remembered without *words*—the handles by which we grasp our world.

* * * * *

Experience is like Electricity, Ideas are like Light Bulbs, and Words flip the Switch. Words articulate the connection between Ideas and Experience.

* * * * *

With the terms JAR, BRIAR, *emotional squirting*, and *migraine mental block*, I am providing "handles" by which you can grasp the world. If you are able to tie these terms to your experience, then you will increase both your *knowing* and your *seeing*. Only through the "electricity" of experience, can you "know" and thus "see" the predictable patterns of the JAR. Yet the value of reading/learning about JAR phenomena *sensitizes* you to "seeing" *new patterns* in the first place—thus experience is expanded and enriched.

Through reading only, the JAR can be reduced to just a catchy acronym, but by allowing this idea to inform your world-experience, a new way of seeing and knowing opens up; thus you will see . . . that the JAR is not just theory. Experience will verify the JAR Principle, as well as other principles expressed herein. Experience is the basis for a philosophical approach called Pragmatism, which is one of five ways for establishing claims to truth (for more info visit: www.CallDrMatt.com/TruthClaims).

Clouded Vision: A Cultural Inheritance. Besides the built-in body bias for favoring our own selfish agendas and the *migraine mental block* that blinds, another reason we fail to clearly "see" the warning signs of betrayal in ourselves, is because of cultural influence; we are taught NOT to "see" the tell-tale signs. Actually, we do "look" but we may not "see" to the extent that our "perception" makes any difference in the way we live.

Many betrayals go unrecognized because *perceiving* is a function of what we've learned lately; sadly, some social institutions spread erroneous ideas that feed and reinforce our everyday expectations. It is fairly common in our culture to think that doing a *bad* thing is OK, if you have a *good* excuse! For example, *screaming and yelling* is generally judged to be bad, but within the context of athletic coaching, *yelling and screaming* is accepted—especially at the highest levels of competition. If a coach does not *scream* at a referee that makes a bad call or *yell* at a player who makes a bad play, that coach is "not doing the job!" Hence screaming is deemed "business as usual" within the coaching culture, and by bad *example* and through *experience* we become acclimatized to the excuse: yelling is OK, if its part of your job description.

There are other societal institutions that initiate and perpetuate an *excuse-making mindset.* It is ironic that the very institution that exists to help you *OUT* of your troubles . . . offers the very intervention that keeps you *IN* your troubles: I'm speaking of It's-Not-Your-Fault Psychology. This single institution plays a monstrous role in misinforming society. When faced with a problem, certain "therapeutic paradigms" teach people to: "blame it on bad biology" or "blame it on a bad up-bringing" and my personal favorite . . . "blame it on the bosanova!" Blame it on anyone or anything but don't blame it on yourself!

It's-Not-Your-Fault Psychology can divert you from doing exactly what would help you most—*own your stuff!* This often means, instead encouraging you to seek the Vote of inner validation that comes by accepting Response-Ability, excuse-making psychology may persuade you to a captivating consolation: do what the masses do, win the popular vote and ride the bandwagon of political correctness.

One of the reasons It's-Not-Your-Fault Psychology has developed to such dismal depths is explained by the influence of another cultural institution that also sires an excuse-making mentality: The Adversarial Legal System! Because massive amounts of money are being paid to "get people off" at any cost, the legal system has a high incentive to seek out every conceivable scheme to accomplish acquittal. Many of those acquittal schemes are directly fueled by none other than: It's-Not-Your-Fault Psychology.

Claiming a "mental disorder" is becoming increasingly more frequent in courts of Law. All you need is a credible psychologist to say: "It's not your fault, you have a mental disorder," and voila—acquittal! In fact "you-have-a-mental-disorder" has replaced "abracadabra" as the most frequently used "magic word." Because big money motivates secular psychology to find plausible alibis for legal defense strategies, there is steady motivation to find new disorders!

The Diagnostic Statistical Manual for Mental Disorders is an ever-expanding volume that legitimizes every nuance of human excuse. When big money defendants need to "get off," *excuse-making psychology* comes to the rescue with a new Disorder. So while you're blaming your bugaboos on a bad brain, bad up-bringing, bad biology, or the bosanova . . . add to this list, *blame it on the Brady Bunch:* "Your Honor, my client is innocent because he suffers from an chronic case of Television Intoxication Disorder." The equally sad commentary is that such "defense" strategies are sometime seen as "brilliant" when they "work," instead of being seen for what they are: dishonest manipulations. "We, the sheep-ple" are being systematically desensitized to thinking that legal proceedings are analogous to a game of sport, complete with plays, tactics, strategies, and victories—a legal game played *as if* truth and justice did not apply.

The "legal-defense-as-sport" orientation was significantly spawned in all its glory during one sensational murder trial, where the national media openly analyzed and debated the "strategies" of an all-star legal defense team. Analysts across the country talked about this murder trial *as if* it were a competitive contest, a game: *"They're going to play the race card,"* announced the experts. News reporters and pundits openly argued the merits of each strategic move in "the game." Thus "legal-strategy-as-sport" became legitimized in the minds of a viewing nation and ingrained into the norms of society.

Why does the media use this tactic? To sell tickets to the coliseum, of course! To increase curiosity to see whether the *gladiators* or the *lions* will win, and whether the jury will give a "thumbs up or thumb down" in the end. Media can't "sell' their product if there is no drama or controversy. Of said murder trial, the media might have straightforwardly reported: "this is the lie that the defense lawyers will try to sell the jury." But who's going to *tune in* if the media simply told the truth? Lies are much more sensational and sell-able!

Politics is another cultural institution that provides clouding influence upon our way of seeing and knowing. The antics of some politicians teach us that it is OK to twist the truth to further an agenda.* Like the "legal game," the beguiling banter of political pundits is viewed as a "political game." As media report the news of politicians slinging *believable lies* back and forth, the viewing audience is subtly and systematically socialized to believing that such rhetorical "strategies," are indeed just "strategies,"—as opposed to being "immoralities." Hence, *truth twisting* is now part of a questionable, but standard job description, and *old-fashioned honesty* is . . . out of fashion.

Because many unwittingly accept the "game/sport" analogy legitimized by the media, . . . lawyers and politicians tend to get a "pass" on moral responsibility: "They're just doing a job, business as usual." Given the cultural impact of politics, the legal system, and It's-Not-Your-Fault Psychology, is it any wonder why some people of this society would have a tendency toward rationalizing, excuse-making, and blaming.

---

* Spinning an agenda means that people cease from sensible consideration of evidence, and stubbornly proclaim their angle on an issue. People who are rabidly and blindly committed to an agenda are called "ideologues." Most ideologues suffer from a Migraine Mental Block: "Never mind the facts, I've already made up my mind!" In contrast, people who Live True will relax, listen, and consider further facts and evidence.

When public opinion is successfully manipulated by an effective scheme (a.k.a., lie), to what extent are politicians praised for a winning strategy? And when guilty litigants go free, to what extent do "we the sheep-ple" praise lawyers for being brilliant and clever? To what extent do we learn from society to seek out *exceptional circumstances* where *bad* behavior has a *good* excuse?

It appears that the moral relativism of secular humanism has significantly infiltrated the media, the legal system, our political system, and thus our culture generally. This is precisely why acts of dishonesty are labeled "strategies," for there is no absolute standard of moral right and wrong from the secular humanist view.

To an associate, I once recounted the story of a man who cheated on his wife and my colleague replied, "what did this man's wife do that drove him to commit adultery?" The underlying implication of this question reveals an *excuse-making mentality* that is fostered by our culture. In contrast, when you do, what you do, with a heart that is true, then you have no need for alibis or blame; this includes the oft invoked rationale *"the end justifies the means"*—a logical maneuver that is just one more insipid *excuse* in a long list of seductive rationalizations.**

Recovering the True You means embracing a "no excuses" approach to Life, a perspective that "sees" bad behavior as . . . bad behavior. While there will always be a context within which our choices are *explained* and *understood*, there is never

---

** Freud identified acts of "rationalizing" as a defense mechanism; a defense "needed" by those who are wrestling with inner conflict. Even Freud—who did not believe in a Creator—asserted that rationalizing and justifying are tell-tale signs of internal turmoil. While he did NOT believe in an absolute source of morality, he did acknowledge a "social" morality via his notion of "superego"—which is equivalent to "conscience."

an *excuse* that turns bad behavior . . . into good behavior. Although our contemporary culture often argues otherwise, there are never any exceptional alibis or rationalizations that make bad behavior . . . un-bad.*

Excuse-making is the opposite of Owning, and Owning your "bad" IS a good way out of the abyss of betrayal! But to clearly see the tell-tale signs of betrayal in yourself and own your "bad," you'll need to push aside the *popular voice* that brazenly persuades *popular ways*—"everybody's doing it"—and instead, listen to the quiet whisperings of your heart.

* * * * *

In matters of Personal Peace,
The only Vote that counts is the one registered
in the Ballot Box of the Heart.

* * * * *

We live in a culture that wants YOU to win the popular vote: to "look good," "be a winner," and "go for the gold." But these garish goals of glory, fame, and fortune can also entice you to live with a self-centered orientation of "ME," as opposed to a compassionate orientation of "WE." When consumed by *selfish concerns* we lose harmony of heart. Changing Your Stripes calls for complete *self-honesty*.

---

* The example of Nephi slaying Laban may appear on the surface to be an example of "bad behavior that was good." But such reasoning disregards the act-as-a-whole, and takes the "slaying of Laban" out of context (1 Nephi 4:10-18). Because the "intent" of Nephi's heart was to "obey God," therefore, the "whole-act" of slaying Laban was an "act of obedience." Intent of heart is what defines the difference between "killing as self-defense" and "killing as murder." In Nephi's case, it was God who directed the slaying of Laban, and it is the Creator's prerogative to give and take life (1 Samuel 2:6-8). Further, this an NOT an example of "the ends justify the means," . . . this is an example of "the Creator justifies both ends and means"—the Creator Justifies.

Rationalize or Recover. As you detect JAR behaviors from the *outside* and BRIAR emotions from the *inside*, you are confronted with a Life-Changing choice:

* *Rationalize . . . or*
* *Recover*

One choice brings peace and the other continues misery. Because *"you can't talk your way out of a problem that you behaved your way into,"* the best solution to the inner imbalance is to behave your way *back out* of the ditch in which you've fallen—*un-do* the very deeds that *spawned* foul feelings in the first place. Of course "back out" means discontinuing the *instigating* behavior—set it aside, put it behind, leave it there!

If you're stuck in the JAR, . . . EXCUSE will be your aim and BRIAR emotions will continue to well within; but if PEACE is your purpose, you will OWN your errors. From each choice, the connected consequence is clear; when you betray your own sense of what is right, two alternatives appear: You can try to *hide it* and *rationalize it*, OR you can be *humble about it* and *own your error.* From the *humble* choice, the possibilities of *recovery* unfold.

* * * * *

Rationalizing defends . . . a stagnant position:
as I RATIONALIZE, I remain the same.
Recovery means:
Owning my Betrayals
and Un-Doing my Dark Deeds;
as I RECOVER, the pathway to Peace
unfolds, the Power to Change is my Possession.

* * * * *

In the end, you don't *have to* own Response-Ability! You don't *have to* change! You don't *have to* feel the euphoric energies of joy! Instead, you can *defend* yourself as you are; you can *explain away* responsibility and *pretend* no wrong doing; you can accuse others and blame your blight on unbearable situations; but then, you *get to* experience all the consequences tied to these choices.

Rationalizing is the *course of least resistance*, yet it only *appears* to be the easy way out—it only *appears* to require the least amount of effort. The truth is the emotional aftermath of rationalizing IS the *course of most misery*. By defending bad behavior—as opposed to backing out of bad behavior—the rationalizing route keeps you stuck in the rut of remaining the same miserable you, and you forfeit an opportunity for growth of character. In this life, *who you become* IS your richest reward; thus, by rationalizing you forfeit your most precious benefit.

There is enormous good news in admitting your errors and embracing change: You are now free to reach the heights of happiness! As you recognize and own your errors, you are free to be . . . the best you can be. Blaming is bondage: "to blame and accuse other people is to choose to empower them, to control you." When you OWN your stuff, only then do you have the *power* to change, and as Heraclitus declared: *"It is in changing that we find purpose."*

When you live your life in blame, you drain yourself of the power to progress personally, and you give that power to those you blame—you become a *Victim* instead of the *Victor!* Owning your stuff is the beginning that brings things back into balance, it leads to the welcome *change* of recovery and renewal. This way may seem *harder to do*—but it's *easier on you.* Living in *peace* is much easier that living in *pain.*

* * * * *

What appears to be Pain in Prospect . . . is Peace in Practice.

* * * * *

Rationalizing uses the fodder of *facts* to fire its accusing and self-excusing cannons. Facts are not always the precious jewels that some suppose. The saying goes, *"Sometimes the truth hurts,"* but I disagree: the Truth always heals. Truth is our highest prize! It is *facts* that are used to inflict hurt and harm. But aren't facts and truth the same thing?

DISCERNING BETWEEN FACT & TRUTH

Facts and truth are commonly equated, but there is an important and practical difference: Consider the way *facts* are used in courts of law to bring about injustice; on this basis alone, Truth needs to be more than a synonym for fact. "Truth" needs its own identity apart from "fact."

Sometimes the word "fact" is used to mean "reality"—the way things ARE, the way the world IS. But then what *word* should *represent* the legal evidence that is used to mislead? In legal arenas, *fact* is often far from a truthful representation of *reality*. Since we already have the word Reality to represent "the way things are," let's use the word Fact to represent *"technically correct words"*—both spoken and written.

* * * * *

Facts are technically accurate statements
made by the mouth or penned by the hand.
Truth is a larger statement, a holistic statement
Truth is not just factually accurate, but also utterly honest.
Truth is the whole statement of one's total being:
a unified expression of word, deed, motive,
and emotion—all of which are True.

* * * * *

Should *"the Truth, the whole Truth, and nothing but the Truth"* be anything less? When a clear distinction is made between facts and Truth, we realize that words can be factual yet *untrue* at the same time; a person's words may be technically *correct* but when inward intent is not *true* . . . then only *fact-speaking* can occur—as opposed to *Truth-telling.**

---

* One of the most obvious examples of fact speaking, while NOT telling the Truth, was when a prominent political figure shook his defiant finger and exclaimed: "I did not have sex with that woman." Because he had a special definition of "sex," he was thus making a technically "true" statement—a speaking of fact (in his mind, according to his linguistic rules). But the "statement of his heart" was false while he was speaking his so-called "fact," therefore, he was not "telling the whole Truth." And Truth IS always Whole.

If the motive behind the message is false, then superficially accurate words are false from their foundations. This is the very meaning of empty rhetoric: words expressed without wholeness of heart. You can't really "tell the truth," unless you are also *Being True* from the heart. Because Intent defines the Act, when motives are not honorable one can actually bear false witness, while *speaking facts.*

Facts can be conveyed regardless of inward intent of heart; again, this means that on the surface words can be technically *correct*—and at the same time—the heart of the messenger can be *incorrect.* Part of the rhetorical game of *fact-speaking* is picking out certain details "from the whole," and just exposing the "the part" that gives factual support to a dishonest agenda. Thus, facts can be used in the service of lies—while Truth cannot.

Truth is whole: heart, might, mind, strength, and soul. Of course, included in this truthful wholeness is being filled with the pure energy of true emotion! Thus, a person who is caught in the BRIAR may make *verbal claims* to truth, but as dark emotions seep to the surface, it becomes clear that such claims are shallow: *Emotions speak louder than Words!*

When Truth is conceived and experienced in wholeness, a different way of seeing and knowing opens up—a new view unfolds. Distinguishing between facts and Truth is vital to Recovering the You . . . that is completely and utterly True.

Being Right versus Being True. Being Right is driven primarily by facts, and not by Truth. Being Right is having accurate descriptions of "what happened." Being Right is about having the facts in your favor; it's about getting *the upper hand* in an argument; it's about winners and losers—for when YOU are *right* then others are *wrong.* And where does than put YOU in relation to others: an enemy, adversary, competitor, opponent, or rival? Being Right is not the best way to "win friends and influence people." Being Right is the booby prize!

* * * * *

No man knows less, than the man who knows it all.
It is Better to Be Kind . . . than Correct.
Being Right makes YOU incorrect.

* * * * *

The real prize is in Being True. Being True is "be-ing" in alignment with Life's inherent harmony—flowing with the guiding Light of Innocence. Being True mean having integrity of character. Being True is the holistic unity and expression of existence: *heart*, *might*, *mind*, *strength*, and *soul.* Being True is more than just speaking factual statements from your mouth, but includes the "statement" of *all that you are!* Being True puts YOU in a positive position in regard to others—a win/win position. For when you are True, then there is Love, to include the rainbow of all *bright white emotions.*

Being Blunt versus Being Honest. You've likely heard this well-worn theme of therapy: *"You need to be emotionally honest . . . and own your feelings."* The rhetoric is right, but the application is often wrong. The distinction between "Truth and facts" lends insight into the difference between Being Blunt versus *truly* Being Honest. Because the wholeness of Truth encompasses intent of heart, when we do not have pure motives, the mere "telling" of candid words is best described as Being Blunt—frank fact-speaking. Since *being honest* includes the truthful motives and emotions of the heart in the moment a statement is given, thus, what is commonly called "emotional honesty" is better described as "emotional bluntness."

* * * * *

Some approaches to Emotional Honesty are not so concerned with really having Honest Emotions, but with bluntly reporting any old emotion smoldering within.
Emotional Honesty is regularly reduced to assertive blurting about foul feelings.

* * * * *

When so-called "honest" assertiveness basically boil down to just being blunt, "emotional honesty" becomes a gross misnomer. The sharp edge of *bluntness* is softened by *benevolence* when assertive statements are accompanied with *honest emotions* (see page 196).

Paradoxically, some helping professionals perpetuate the practice of blunt blurting about *black* and *gray* emotions; they teach clients to send "I" messages that can easily be laced with foul feelings. The "I" message system mostly involves ME telling YOU . . . that YOU are making ME ANGRY: "I feel very annoyed when you chew your food that way!" This is done in the name of "owning your feelings," but regrettably does NOT include . . . "owning your betrayals."

The *false application* of "emotional honesty," likely occurs due to the *false assumption* that emotions are morally neutral, and thus feeling emotion in any form is a *natural* occurrence. Of course, naturally flowing with one's nature is a good thing, but from which "nature" is the "flow" coming from? (see page 205). By failing to make a distinction between pure white emotions *versus* betraying emotions of black & gray, therapists unwittingly validate foul feelings; curiously, it never occurs to some *helping professionals* to "help" clients *get rid of* dishonest emotions at the *root* (see page 136).

The truth is that "body physiology" IS INDEED morally neutral: the flow of adrenaline that makes the heart beat faster IS neither right nor wrong. Nevertheless, aspects that comprise *whole emotion* (thoughts, words, deeds, intentions)—that *happen with* physiological flow—ARE absolutely morally loaded; this means those same thoughts, words, and deeds will *impact self and others* to either *betterment* or *detriment.* The Heisenberg Effect applies: *inescapable impact always!* In every human act . . . there is impact; people cannot NOT influence others in the course of human relations. When viewed in a holistic way, every *emotional expression* will inevitably land on either side . . . of a moral divide.

Body physiology is only separate from *conscious experience*, *behavioral action*, and *spiritual integrity* at the level of words and descriptive analysis. Words create the illusion of separation. While we can separate the *construct of emotion* at the "symbolic" level, we CANNOT make the same separation at the level of "living reality." Therefore, *whole emotion* is ever and always morally loaded—there are NO NEUTRAL emotions. And why should emotion be thus conceived? Because that is how emotion occurs in the wholeness of directly-lived experience!

* * * * *

When understood in its richest sense,
Emotional Honesty includes Emotional Honorableness.

* * * * *

Being honest is inseparable from *expression of whole being. Being Honest* is a facet of *Being True* . . . otherwise the term "emotional honesty" is reduced to a superficial meaning that falls far short of an honesty that is unified and complete. Therefore, when people convey *frank* reports of *feelings* that are *black* or *gray*, and call that report "emotional honesty"—you see the problem! What they have really done is give an accurate report of dishonest emotions, which isn't be-ing *emotionally honest* at all—for be-ing *honorable* has been excluded.

THE MYTH OF EMOTIONAL SCARS

Years after experiencing a trauma, some continue to claim emotional pain due to that difficulty; they blame their *present pain* upon a *past aggravating event.* In their mind, they think the past situation "caused" the pain they still feel years later. This could be the case if bodily contact occurred and physical damage was done, but if the pain is *purely emotional*, then the principles governing this "pain" are different. The following discussion deals with emotional anguish only; it addresses the "emotional scar" phenomenon: The lingering, long-term emotional "mark" that *supposedly* never goes away and never completely heals.

Obviously, the idea of emotional scars got its impetus from the tangible reality of physical scarring. Physical scars occur when bodies are battered or broken, and as they heal, the evidence of abuse or accident remains in the flesh. The theory behind "emotional scarring" is similar, but it is the inner person that is battered and broken; thus, the parallel assumption is that emotional scars—like physical scars—leave a "mark" that never goes away.

* * * * *

The physical flesh has its own realm of reaction,
uniquely different from the emotional realm of reaction;
while it's commonly assumed that "emotional scars"
never completely heal and never go away,
such is a Flat-Earth Assumption.

* * * * *

For a victim to conclude, "I've been emotionally scarred for life" is comparable to this false alarm: "Help, I'm falling off the edge of the earth!" When we get completely clear about Cause as opposed to Constraint (page 3), we see that it is impossible for a situation to "cause" *emotional pain* after the initiating event no longer exists—just as water can no longer flow from a faucet when the valve has been shut off. Any emotional pain that is felt *after* an aggravating event has long since ended, is *self-inflicted*. Thus, when assumptions are OFF about how emotional traumas initiate, continue, and end, then the victims that hold erroneous ideas will *live like* they are falling OFF the edge of the earth.

Here's the truth: The earth is *round* AND all people who have experienced *emotional trauma* can be healed and made *whole*. Emotional scarring is the *optional extension* of emotional trauma, and originates via OFF *assumptions*, thus OFF *perceptions:* W.I. Thomas affirmed, "that which you perceive as real . . . is real in its consequences."

Even though the initiating event has ended—like a faucet that has been completely shut off—still some people manage to keep bitter waters running, anyway! How is this done? Beyond the physical *effects* that linger due to actual *causes* inflicted to the body, YOU are the *cause* of all other *responses* that come from YOU. Emotional suffering can only continue with your *permission* and active *participation.*

Life is a Set Up that supplies hard-to-bear adversities, yet, Inner Liberty remains: You possess "final freedom" to choose inner responses of heart, mind, and soul; thus, while physical pain may be *necessary*, emotional suffering is *optional.*

* * * * *

When physical flesh is bruised and broken, a visible mark may remain: Physical Scars are "Permanent." In contrast, emotional scarring is not an effect that is caused; ultimately, . . . it is a chosen response in answer to a constraint: Emotional Scars are "Optional."

* * * * *

While the constraints that press upon you may be very compelling, emotional "marks" remain only through your continued culpability; still, this active, willful creation of today's emotional scarring does not discount the *initial trauma* that was *hard to bear* when yesterday's afflicting faucet *was* turned on. Situational Suffering is real, and occurs beyond the choice and perceptual participation of the afflicted; meaning, the afflicted person is NOT choosing to make it bad—it just IS bad. Yet while suffering may be *necessary*, the degree to which that suffering is felt . . . is determined by the disposition of each individual.

* * * * *

Your personal P.Q. comes into play: Situational Suffering is inevitably amplified or diminished by the condition of your disposition.

* * * * *

There are two foundational reasons why mistreatment need not leave an emotional mark. One reason is *psychological*, and the other is *spiritual.* The psychological reason has to do with the way you perceive reality in the first place, as Stephen R. Covey affirms: "You don't see the world as it is, you see it according to who you are."

Reality is subjectively *constructed* from the perspective of the perceiver; one's perspective in the present moment is a function of knowledge and maturity. This means that you *see* and *interpret* reality on the basis of what you've learned lately. Dostoevsky writes: *"Reason only knows what it has learned yet."* Harboring *false assumptions*, leads to drawing *false conclusions.*

* * * * *

The World does NOT simply speak to you, and tell you What Is Happening; instead, you "bring" to the world an Interpretation according to your Learning, Experience, and especially your Disposition of Character.

* * * * *

This explains why some people at a perfectly good party will be having a ball while others may say, "this bash is boring!" The explanation of what is *happening* at a party has *more* to do with the people attending the party, than the raw content of the occasion. The fact is that boring people bring themselves and their boring perspective to a perfectly good party and surprise, surprise, *a boring party* is perceived—no matter how creative the curriculum. But EVEN IF the content of a party IS a tad retarded, people who live *truthfully* still find great pleasure in face-to-face associations; to them, this is the curriculum that counts—bells and whistles are not required to make an event enjoyable.

Objective observations of life clearly confirm that two people who endure essentially the same tragic situation can *respond* in diametrically different ways; while one person may be tormented by a traumatic situation for years, in contrast, another person may live happily and productively as if the adverse event never happened. But the event did happen, . . . so what's the difference?

* * * * *

Without changing any physical facts of the past,
one difficult misfortune can result in
two very different memories.
A Re-Membering that is colored with Compassion versus
A Re-Membering that is tainted with Contempt.
As I am mired in today's Contempt,
I cannot access or even imagine
Compassionate Possibilities. The meaning of
yesterday's facts Change . . . as I Change in the present.

* * * * *

The dividing difference does not happen by means of a mental trick—*pretending* like it never happened—nor is the difference due to *re-programming* one's so-called *neuro-computer*. No, that's definitely not it! The difference is determined by matters of the *heart*, and not the *head*. A trial or tragedy will be a "stumbling block" for those whose *heart* is tainted with contempt; conversely, a tragedy possessing the same physical facts will be a "building block" for those whose *heart* is filled with compassion—"the good treasure of the heart" (see page 89).

When I use the word "contempt," that emotion may overstate the sentiment felt by some who *hang on* to emotional scars; to be clear, "contempt" is a word that represents an entire category of *negative emotions* that fall short of *bright white purity*. Those that cannot "see" what suffering *was* willing to teach and still *is* willing to teach, are those whose *hearts* harbor black & gray emotions—emotions less-than-love.

* * * * *

The Living Reality that you experience,
the reality that IS your world—Past and Present—
is constructed according to Today's Interpretations, which
are in turn determined by your Disposition of Character:
The Good Treasures of the Heart.

* * * * *

Re-Membering the Past. Since "memory" is a noun-word, it has a "thing-ish" meaning in the minds of many and the "thing" that memory is commonly compared to is a "computer hard drive." When conceived as a *noun*, memory is regularly *reified* into a thing-ish container of historical data. But this not the best way to conceive memory, for memory is really *activity*—not entity. In the *case of computers*, records are retrieved in the exact same form every time; but in *matters of memory*, past happenings are re-called creatively, interpretively, and variably.

* * * * *

Memory is not a "thing" that contains facts; instead,
Memory is "an activity" of Re-Constructing
the Meaning of What Happened.
"Memory" is a noun-word that represents verb-activity,
Memory is really . . . Re-Membering.

* * * * *

The hyphenated word "Re-Membering" symbolizes what is actually happening as one Re-Members yesterday: the "members" are "put back together," they are "assembled again." Thus, one does not retrieve *the past* like *data* from a computer *hard drive*—the past does not exist like unchanging data stored in a brain-container. In reality, *the past* does not have a life of its own apart from your *re-membering*.

* * * * *

What is called "The Past" literally lives
via Re-Membering done Today.

* * * * *

If you don't drag yesterday's dreary details ahead, day by day, they tend to go away—especially as you have better and brighter projects to pursue! More specifically, what "goes away" is the "painful meaning" you *used to bring* . . . to what happened; that old *painful* meaning is then replaced by a new *productive* meaning, a *re-membering* that doesn't hurt—a new meaning that literally builds your strength of character.

Re-membering means that a person *actively and creatively constructs* the past from the perspective of one's present day experience, maturity, and character. The facts of the past do not speak for themselves, they must be interpreted. "The past" is perceived in essentially the same way "the present" is perceived, but in constructing the present, *empirical facts* are typically before you; whereas, in *re-membering* the past, you only have *your imagination* before you. In either scenario, you can put on "The King's New Clothes" through the *creative* re–construction of both past and present happenings.

Through the *activity* of "re-membering" you can create interpretations that don't really exist, . . . except as "really" erroneous mental myth-making. For some, such creative embellishments occur "intentionally," and for others, *creative contrivings* occur "unwittingly." Either way, re-membering is always a subjective, interpretive activity. In matters of memory, people are simply, sincerely, and easily . . . mistaken!

Even perceptions in the present can be elusive: Imagine being at the scene of a car crash; in a one explosive moment, an accident occurs and because it was unexpected—careful attention was not paid. Thus, even in the "now" . . . present events drift into vagueness. The "crash" was right before you only seconds ago, yet you must now *re-member* this present happening, just as you would *re-assemble* yesterday's history. So even though today's creative construction of "the crash" is fairly fresh, you can still put on "The King's New Clothes," in the way you sincerely, but mistakenly re–construct "the meaning" of the present moment.

Your *experience of reality* does not exist apart from *the meaning you make of it.* This is such an important truth to internalize that it bears repeating, with a stunning application:

* * * * *

Your experience of Reality does not exist apart from "the meaning" you make. Reality will mean . . . according to the interpretations you bring.
When the Facts of the Past "mean" something different today, than they meant yesterday, then the Past has changed!

* * * * *

This is because "the past" was never just the raw facts, but *the meaning you bring* to those facts. Again, "facts" do not speak for themselves; they require interpretation by YOU. The activity of re-membering is a "bringing of meaning" to past happenings by YOU. Yet, you can't simply choose to interpret "the past" or "the present" any way you want; instead, your interpretations *spontaneously flow* from *who you are;* your *way of seeing* flows from the "abundance of the heart"—or lack thereof.

* * * * *

Who You Are determines how you perceive your world,
there is more than one Reality for you . . . to view.
One is seen through the Eyes of Innocence,
another view is tainted by contempt.
Bright White Reality comes to view
as your response to "The Past"
is completely & purely True.

* * * * *

If you're living in spiritual disharmony today, you will be fraught . . . with a *migraine mental block;* this means you are destined to re-construct the past using a *defective perspective*—an outlook fixated upon the facts, yet fails to honor the Truth. And just like the boring person who brings himself to a perfectly good party, . . . surprise, surprise, the past is *made* bitter, by a bitter mind.

* * * * *

The Past, the Present, and your anticipations of the Future
are all at the mercy of Who You Are, and how
You assemble the "members" today:
how you Re-Member.

* * * * *

Since your *only view of the world* comes via interpretations you *bring*, thus, the past is *re-constructed* according to *who you are* in the present. If YOU are presently a resentful and bitter human being, you will re-member only one *possible* version of "the past"—you will re-member the bitter version! Not because that is the "way it was," . . . but because that is "the way you are." This means "the past" can be and IS regularly resurrected through the perceptual filters of resentment.

When you *re-construct* the past through the bitter filters of resentment, you climb into a boiling pot that YOU yourself have pushed into the fire, and being up to your neck in the hot water of mean emotions, YOU *stew* and *ruminate* upon past calamities. "It's-Not-Your-Fault" Psychology calls such torment "Post-Traumatic Stress Disorder," . . . but I call it "Post-Traumatic Stew" and YOU are the Soup Nazi makin' the brew!* As we anxiously *stew* about yesterday's unfair adversities, we engage in a *faithless fretting* that suffers from *near-sighted* vision. We fail to "see" the *far* picture and purpose of existence: The Creator will absolutely answer all injustice with perfect judgment, justice, and mercy.

* * * * *

Stewing in Hostility and Ruminating in Resentment is like choosing the Misery of Eating Mud, while refusing the Feast of a Healthy Meal.

* * * * *

The distorted thinking goes like this: If I can actively *resent* and hold a *grudge* today about injustices of yesterday, maybe I can launch some psychic arrows toward my abusers to *get back, to punish, to reap revenge.* Re-sending resentful energy is an enormous waste of time and effort; the person that suffers most from this exercise IS . . . the person doing the resenting—the re-sending! Remember: Resentment is the poison that *you* drink, while expecting your abusers to die, from the poison that *you* drink.

Think this through carefully: A tragedy that happened *yesterday* is no longer happening today, the afflicting faucet has been turned off. So, the only torment to experience *today* IS

---

* The Soup Nazi is a character from the sit-com Seinfeld: He is a renowned master soup-maker who is extremely strict and authoritarian in the way he dishes out soup to his customers—hence, the Soup Nazi.

the torment of "re-thinking" past tragedy over and over in your mind, and instead of choosing a better way today—instead of embracing *bright white reality*—some engage in the *voluntary re-construction* called "emotional scarring." Instead of feasting upon the freedoms and opportunities that a *new day* affords, they fret and brew . . . in Post Traumatic Stew, and with small-minded rancor they resentfully ruminate upon yesterday's injustice—with self-absorbed alienation, they gnaw upon yesterday's dead bones! As Mother Teresa advised: "Yesterday is gone. Tomorrow has not come. We have only today. Let us begin."

Emotional Scars: Exactly what are they? People who claim "emotional scars" live life in a "marked" way. But exactly what is that mark? To understand what an *emotional scar* might be, first we need to correctly conceive "emotion" (see The Emotional Self, page 105). In review, *emotion* is a word to describe moments when heightened bodily arousal augments the perceptions of a given moment. Emotion is a word to represent a situated activity of spirit-mind-body-behavior—"situated" means that *being-emotional* always occurs within a particular living context.

When correctly conceived, the noun-word "emotion" will translate into verb-activity. Thus, the image of emotion should never evoke a general construct, or ethereal essence; instead, the word "emotion" should bring to mind a *specific emotional moment* enacted by a particular person.*

* * * * *

As I fail to "see" Emotion in the specific context of living reality, by default, my conceptions end up floating in metaphysical La La Land, a.k.a., Generalville, a suburb of Esoteric City, within the State of Mind.

* * * * *

The "world" in which we have *being* IS specific, detailed, situated, and alive! In contrast, the spoken and written "word" that is used to describe the "living world" IS general, categorical, abstract, and symbolic; thus, there is a natural tendency to conceptually confuse the general *category* of "emotion" with the specific, situated *reality* of emotion. Remember, every-thing that is real, is either a "thing," or a "thing-in-action"—else it is "no-thing."

* * * * *

Emotion is a noun-word that represents verb phenomena;
Emotion is a word to describe Human Activity
and not metaphysical Essence or Entity.

* * * * *

Simply put, emotion is a "thing-in-action," and YOU are the thing! Emotion is the activity of *you-being-emotional.* Now, there is a practical reason why it is important to correctly conceive *emotion* as something humans are *doing* and *being:* THE VALUE OF THIS INTERPRETIVE EFFORT IS to make sure that "emotion" is not reified into a "thing" possessing power over you; instead, YOU are the "thing" possessing power.** You possess the power to choose; a power that expands in freedom as *You . . . Live True.*

Although it sometimes feels like emotions do . . . over-power you, the truth is that you are the one that empowers compelling emotions in the first place: You set-in-motion,

---

* It takes many months . . . or even a few years to finally STOP turning tangible verb-activity into metaphysical essences endowed with independent power. To do this, one needs to swim upstream against the influence of scientific talk, variable/factor talk. Here's an example of what I call science-speak: High Self-Esteem is negatively correlated to Depression. Self-Esteem as a scientific variable only has a "general existence" in your mind, as a "word/construct," but its real existence in the world is a "thing-in-action," more specifically, a particular person esteeming himself or herself in the moment. The reality of "Self-Esteem" IS the specific activity of "evaluating" oneself in that very moment of self-evaluation.

** Because humans are "alive" and "living," they are more than just a "thing," but a "thing-in-action." Philosopher Chauncey Riddle refers to Human Beings as . . . Thing-ings; a word that captures the traits of both "noun" and "verb"—both substance AND the living activity of substance-in-action.

your emotions—to include the tormenting emotions called "emotional scars." Your physiology is following you by virtue of a pattern of choices made in prior weeks, months, and years. You are the one who hurls *emotional stones* that must *land* at some future time. The "landing" of *your emotional responses* represents *living exclamation marks* that call attention to how well you have chosen—or not.

The emergence of today's *black* and *gray* emotions is a self-correcting clue, that you . . . have not been True. From the fountain of spiritual disharmony flows the polluted water of scarred perceptions.

* * * * *

The term "Emotional Scar" . . . IS . . . literally:
Today's scarred way of thinking about Yesterday;
It's a Re-Membering of the Past . . . done in the Present,
that is tainted by the falseness of the
person who Re-Members. Scarred Thinking
and Scarred Emotions flow . . . . from Being False.

* * * * *

Believing a Lie: The King's New Clothes. Emotional pain attributed to past trauma is really re-created by *stinkin' thinkin'* in the present. It's the same kind of *thinkin'* that creates *the King's New Clothes.** After the afflicting faucet has long since been shut off, claiming emotional pain today is like wearing *the Kings New Clothes*—you *think* you've got clothes on, when really . . . you're buck-naked.

---

* The King's New Clothes refers to royal garb cleverly crafted for a King who was particularly hard to please. After being befuddled about making a perfect new suit for "His Maniacal Majesty," an ingenious Tailor decided to weave a psychological suggestion for "Your Highness"—a suggestion that was reinforced by the people of the Kingdom, who were "in on" the ruse. Thus, the King was given "nothing" to wear . . . but was told by the Tailor that he really was wearing a stunning new suit. Even though, the King was buck naked—not wanting to be thought of as crazy by all who adored and praised his "new clothes"—the King convinced himself that he was really wearing something . . . when "nothing" is what he really wore.

Like the King's New Clothes, optional emotional pain is woven on the loom of *imagination.* Different from physical scars, there are no actual emotional "marks" left behind due to tragedy and trauma. In the re-membering process called "emotional scars," there is just a "marked" way of thinking and a "marked" way of living—dysfunctional thoughts and behaviors that YOU are doing in the present.**

It is YOU who re-constructs the King's New Clothes via your poisoned perspective—a way of seeing the world that is marred by a *migraine mental block.* So, when victims say, "my life has been ruined," ironically, this "ruining" IS directly due to the continued drinking of a toxic brew: the homemade moonshine of BRIAR beer, served in a JAR.

To make matters worse, certain cultural institutions of science and therapy actually reinforce the continued *wearing* of unnecessary emotional pain; these institutions legitimize mental *disorders* and *diseases* that supposedly inflict victims like the Flu—meaning, your suffering has nothing to do . . . with you. Because some people are led to believe that the pain they "wear" is caused by bad environment and/or bad biology, and they are diverted from the very thing . . . that will bring emotional healing: Owning Your Stuff!

Inner Liberty Revisited

It is essential to grasp the reality and power of what Viktor Frankl calls "inner liberty." Without this liberty, Frankl himself could not have been *lifted* above his tortured past, that the Hope of a new day could heal his suffering.

If anyone should have been "emotionally scarred" through all the afflictions he endured, it was Viktor Frankl. Because of the reality of Inner Liberty, Frankl was able to embrace inner peace amid horrific abuses; he possessed a

---

** There may be directly-felt and directly painful emotional feelings, BUT these are the psychosomatic offspring of scarred thinking: Your feelings are . . . following you!

personal peace that could not be crushed, even by the extreme constraints and causes of a Nazi death camp. Forward-thinking in the face of affliction is the basis of Frankl's "logos therapy"—a future-focused approach that is diametrically different from the *widely-applied* practice of dredging up the dreary history of yesterday's abuse, a.k.a., "mental health therapy."

By embracing Inner Liberty, Frankl matured in wisdom and character *directly because* of his suffering. Strength of character is forged in the furnace of affliction; it is *directly because* of our sorrows that we learn unique lessons that *only* tough times can teach—precious lessons that are central to Life's meaning and purpose.

This is where Viktor Frankl's forward-oriented logos therapy looms large: Instead of focusing upon the past, Frankl fixed his focus upon the *hopes* of a bright new day. Through his direct experience, Frankl discovered that the motivating potentials of a bright future . . . can *lift* people out of yesterday's torment and tragedy, into bright white reality.* Frankl learned that the *productive possibilities* of a new day can generate *renewing energies.*

Because Frankl *walked his talk*, he wasted little time to lament the unfortunate abuses of his tragic past; instead, he opened himself up to *"making use of the opportunities of attaining the values that a difficult situation may afford."* Frankl invoked his "final freedom" and was *lifted up:* He stood upon the very rock . . . that could have been his stumbling block.

---

* Don't confuse these hopeful energies with "fake-it-till-you-make-it" positive self-affirmations. NO, that's not it! The productive energy of which I speak IS the "Energy-in-Motion" that we set-in-motion by directly choosing to honor the Source of all living energy! It is the Creator who energizes, enlivens, redeems, and makes new!

* * * * *

Tragic events do not cause emotional scars necessarily. Different from physical scars, emotional scars are optional. Emotional Scarring is a direct result of "Scarred Thinking," A kind of thinking that refuses to learn what past pain and suffering is willing to teach.

* * * * *

Even after all the tortured conditions Frankl endured, he declared: "There is only one thing I dread: not to be worthy of my sufferings." Clearly, Frankl allowed tough times to *teach* him—instead of *torment* him. It is wise to reflect upon yesterday's misfortunes *long enough* to learn from them, working through old issues to discover what tough times will teach. But thinking upon past troubles is only useful to a point. Mark Twain offers this sage advise:

> *We should be careful to get out of an experience only the wisdom that is in it, and stop there; lest we be like the cat that sits down on a hot stove-lid. She will never sit down on a hot stove-lid again—and that is well; but also, she will never sit down on a cold one either.*

As we choose well and keep Inner Liberty, the past can be a building block upon which we stand tall; OR, as we choose less-than-well, the same adversity *will be* a stumbling block over which we fall. Attaining the values that a difficult situation may afford is to be a Victor, and NOT a Victim.

Those who "perceive" themselves as victims of environment . . . *will be* victims of environment. The Thomas axiom applies: "that which you perceive as real, is real in its consequences." This means, the cause & effect assumptions of being *chained* to your past DO practically apply to people who fail to "keep inner liberty." Shackled by their own erroneous assumptions, they are *not free* to "see" that environment is *not causing* a necessary destiny.

Delving deeply into a person's past, supposing that such dreary dredging is *required* to reach healing and happiness, is the incorrect assumption of some therapies; this approach is exactly opposite from the principle applied by Viktor Frankl. Stirring up yesterday's dirt—dusty details better left settled, learned from, and forgotten—is commonly done because of the *widely-taught* traditions of cause & effect psychology, and the associated assumption that a "causal chain" *pushes* people into a *necessary* destiny.

If there really IS a causal chain that forces behavior into a predetermined direction, . . . then why should *talk therapy* do anything to change this? Some therapists play both sides of the ontological fence: "determinism," when it enables victims to feel absolved of response-ability for their emotional plight, and "free will," when it time to sell the *talk therapy* service.

However, there IS a *chain* that pertains to a person's emotional destiny, but it's not a *mechanical* chain of rigid metal links that *necessarily attaches* past influence to today's craziness; it's not a *cause* & *effect chain* that causes *inevitable* effects upon *who you are* today; instead, it's a *meaning-full* chain of *constraint* & *choice* that we, the meaning-makers, mitigate via variable perception and *creative imagination* according to free will.

If "free will" is real (and it IS), then your personal fate is NOT found in *the stars* or in your *palms* or in the *cards* or in your *bad upbringing* or in your *bad biology;* instead, your future fate is yours . . . to choose. Because people are free to make "bad" choices, this explains why: "Everything Doesn't Happen for a Reason"—at least not a *good* reason! Contrary to popular opinion, the reality of human life is better stated this way:

* * * * *

There is human "reason" in everything that happens, and sometimes that "reason" IS un-reasonable.

* * * * *

Un-reasonable destinies are the un-necessary ditch in which we wallow, while erroneously imagining that such dark destinies were *"written in the stars."* By making un-reasonable choices—choices that go against Life's inherent harmony—we become blinded to thinking that "my-way" . . . is better than the "High-Way." Thus, a *migraine mental block* blurs our ability to "see" the *higher Reasons* available to us, so we choose *lower reasons*—un-reasonable reasons. The root source of all "emotional scars" is invariably traced back to a history of selfish and short-sighted reasons.*

In terms of human behavior, much of what is thought to be "cause," is really "constraint." Throughout our lives we stand at numerous, constraining cross-roads—each a point of transition where either the High Road OR an array of lower roads can be chosen. With each choice comes a connected direction and destiny; when we don't proactively choose the High-Way, by default, we are dumped in the ditch of a lesser destiny. Amid the most compelling constraints of accident or abuse, we still possess the power to travel the High-Way to a Bright White Destiny—this is Inner Liberty!

* * * * *

Inner Liberty includes the Freedom to quit dwelling on yesterday's dreary details, and the Freedom to see productive possibilities of a Hopeful Future, and to fully realize them.

* * * * *

When you go against your own sense of what is right, you will impulsively look to the past to place blame upon other people or situations; hence, with an eye firmly fixed upon the past, you become vulnerable to *the false view* . . . that the past is tormenting YOU. Betrayal binds and blinds you from being able "see" with bright white clarity; contrastingly, when you choose to "keep inner liberty," you naturally enjoy the *Hopes* and *Freedoms* that flow from that *Faithful* choice.

---

* Living an "emotionally scarred" life IS the un-necessary destiny for those who fail to "keep inner liberty" and embrace Bright White Reality. Emotional scars are "worn" when one's focus is firmly fixed upon the past.

While you are NOT chained to the impact of past constraints, you ARE "chained" to the consequences of your free-will choices. To assure that Life is Self-Correcting, you must necessarily feel the fruits of your choosing—else, how would you know that you're choosing well? In the end, we will all give an accounting of our choices before our Maker. George Ritchie gave such an accounting when he visited a realm beyond mortal death and was asked the following questions by *a Man made out of light:* "What have you done with you life?" . . . "How much have you loved with your life?

* * * * *

In this Life, I am not only Response-Able for all Thoughts, Words, and Deeds that proceed from me, but my Highest Response-Ability is to ultimately learn . . . to answer every adversity with the Motives and Emotions of Love.

* * * * *

Who's Creating the Wake? Visualize a boat upon a lake moving through the water ahead. As the boat travels forward across future waters, there is a trail of ruffled waves that fans out behind called "the wake." In this image, it's completely clear that *the boat* is powering its way through the water . . . and to imagine that "the wake" has any power to propel the *drive* or *direction* of the boat would be ridiculous!

The wake that trails behind the boat is analogous to your *past happenings*, and *you* are in the driver's seat of life, . . . steering your course. Your forward progress into the future is directly determined by the decisions you make at the wheel. You are creating *the wake* that trails behind, and EVEN IF you pass through waters of adversity, . . . you still determine "the wake" through *your steering responses* to turbulent conditions.

In each new day, . . . you may return to the driver's seat and navigate your chosen course through future waters. Further, this is what you *will do* when you are Being True; and when being false, you may—with eager help from unseen forces—entertain and espouse this kind of *scarred* logic: "because of the wake behind me, I am permanently impaired in my ability to steer my boat."

Those who harbor *emotional scars* say it this way: "I've been scarred for life, and I'll never be the same." It is true, you *will* never be the same, . . . but that is also true even when cruising through everyday waters. Whether constraints are passive or compelling, typical or traumatic, the Heisenberg Effect establishes that there is inevitable impact always. Every Life experience impacts you in some way; thus, you will never be the same *anyway* thru the normal passage of time and the passage of common occurrences. At every crossroad of choice, an essential decision confronts you:

* *Will you learn from past experience and stand taller, thus expanding your character to something better? Or,*

* *Will you blame past tragedies and remain smaller, and contort your character to the deformities of being bitter?*

Choosing the latter option is analogous to imagining that "the wake" is propelling the drive and direction of a boat. Yet such is a prominent indoctrination of behavioral science; people are the "cause & effect" products of the past—*who you are* is the necessary result of environmental inputs. But here's a most fascinating twist: The assumptions of "Behaviorism" are absolutely false, . . . yet at the same time, completely true—depending upon whether YOU . . . are *being false* or *Being True.*

If your *way of being* is false, then you *will* be a "victim" of your past and you will be propelled and piloted by "the wake" in your muddled imagination; but if True, . . . you will be the "Victor" of your past and you will be free to steer your future course to your best Destiny.

People who *Live True* are proactive about the hopes and dreams of a new day; they assertively steer a boat that powers forward into a Bright Future. Whereas, people who *live false,* who do not heed the hopeful encouragements of the Heart, will float along in a boat with no oars, engine, wheel, or rudder; they passively drift in directions determined by the external influences of wind and wave. But here is the most fascinating fact: They did not directly choose this aimless dismal drifting; instead, they directly chose to be false, and *from that falseness* flows the mindset that imagines that *the wake* is propelling the boat to its dark and dreary destiny.

* * * * *

The Goal within Your Control is Becoming Loving and True.
As You put your Whole Soul into this Single Goal,
You will be Released and Relieved from
the Self-Made Misery called
Emotional Scars.

* * * * *

Where did the Past Go? When *memory of the past* is correctly conceived in terms of *re-membering*, the theory of a "time continuum" is blasted into oblivion. One version of the time continuum is that the *past* and *future* are happening simultaneous to the living moment called the *present.* Of course, entering into this "continuum" only happens by accessing an available hypothetical, theoretical wormhole. But once that elusive entrance is found, then one can go backward or forward IN TIME . . . as if "Time" were a big "Tube" you slide through—cowabunga! Of course, getting *into* the elusive *time continuum* isn't as easy as climbing up a ladder and shooting down a slide—you need a Time Machine. Then, you can *warp* your way "Back to the Future."

Time travel is great *escape* entertainment but should not be confused with reality. The truth about *time* is this: "Time" is yet another *noun-word* to describe *verb-activity.* Time IS a description of the "passage of life," . . . Time is a word that points to "living activity," from moment . . . to moment. The reality of *embodied beings living on a substantial earth* IS the "thing-in-action" measured by descriptions called . . . time.*

Because, the past ONLY lives as you *re-member it* in the NOW, you may be asking yourself, "where does *the past* go if I don't re-member it?" Answer: It goes away! It disappears into thin air . . . with two exceptions:

* Certain descriptive pieces of "your past" are re-membered by the minds of other people, and
* A complete accounting of "your past" is perfectly Known by the Mind of your Maker.

As to past details you'd rather "forget," the exciting news is that the "forgive and forget" principle IS part of the Prime Mover's Plan. He has promised to *"remember no more"* all dark deeds that you *humbly own* . . . and altogether *un-do.* This means, the Creator's comprehensive account of your life has all the *repented parts* edited out (Isaiah 43:25 & 44:22).

So, if there are dirty details of "your past," that you wish would go away, . . . they can! And when you don't remember . . . and others don't remember . . . and when The Creator "remembers no more," then where did that particular piece of the past go? It goes away, completely, absolutely, and perfectly! Would the Creator accomplish anything less

---

* However one conceives past, present, and future, it must be done while keeping "Free Will" intact and avoiding doctrines of predestination. There are many written accounts of people seeing a "vision of the future." However, such a vision is NOT seen because "the future" is happening simultaneous to "NOW" . . . at another location on the "Time Continuum." Rather, visions of the future are an "Artist's Conception" of how the future will unfold according to promises made by the Artist. In fulfilling His promises, the Creator doesn't force the future to happen, instead, He "invites" it to happen through those who are willing to hear and heed. As to "visions of the past," the Creator owns a large video library, . . . home movies of his children (with all the "repented" parts edited out), just what you would expect of an infinitely loving and resourceful Father . Thus, "visions of the past" are not seen because the past is happening NOW, . . . but are viewed because the Creator can show the video . . . NOW. George Ritchie's "death" account speaks of having his entire life flash before him in ONE moment in time; a feat accomplish by "a Man made out of Light," who was "power itself."

than a perfect forgetting? Through the Creator's infinite power, a perfect forgetting also occurs in the minds of all who joyfully bask in Pure White Light.**

Changing the Past. The phenomenon of emotional scarring is the residual suffering that remains AFTER the inflicting faucet has been shut off. Today's re-membering is informed and fed by the person you've become from the time a past trauma occurred . . . to the present day—the day in which you do your re-membering. It is said, "the only constant is change!" Thus, you will *always* re-member "the past" differently as you continue to "change" in the present, as you *progress* or *regress* in maturity and character. Remember, *perception* is a function of what you learned lately, so *emotional marks* necessarily change over time, as YOU change over time.

* * * * *

While there are Physical Realities
that exist independent of how you perceive them,
still, the only World you know is the one that you experience
through your Interpretations, from your Perspective.
As You Change, Your Perspective Changes.
As You Change, the Past Changes.

* * * * *

Through greater present-day insight, the past will inevitably "mean" something different today, than it "meant" back then. Some *changes of the past* can even occur solely through psychological effort; for example, imagine a man

---

* As for those who re-call and resentfully re-member dark details of "your past" through the distorted view of a Migraine Mental Block, if they continue to harbor such accusing and bitter thoughts and refuse to let go, they will die from the resentful poison that they drink; they will be "paid" the "wages" of a spiritual death and their enjoyment of a Bright White Future will be in jeopardy. Further, as the scriptures teach, the Creator can protect those that obey him by taking "away out of their minds to bring affliction upon you." So, where does a "dark past" go, when one repents? It goes away . . . perfectly and completely.

trying to open a door, he struggles to *push* the door open, but the door will not budge. Futile attempts to *push* the door open continue for many hours. In the man's frustration, resentful thoughts of passing moments quickly accumulate! Utterly baffled, the man curses, "you dumb door!" Just then, a passerby notices the man's bewilderment and tries to help. The stranger suggests *pulling in* on the door . . . instead of *pushing out.* Voila—the door opens!

Now that the man realizes that it was his own *ignorance* that generated the negative emotions associated to his moments of frustration, how might memories of the *innocent* door be recalled and re-membered? In light of new information, how might the "meaning" of the past change? The man could harbor resentment towards the door for many years to come? Every time he sees a similar looking door, he could "flashback" to frustrating memories. The tormented man might even hire a psychotherapist to tell him that his traumatized condition is . . . "not your fault, because you *have* P.T.D.D.—Post Traumatic Door Disorder."

The traumatized man could remain in a confused state of *complexity*, OR . . . he could enter the world of *clarity* and *simplicity* by owning his opaque ignorance for creating all his negative emotional energy. He could also allow the door to be as *innocent* as the door was and is and ever will be. Who in their *right mind* would harbor resentment towards an inanimate door for not opening, when the "opening" procedure was misapplied? Yet the blameless door received the initial brunt of the blame anyway.**

** You will eventually come to understand that EVEN IF the "door" were guilty of something, . . . blameworthy of something, still, your response to the door IS all that matters when it comes to the question of Truth! For Truth is not about Being Right—getting the facts straight and making sure all accusations and litigations are "in line"—rather, Truth is about YOU Being "In Line." Truth is about "how you respond to What Happened."

Black Elk's wisdom applies: "It is in the darkness of their eyes that men get lost," and Terry Warner adds: "When we cannot see our way, we think darkness is shrouding our pathway, when really the darkness is in ourselves." Owning our ignorance is liberating: It frees us to see *new* meanings in *old* events—it frees us to *change the meaning* of the past.

* * * * *

The Past is not just structural facts,
the mere occurrence of physical things, instead,
the Past IS what those facts "mean" . . . to perceiving beings.
Thus, the Past will necessarily change, as perceiving
beings change—for better or for worse.

* * * * *

When psychological efforts are coupled with *spiritual integrity*, "Changing the Past" becomes even more profound. This means "emotional marks" will change over time and will eventually disappear as a people cease to *re-member* with a bitter mind.* As one's *way of being* changes, so does the *way of re-membering*. Because the past only exists by virtue of today's conscious re-membering, what the past IS . . . is what the past "means" to the person who perceives in the present.

The emotional scar IS the *activity* of perpetually hanging on to a false way of re-membering—clinging to a false "meaning" that strives to be factual, but fails to be True.

---

* Even though a physical "mark" may remain in your flesh, . . . even then, the physical scar will absolutely "mean" something different over time too! In some cultures, having a scar in the flesh can be a promotion, a "badge of courage." Constructive "meaning" can be brought to the way we "see" even physical scars.

** "Mind" is yet another noun-word to represent verb-phenomena. While the "Brain" is indeed a tangible "thing," in contrast, Mind is "the living activity of conscious awareness." John Dewey referred to this conscious activity of perceiving one's world as "Minding." When "brains" are dead and have returned to the dust, . . . the immortal "Mind" continues. Thousands of "near-death" accounts affirm that consciousness does not cease when mortal bodies die, and brains are obliterated. Conscious awareness is a function of the immortal Soul.

Emotional scars are not *fixed* . . . but *fluid.* They are the false, yet flexible, *meanings* that necessarily change as you change—especially as you *recover innocence* and *live true.* And when you see the past differently, *re-member* it differently, the *Mind aspect*** of the *mind-body activity* called "emotion" will let go of the *old meaning* attached to a *traumatic experience*—the tragedy that supposedly caused the emotional mark. Once that "old meaning" is let go, the *Body aspect* of this *mind-body activity* is altered; hence, your *old feelings* about a past event change, as the *meaning* you bring to that past event changes, and all *distressing physiology* that arose psychosomatically . . . disappears psychosomatically.

* * * * *

Your state of Mind flows from
Spiritual Integrity—or Spiritual Disharmony;
a fundamental Change of Mind requires a Change of Heart.

* * * * *

Continuing to maintain *emotional scars* of the past means hanging on to *distorted thinking* in the present—*stinkin' thinkin'* that flows from a *migraine mental block.* When scarred thinking goes away, so does "emotional scars." Scarred thinking naturally disappears when bitter cold memories, born of betrayal, are melted by the glowing Hope of a new day. So the key to melting away yesterday's memories IS to bask in the warmth of the Light, and as the Sun makes you a new creature, you are able to *bring new meaning* to past adversity—those exact same *moments of misfortune* become the very events from which strength of character is forged!

* * * * *

Memory IS Re-Membering! It is You that Re-Members.
It is your Way of Being in the present that determines
your Way of Seeing and Re-Membering the Past.
As your Way of Being Changes in the Present,
Your Way of Seeing the Past also Changes.
When You Change the "Meaning" of
the Past, . . . You Change the Past.

* * * * *

Changing the Past is not a *fake-it-till-you-make-it* mental trick of talking yourself into things being different and *pretending* that things are different, it's about a real change. Changing Your Stripes and Becoming a New Kind of Creature has little to do with *positive self-affirmations* or *brain-programming.* Changing Your Stripes is about *genuine change* from the *Heart.*

Your reality of present and past has always been the interpretive "meaning" you bring to What Happened; thus, after you *Recover the True You*, your interpretations of Life are not *contrived* by the Head . . . but are *true* from the Heart. Because perceptions now flow from the abundance of a *pure heart*, with new eyes, you are able to "see" past tragedies as being the very events that have built a better you!

Recovery through adversity means you are *better* than before. Today is better, tomorrow is better, and amazingly yesterday is better, because the "meaning" of past trauma has changed—through your *change of heart. Being new* and *seeing new* means that you no longer participate in re-membering a scarred past, for the past is no longer your *tormenter*—it is your *teacher.*

The counterfeit of Being True . . . is Being Right—a mindset consumed with capturing facts. Seeking to precisely perceive the facts of *what happened* yesterday is the wrong question to ask of Life. The pursuit to capture accurate facts is entirely trivial in contrast to the rich purposes of Truth; especially Being True in response to *what happened* yesterday—Being True in response to the very event that *was* the object of "resentful recall." The pursuit of "Truth" is not just about *perceiving accurately* (getting the facts exact to the "t"), but in *responding compassionately.*

* * * * *

The tendency to fretfully fuss and flatulently yammer about the smelly details of what happened yesterday IS the cultural inheritance of a litigious society fixated upon the "facts" . . . to the exclusion of honoring the "Truth."

* * * * *

The pursuit of *facts* and *being right* is the booby prize; in contrast, the pursuit life, liberty, and happiness depends upon whether we embrace the true prize, . . . the grand prize: *the Truth of bright white reality, . . . the reality of bright white Truth.*

RECOVERING THE YOU THAT IS TRUE

Two Alternatives Only. Amid the routine blur of a thousand everyday decisions, there can be simplicity and clarity. In any given moment in time, there are only *Two Fundamental Alternatives* from which to choose, and only *One Fundamental Choice* that is directly pertinent to the fulfillment of Life's purpose and meaning:

* *Be True* . . . Or

* *Betray.*

Most daily decisions we make in life are cosmetic window dressing in comparison to the choice made between these *two basic options;* choosing either "Be True" or "Betray" is at the heart of *every* decision we make at the surface—which car to buy, what clothes to wear, which movie to view, what career to pursue, and what's on the menu. The basic choice between "Be True" or "Betray" underlies the broad diversity of *all human doings.*

* * * * *

Being True brings the natural consequence of "better,"
and the choice to Betray naturally delivers
the consequence of "bitter."
These are the fruits that spontaneously grow,
according to the seeds we sow;
this IS . . . . the Law of the Harvest,
the Law that makes Life Self-Correcting.

* * * * *

These two foundational choices carry with them two connected consequences: How else would you know that you're NOT doing the things that bring personal peace, unless the results of your doings were . . . "bitter?" And how else would you know to continue what you're doing, unless your *productive doings* resulted in things being . . . "better?"

Choosing *better* over *bitter* . . . that's a no-brainer! Of course, anyone would logically choose to eat *a healthy meal* over *a pile of mud!* But the fact is . . . you literally can't choose the *meal of goodness*, if you're NOT the kind of creature that naturally gravitates to goodness. You don't really choose bitter or better directly . . . for they are the *end products* of the two foundational choices of Be True or Betray; thus, to reap the most coveted consequences you must go to the well that supplies the water.

So, why doesn't everyone simply choose to Be True, when this choice brings the richest rewards? Answer: Because they can't, . . . it's not "in" them to choose it; they are NOT yet the kind of creatures that are capable of *seeing* the virtue of true choices—let alone *making* those true choices. They may be able to logically reason and admit, . . . *"I ought to Be True,"* but when it comes right down to it, the desire to Be True is not burning in their bones. So they choose something *less*, because *less* is what is "in" them. At certain times in life, "less" is what is "in" each of us; this means our inherent potential to be "more" lies dormant within us, waiting to be recovered.

Throughout life, we are inevitably impacted by every event and every interaction, and whether that impact is tremendous or trivial, in the end, the test of Life is about *how we respond to what happens.* Thus, in every moment we stand at a point of transition, a junction of choice: Be True or Betray. Whichever way we choose, . . . we will "never be the same."

On the "Betray" side of "never being the same," the behavior that flows from us will be *bitter* and resentful; we will easily and frequently be *upset* by the *setup* called life. Differently, on the "Be True" side of "never being the same," the empowering energies of being *better* are before us. To understand why people don't simply choose "Be True," when the benefits for doing so are obvious and abundance, we must become *clear* the following possibilities:

- *People who sense they are Being True . . . and are Being True.*
- *People who sense they are Being False . . . and are Being False.*
- *People who think they are Being True . . . but are really Being False.*
- *People who think they are Being False . . . but are really Being True.*

The last combination isn't really *possible* to do in *directly-lived reality*; it only exists as a permutation of systematic *word arrangement* (yet another example of how words can mislead). This 4th permutation is not possible because when one wholly embraces the Light, all clouds of doubt disappear: Being True means Being Clear! So it is impossible to "think" you are Being False . . . when you're really Being True. Truth is Whole: All aspects of what it means to be human combine together into One unified reality: Heart, Might, Mind, Strength, and Soul. Again, being clear in "Mind" intrinsically goes with Being True. When plagued by clouds of doubt, this condition and consequence . . . points to the sower of a doubtful seed: You are not fully and wholly . . . Being True.

As applied to *emotional scars* and *scarred thinking*—as well as an array of *JAR behaviors* and *BRIAR emotions*—attention needs to be paid to the 3rd possibility: *"People who think they are Being True . . . but are really Being False."* This condition (along with the 2nd combination) is called "fooling yourself" or "being blind." These two conditions of *self-deception* are made possible by the real existence of *Unseen Evil;* conversely, the 1st possibility exists directly because there is a Creator, who is the *First-Cause* or *Prime-Mover* of all that is Good.

The Reality of Unseen Evil. By using terms like *self-deception* and *fooling yourself*, a misleading monolithic image is implied, *as if* you do your deeds of darkness by yourself—solo! The individualistic idea inferred by such terms is an illusion (words playing tricks again). From the beginning of human history all acts of self-betrayal and self-deception are actually done in . . . duet. A law of physics applies:

> * *An object that is set-in-motion will remain in motion unless acted upon by an Outside Force.*

While Newton's Law primarily pertains to predictable patterns in the material world, there are applicable parallels to the behavioral world, as well: *Human doings* and *be-ings* are *highly habitual* precisely because the consequences of our choices *set-in-motion* behavioral momentum that *will not* switch course . . . unless acted upon by an *Outside Force.*

From birth, pure innocence was the natural "motion," in which we were "set," . . . and we continued to move in this unwavering *orbit of innocence* until an "outside force" pushed, pulled, or persuaded us off course. Different from the *mechanical* movement of cause & effect between physical objects, the *meaning-full* movements of mind, motive, and emotion are only *constrained* by "outside forces." Such constraints can *pull* you off course ONLY with your *permission* and co-operative *participation.*

Your entrance into an opposing *orbit of betrayal* can only occur be-*cause* an "outside force" supplies a *reason* to deviate, and you willfully yield to that *reason.* In other words, you must *consent* to diversions from your primal "motion" of purity—the motion that flows from you naturally.

Satan IS the initiating "outside force" of all that goes against goodness, love, and light; thus, when you choose to Betray, . . . you are being assisted, every inch of the way. People are deceived daily by *the devil on their left shoulder*—often unwitting and unaware. Because they can't "see" the devil and his minions, some *discount* or *disbelieve* the real existence of *unseen evil* and thereby grossly underestimate its influence; thus, skeptics are vulnerable to deeper depths of deception.

* * * * *

Stuck in an orbit of dark thoughts & deeds, an orbit that feeds . . . further dark thoughts and deeds; such contrary "motion" commences by permission and participation with unseen evil—the Outside Force that knocks you off course.

* * * * *

Referring to the four possibilities listed previously, those that *sense* they are *Being False* . . . and ARE *Being False*, these people don't deny the reality of unseen evil; instead, they sell themselves to it and willfully enter an orbit of evil. The "outside force" of darkness *knocks them out* of the orbit of Light by *permission* . . . and for *reasons*. When living in the confused complexity of darkness, the world is perceived thru a blinded mindset. Making anti-establishment statements and being contrary IS the natural *motion* of this ominous orbit; rebellion against the "powers that be" is the fad and fashion for those who *sell* themselves to darkness.

On the other hand, *rebellion* against powers of tyranny and oppression IS the kind of "good rebellion" that brought about the birth of a great nation. So what's the difference? "Bad rebellion" is consistently coupled with the dark motives and emotions of the BRIAR—this conspicuous tell-tale sign supplies the distinguishing difference.

While rebellion against established earthly authority is how "bad rebellion" manifests at the surface, . . . at the heart is sedition against the unseen "establishment"—a rebellion against the spiritual powers that support and persuade the primal motions of purity. Those who wear darkness, and worship darkness, may admit that they're doing bad or being rebellious, but if you ask them "why," . . . they will deliver a logical lie. They "spin" a *rationalizing reason* that only makes sense to a mixed-up mind . . . that is blind, yet they don't pretend to be doing good, they simply pretend to be *justified*—"the end justifies the means."

If you carefully research the pernicious pedigree, Satan IS the ultimate initiator of every evil act and idea. The devil is called "the father of all lies" (Moses 4:4) because he is the very first influence to suggest *ideas* contrary to the way of goodness. Satan IS the "outside force" that impacts and persuades human beings out of their *primal orbit of innocence*—with willing or unwitting consent. The evil equation happens this way: Satan's Constraint + Our Consent = An Opposing Orbit. The fact is no one can enact an evil deed . . . unless that act is first conceived; without Satan dispensing deviating ideas, human beings would simply stay in their Orbit of Innocence—given Newton's Law, how could it *be* otherwise?

* * * * *

All diversions from a Physical Orbit require
an outside "Cause" to force . . . a different course,
and all diversions from a Be-havioral Orbit require
an outside "Be-Cause" to initiate a new direction.

* * * * *

Innocent and pure people stay . . . "unless" they are given a *reason* to stray—betrayal requires an *outside reason*, an *outside be-cause.* Human beings were NOT born with an evil rationale or evil reasons within them, such must be *learned.* From the earliest accounts of human history, it was Satan who inspired the first "idea" to commit murder. Satan was the *sufficient cause* that *initiated* and *inspired* Cain's contrary logic that killing Able would be advantageous. Cain did not come up with this *evil idea* by himself! In this way, the devil is the prime-mover of all dark deeds.

Nevertheless, the devil did not *make* Cain do the *evil deed*, he simply supplied the *initiating idea*—the tempting influence. Cain's act of killing Able was a "duet" done with the devil; like a *halfback* requires a *quarterback* to enable a "hand off," Satan extended Cain a dark and deviant "handoff," and Cain received it and ran with it! Each partner in a dark duet is

Response-Able for the *deed* that is *done* directly: The Devil *does* the deception . . . and You *do* the deviance!

Again, human beings are NOT born with evil rationales or evil reasons within them, they must *learn* the ways of darkness . . . one devious deception at a time. When people are sufficiently blind, they actually choose *bitter* over *better* for "reasons" that only make sense to a person racked with a *migraine mental block*. *Bitter* is chosen over *Better . . . Be-Cause:*

* *You don't "think" you are really choosing bitter over better—you are deceived.*
* *Your mind is incapable of seeing Bright White Reality, for in betrayal you've lost the illuminating Light of Innocence, and thus*
* *You are left to the darkness and deceptions of "the devil on your left shoulder."*

Yet, you cannot claim, "the devil made me do it." While the devil is "allowed" to *constrain*, he cannot *cause*—unless you sell your whole soul to darkness and thereby become completely calloused to the invitations of Light.* As long as you still have a sliver of Light shining within, the devil cannot cause but can only constrain. Even though you *get to* totally take responsibility for your own bad behavior, remember, doing *your bad* is never a "solo," you've always had help every step of the way, from forces both seen and unseen (recall Human Doings, p. 54). Outward Doings emerge from a co–operative context in all cases—this is Sufficient Cause.

---

* From the beginning of human history, God warned, "My Spirit shall not always strive with man" (Genesis 6:3), and clearly kept that promise on one occasion as millions bloodthirsty beings plundered each other into complete annihilation (Ether 15:19). When people consistently push away the gentle invitations of Light—again and again—and persist in doing dark deeds intentionally, then, those people become "passed feeling" (Ephesians 4:19; Moroni 9:20). And when they can no longer "feel His words" (1 Nephi 17:45), such people are left to the bondage of Satan's full power over them (Mosiah 16:5)—a concept critical to understanding "addiction," & why the "AA" model is the most effective therapeutic approach for curing addiction.

* * * * *

What You "Do" . . . is explained by
What You are Responding To,
but What You "Be" . . . is entirely up to Thee.

* * * * *

Our outside "doings" get persuaded, pushed, and pulled every which way by the invitations, assignments, and oppressions of others—yet our inside "motions" of mind, motive, and emotion possess "final freedom." This means, when we divert from Inner Liberty, we do so by contrary consent with an unseen dance partner. Even though all betrayals are done in "duet," . . . you still *get to* own moral responsibility for "dancing" your part.* Every diversion you've ever dreamed began with a satanic whisper, an evil invitation to dance with darkness, somewhere along the line.

To resume your original orbit of innocence, it is highly helpful to comprehend the extent to which Unseen Evil impacts human life; knowing the antics of the enemy is advised, else that enemy will have the upper hand. It is vital to know that the devil is extremely *good* at bartering *bad*—he is even *good* at making *bad* "look like" something *good.* Satan can sell you *pile of mud* and make you think that *chocolate moose* is on the menu! Because Unseen Evil really does exist and

---

* There are a myriad of excuses, reasons, and rationalizations to dodge responsibility, . . . and those that do such "dodging" reveal their departure from the Light. Owing complete Response-Ability is how the Creator designed our existence, and being infinitely wise, He provided a way to escape evil influence at every turn: The Apostle Paul taught that God will never allow "you to be tempted above that ye are able" (1 Cor. 10:13). This means that Satan's influence upon you is ever and only "constraint," UNLESS you sell your whole soul to Satan, in which case your dark bondage will occur via "cause." This is the helpless state of both "addiction" and "insanity," and the only way out is to be . . . "saved." When selling out to Satan, people become insane: This dark condition directly explains "how" people come to commit sickening and vicious acts of violence; nevertheless, they are accountable for all . . . to include the selling of their soul, and their resultant insanity.

really does *knock people off* their orbit of innocence, many people paradoxically choose to eat a *pile of mud* instead of feasting on a *healthy meal.* This paradoxical decision is detailed by C. Terry Warner:

> *"We devise and hang on to our emotional problems for a purpose, a purpose more important to us than our happiness. And we deceive ourselves about the fact that this is what we're doing. We participate in the creation of our emotional troubles and deny we've had any part in it."*

Satan tries to sell enticing "reasons" to *hang on* to our emotional troubles. Satan sells us a "purpose" that becomes *more important* than personal peace. One palpable purpose that he sells is the enticement to retain *the evidence* that confers credence to a crusade of victimhood (see page 27). After an afflicting faucet has been shut off, the temptation to continue victimhood is a *handoff* of unhappiness *held out* by Satan.

This is the same "handoff" deceptively placed in the belly that enables the act of *hanging on* to stinkin' thinkin'—the impetus to *retaining* emotional scars. And when we don't get *scarred thinking* straight from Satan's unsavory *handoff*, . . . we get it from a noxious genealogy of foul ideas, passed down by people previously deceived by the primal force of foulability. There really IS a devil on your left shoulder and that *evil being* IS the prime-mover** of stinkin' thinkin'—the *marked way* of re-membering called "emotional scars." It is the "outside force" of *unseen evil* that incites you to do . . . dis-ordered and dis-eased re-memberings; it is the power of darkness that helps you *hang on* to scarred thinking.

The raw reality is this: People beset by the torment of mind and emotion are *mostly* and *really* engaged in a dialogue

---

** The "prime-mover" principle implies "cause and effect," but Satan's temptations come under the category of "Sufficient Cause," or a "Be-Cause that conquers you"—with your permission, of course. The governing principle that applies directly to human behavior is . . . Constraint & Choice, and not Cause & Effect.

with the devil; for example, the foreboding flashbacks that psychology calls Post Traumatic Stress Disorder are *actually* and *literally* "the devil messing with your mind." Thus, how can a therapist, who's bought into the mental illness illusion,* possibly hope to fix this "Dis-Ease" when the diagnosis for its origin is so drastically off?

Especially in regard to functioning humans who can hold down jobs and consistently keep appointments, the diagnosis and application of "mental illness" is *mostly* and *really* . . . the King's New Clothes—what you "think" is there (a mental disease) . . . actually isn't there, and what you may not *believe* is there (the devil messing with your mind) . . . really IS there!

* * * * *

Permission and Participation with
Unseen Evil . . . . explains Mental Dis-Ease.
Your willing or unwitting Co-Operation with Darkness
IS the fundamental reality behind Mind
and Behavior Dis-Orders.

* * * * *

By denying or dismissing the existence of the *unseen enemy*, you expose yourself to attack; you are more vulnerable to doing dark diversions and being blind to your blunder. For instance, it's quite common to *think* that the voice in your head is "just me talking to myself," but the devil enters into this mind monologue much more than you might imagine.** What you think is a "monologue" is really a "dialogue"—this is especially so, as thoughts are mired in BRIAR emotions.

In moments when you genuinely feel like you are *not trying* to intentionally think bad thoughts or bring up an

---

* The word "illness," when used in the term "mental illness" has a misleading implication: that mental illness happens like physical illness—as if by a germ, bacteria, or virus; thus, the Mental Illness Illusion IS about the origin of a Mentally Dis-Eased condition, and does not deny the fact that people really are Dis-Ordered in Mind and Emotion.

unproductive past, . . . guess what: Quite often you are NOT the initiator of such unproductive ideas, and it's really the devil inviting you to dance. People who *hear voices* or *think obsessive thoughts* often lament, "but I don't want to think these thoughts, . . . I am haunted by my memories." Bingo! That IS what's happening! Indeed, "haunted" is the right word. People do feel haunted, precisely because they ARE haunted by the devil on their left shoulder.

For this reason when psychotherapists explain that the *voices in your head* are a function of an illness (they say you're beset by bad biology), they do more harm than help, for they *unknowingly enable* Satan to do his deceptions, undetected. When you dismiss the reality of unseen evil, you become easy prey for the devil's dirty tricks. The Apostle Paul warned:

> *"For we wrestle not against flesh and blood, but against principalities, against powers, against the rulers of the darkness of this world, against spiritual wickedness in high places"* (Eph. 6:12).

The proof of Paul's preaching in the pudding: the real existence of dark "powers" is the only coherent explanation for "why" terrible atrocities occur. Try to explain "how" the holocaust could have happened if not for the intervening influence of unseen evil? Further, try to explain the reason "why" a dozen suicide hijackers intentionally killed thousands of innocent Americans on September 11, 2001, and "how" they could claim this killing was for a good cause?

Secular psychology's explanations for such atrocities include Bad Upbringing and Bad Biology, and under the latter category comes . . . the *Mental Illness Alibi.* Are we to conclude that extreme acts of terror, violence, and abuse are perpetrated by people who are *not really responsible* for their actions, because they HAVE an illness? Can we say with all confidence: "It's not their fault for they suffer from a Mental Disease that makes them, forces them, to do crazy things?"

** Refer to "Satan is in the Self-Talk" at www.CallDrMatt.com/SelfTalk

* * * * *

If you apply the Mental Illness Alibi,
it must occur by necessary Cause & Effect,
for if the intervening bad biology is Constraint,
then individuals remain Response-Able
for their crazy behavior.

* * * * *

Another secular explanation for *evil action* comes from the *Bad Upbringing Alibi*—the "cause & effect" conclusions of Behaviorism. Think this through very carefully: If human behavior occurs mechanically due to external causal forces, then why does society put people in prisons and hold them accountable for their unlawful acts? The notions of guilt and blame are *good-for-nothing* unless humans are somehow "responsible" for their actions. It follows, that in order for people to be morally responsible, they must possess free-will to choose between alternatives. Such a conclusion seem so obvious, yet whenever the *Bad Upbringing* or *Mental Illness Alibis* are invoked—which is every day in courts of law—free-will is essentially tossed in the trash!

Final Freedom. In his classic book, "Man's Search for Meaning," Viktor Frankl describes his experience as a prisoner of Nazi death camps. He observed how a few fellow prisoners rose above the oppression of their situation to choose a compassionate response; he writes:

> *The men who walked through the huts comforting others, giving away their last piece of bread. They may have been few in number, but they offer sufficient proof that everything can be taken from a man but one thing: The last of his freedoms—to choose one's attitude in any given set of circumstances.*

Final freedom is NOT merely the liberty to conjure up *any attitude;* instead, because Life is a Set Up, final freedom entails choosing one's eventual attitude *in response* to what happens—"in any given set of circumstances." This is why the superior paradigm for explaining and understanding human behavior is *Constraint* & *Choice*—not *Cause* & *Effect.* "Constraint" represents the realities to which we respond—to which we invoke our final freedom. Even though tragic situations may oppress our flesh, *causing* physical harm, still mortality's most eminent "wrestle" is with an invisible constraint—an unseen enemy.

What it means to be human is to be constrained by every element within your immediate world, to include the constraints of your own body and be-ing. For this reason, every thought you *initially* think is introduced by these very elements, these constraints. This means, you are literally NOT free to NOT think about what is before you—even the act of ignoring is to *think about* that which you are ignoring.

* * * * *

While Constraints do "Cause" me to pay attention for a time, they do not "Cause" the color and character of my ultimate Response.

* * * * *

Satan is "allowed" to constrain your world. The devil IS the co-author of all dark thoughts and deeds, and here's the part you play in this dismal duet: You are listening to Lucifer's lousy logic and you are buying his pathetic product. You decide whether the devil's CD's get further playing time . . . in your mind. While you are NOT always responsible for the *entrance* of a satanic sales pitch, you ARE completely responsible for the *exit.* You are the final editor of the text that trickles into your head; you possess potential *veto power* to edit out every evil idea. A potential that is realized more fully as you move from the shadows and into the Light.

Only as you receive the Light with a humble heart can you stop the stinkin' thinkin' that leads to doing dark deeds. Only when living in the Light are you empowered to *eject* the devil's CD's . . . and quit playing his sorry songs entirely—well, almost entirely. Because Lucifer is "allowed" by Divine Design to deliver temptation's test, you will need to endure Satan's pathetic *sales pitch* that pushes his latest *release.*

Again, while the pitch may enter your mind, you possess the "final freedom" not to *buy* his pitiful product—that's the good news! Now for the bad new: Your ability to *reject* and *eject* the devil's CD's depends upon your present condition of character; the extent to which you live in the Light. In which case, you *may not* be able to easily or immediately quit playing Satin's sorry songs.

If you have a High PQ, . . . you are "toast," and if you resist *recovery* and maintain your High PQ hair-trigger, you will habitually listen to more of Lucifer's lousy lyrics . . . like: *"I'm an Obsessive-Compulsive critter, and that's why I fritter. How do I know? My therapist told me so!"* Consequently, if you fail to escape this High PQ orbit of agitation,* you'll be more than a *fritterin' critter*, . . . you'll be a *crispy critter.* Hellfire's heat will *toast* you up in a hurry. Having a High PQ means you will get *stuck* in the broken-record-rut of playing the detestable tunes by *the artist otherwise known as* . . . Satan!

You may be asking, "what is the reason Lucifer is allowed to tempt and entice?" The answer begins with this: The Creator wants to know who will *be good* when tempted to *be bad.* Further, human beings could NOT even choose to be good unless placed in a context where they are enticed to the opposite possibility. Here's the reality: Goodness is only "possible" if the opposing option is *actually available* to an exercise of will. It is precisely because free-will is real that people can choose to commit acts of terror, violence, and oppression. The possibility of Goodness *only* exists against

---

* What Psychology calls "Obsessive-Compulsive Disorder," IS literally the Devil messing with your Head. Because of an entrenched pattern of dark decisions, negative energy is set-in-motion to such an extent that evil inertia becomes overwhelming. Even if you "locked up your behavioral brakes," you will not be able to immediately stop "OCD-ing," just as a train cannot immediately stop when brakes are set. The *way of being* called OC. is not merely a Head Dis-order, but a Heart Dis-order. Obsessive Compulsive patterns ARE a consequence of dis-ordering Life's Inherent Harmony.

the real possibility of Evil. Earth life is a moral context within which we tried and tested: to see who will hear and heed the *angel on your right shoulder* or the *devil on your left.*

Without opposition to goodness, life would not be a true test of character, nor could it be a school where the refining lessons of pain and compassion are taught; instead, the world would be as secular humanists maintain: there is no Creator, there is no devil, and "morality" is whatever people socially negotiate. But moral relativism is NOT the reality of this world, and there is a train-load of empirical proof to persuade otherwise.

The Creator has given humanity the guiding *Light of Innocence* to lead the way—patient, persistent whisperings that prompt the principles of fulfillment. The pervasive presents of this *spirit voice* is clear evidence of Divine Design. Further, the fact that *Life is Self-Correcting* is powerful proof of *the plan* that Father has put in place.

* * * * *

The Creator's Self-Correcting Cycle
is consistently real and clearly observable:
Dishonest Deeds cannot return Happiness, anymore
than Bad Seeds can bring forth Good Fruit.
Life will teach you this lesson
again and again, until
you get it right.

* * * *

Reality Check: Ditch Dwelling. At many moments in life, you will find yourself in one of two grooves: The *ditch* in which you've *jumped*, OR the *ditch* in which you've been *dumped.* The ditch in which you've been dumped—Situational Suffering—does not necessarily involve a dialogue or dance with the devil; it is misfortune that can occur by no fault of your own and is not necessarily connected to the life-balance boomerang called "karma."

Misfortune can come upon people who are Being True. Situational Set Ups (see page 2) will happen to people who have done nothing to deserve it. An idea captured in these words by Sheri R. Barr:

* * * * *

Thinking that Life will treat you fairly, because you're a good person, is like thinking that an angry bull will not charge you, because you're a vegetarian.

* * * * *

The Creator allows *bad things* to happen to *good people* for the purpose of personal refinement, . . . character building, for *who you become* IS Life's richest reward. Life is a Set Up: Situational Suffering happens. This is the ditch in which you've been dumped by no fault of your own, yet there is opportunity amid adversity.

In contrast, the ditch is which you've jumped, Self-Inflicted Suffering, is misfortune that occurs in consequence of doing ignorant, unwise, or dishonest deeds; this suffering is felt directly due to the corrective clue called karma. The ditch in which you've jumped IS a self-defeating dance done with the devil—unless your just being dumb, in which case your not doing a dark duet, . . . yet, karma will kick your *rear end* anyway. Self-Made misery is the dubious ditch that you dig and then dive into! Even though you "choose" this misery into existence, still the suffering is NOT *imaginary*, it's simply *unnecessary*. Self-Inflicted Suffering, though *real* . . . is also *really* optional.

Because Life presents the possibility of two grooves, you either need to *endure* and *escape* the ditch in which you've been *dumped*—the difficulties of which you are a victim. OR you need to *climb out* of the ditch in which you've *jumped*—the difficulties for which you volunteer. Mortal life is a Set Up for ditch dwelling, one way or the other! * So whether your suffering is *self-made* or *situational*, . . . satisfying solutions need to be applied.

Satisfying Solutions: Head vs. Heart. All human beings are in urgent need of a good "exit strategy" from the ditch in which they dwell. This is where beginning right and asking the best questions will lead to superior solutions. Two basic beginning points are thus:

* Solutions contrived by the Head,
* Solutions that flow from the Heart.

When facing Life's most perplexing problems, seeking solutions via *figuring* and *facts* will just keep you stuck in Einstein's Mind Bind: where the defective *head* that created a problem is used to solve that same problem—an exercise in futility. Additionally, superior solutions will not focus upon changing others or altering circumstance, but upon *changing you* to meet the challenge of circumstance.

Change from your core only occurs thru the *permission* and *power* of Heaven; with no help from Heaven, people are left to the puny solutions of the Head. Of the many Head remedies available, the single most prominent approach is *programming* your head with positive self-affirmations. *Thinking* that your *thinking* can *change you* sufficient to solve Life's largest dilemmas, is to *begin wrong* from the start. Intellectual gymnastics, no matter how impressive or appealing, CANNOT bring about a genuine, lasting change.

With one simple question, Jesus established a profound principle: "Which of you by *taking thought* can add one cubit unto his stature?" (Matt. 6:27). The truth is you really can't chant enough affirmations to change yourself into a person of higher character, nor can you *think* yourself into being happy.

---

* The "ditch" metaphor represents a relative location: Compared to some people's predicaments your personal adversity may look like a "mountain top." But also "relatively speaking," . . . when you compare your personal progress against the Standard of Pure White Light, your location in life may look pretty "ditchy."

Cognitive therapies of "mental programming" may alter outward appearances, but *who you are* from the heart remains unchanged. Like ripples that undulate from a pebble cast in a pond, leaving the pond unaltered at its depths, the superficial effects of mind power eventually dissipate and disappear. It is true that *positive attitude* and *vivid visualizing* may raise your bowling score, improve your golf swing, or make you a dazzling dancer—but the same *cognitive conjurings* cannot increase your character or bring peace to a troubled soul. By using *Head remedies only*, even the strongest mental determinations to be a better person will not work.

The futility of focusing upon your own *figuring* and *affirming* self-talk is reinforced by another truth that Jesus taught: "Watch ye therefore, and *pray always*, that ye may be accounted worthy to escape all these things" (Luke 21:36). When examined in the whole context of Christ's teachings, it is clear that Jesus literally meant that we should engage in continual communion with the Light to receive the promised "escape." As opposed to pumping yourself up with positive self-affirmations, the Pray Always Principle is the best *exit strategy* to escape each and every dose of ditch dwelling.

About three thousand years ago, King Solomon wrote these wise words: "Keep thy heart with all diligence; for out of it are the issues of life." Because the physical heart is a life-sustaining organ in the body, matters of *heart* refer to that which is vital and central and life-giving. With the words "keep thy heart," Solomon encouraged a close and constant conversation with the Creator. Expressing a complementary concept, Viktor Frankl used similar *wording* in regard to final freedom: "keep your inner liberty."

Fundamental change occurs as true principles are loved and lived, yet how can YOU possibly love and live principles of truth unless the disposition to do so . . . is *in* you? Thus, you need a new Heart that inherently feels to love and live the truth. You need a change of Heart, . . . there is no other way. Terry Warner writes:

* * * * *

The only change that matters is a change of heart,
every other change alters us cosmetically
but not fundamentally, modifies how we appear,
what we do or what we say,
but does not change who we are.

* * * * *

"Heart" is not really something *in* you, rather it is an activity you are *in*. Self-introspection of the *body-self* in not something you can actually do; this look "inside" yourself is just a *way of talking* (words playing tricks again). If you take a literal look "inside" you will only find a couple of kidneys and a lung or two; hence, personal guidance and fulfillment is not really found inside of you. In contrast, the look "inside" the *self as be-ing* can be literally accomplished—an examination of your relations.

"Heart" is a metaphor that represents your relational harmony with spirit realities—all which exist outside of you. On the *Light side* of harmony is clear communion with the Creator; and on the *dark side* sings a sinister harmony, a duet with the devil. This dark duet is the reason and reality behind the words: "hard heart." So to start with the *best questions . . .* that will lead to the *best solutions*, it is best to focus upon the *vital communion* you are *in*—this is the meaning of "Heart."

Mortal life means *living in a dialogue* with all living beings and things: a conversation with people, plants,* animals, the earth's physical features, material property and possessions—

---

* How does one "converse" with a plant? To begin with, you cultivate and weed around it, you fertilize and water it; and how does a plant reply? By growing and blooming and bringing forth fruit. You "converse" with a plant by eating and enjoying its fruit; you continue to converse by "hearing" the plant's beauty—exterior appeal in direct response to your nurturing expressions. This is the delightful dialogue you may have with a plant. A similar conversation happens between you and the geological features of the earth; you get to "hear" its natural beauty, and you get to "speak" to the earth, by tending to it, and taking care of it.

and permeating every moment of this empirical conversation is the *inescapable dialogue* with spirit beings of both darkness and Light. Contrary to common belief, thinking is never really done alone; it's always done in duet! So when focus is mistakenly given to an *individualistic mental monologue* of *self-talk affirmations* and *brain programming*, three things occur:

* Focus upon YOU defeats true self-discovery,
* The Divine Dialogue is disconnected,
* By default, you dance with the devil.

I'm exposing the conspiracy! The devil's cover is totally blown, for truth be told: Satan IS in the Self-Talk! For all these many years you may have passed off countless moments of mental chatter as routine thinking: *just me talkin' to myself.* The devil delights in this naive assumption—and exploits it to his evil ends. The devil and his minions desperately want you to think that YOU are simply talking to yourself in moments of *ordinary thinking.*

But sometimes our thinking IS ordinary and innocuous; for example, you might say to yourself, "let's see, I need to pick up a loaf of bread and a gallon of milk at the store." Yet, if you're Being True in this moment, even routine thoughts about daily details can be done with an *attitude of prayer.* When this heart-felt attitude is not consciously and sincerely chosen, you dance with the devil by default. While you may not hear him immediately, Satan is lurking, blending in, silently strategizing his best entry into your *supposed* mental monologue—you're doing a duet, yet you don't know it!

The beauty of the Pray Always Principle is this: Whenever you are praying, you will *always* and *ever* Be True—pure water proceeds from a pure fountain. Mark Twain alluded to this principle thru the words of Huckleberry Finn: *"I was trying to make my mouth say I would do the right thing and the clean thing, . . . but deep down in me I knowed it was a lie, and He knowed it. You can't pray a lie."* Dark thoughts and deeds can only be done, when we leave the dialogue of Light.

"Satan in the Self-Talk" is the dreary ditch in which we dwell through moments that we consciously *commit* acts of evil, or as we *omit* a continual and true communion with the Creator. This is precisely why the scriptures admonish: "Pray always."

Again, thinking is never a solo . . . but always a duet: It's either You-and-Satan-in-the-Self-Talk OR it's You-and-God-in-Prayer. When you fail to consistently commune with the Light, *automatically* you enter the dialogue of darkness. Accordingly, there are *predictable emotional patterns* that spontaneously appear with self-talk that is unwittingly co-authored by Satan—the black and gray emotions mired in the thorns of the BRIAR.

But short of self-talk that is saturated in obvious black BRIAR emotions, self-talk also occurs in muddy shades of gray: Self-talk that seems like normal, innocuous, everyday thinking, but it fails to rise to the level of pure white Light. By default the dialogue of darkness is yours, yet you may say to yourself, "I did nothing wrong to deserve this." Aside from directly doing wrong, the other reason you and I enter a dark dialogue is this: we fail to do something right. Though we clearly *hear* it, when we fail to *heed* the crystal whisperings of Light in any moment, we betray the Light—and darkness enters in.

Whether he is able to entice you to *commit* evil or *omit* good, the devil endlessly endeavors to deceive you by any subtle tactic he can devise. To keep you . . . from Being True, Lucifer wants to bamboozle you in such a covert and clever way, that you don't know you're being bamboozled! Satan's best lies, are the lies that we don't know are lies! What better *deception* could Satan design . . . than a *deception* that is not perceived as *deception?* One of his most popular ploys is to use the facts to divert you from the Truth:

* * * * * * * *

Living Life Logically from the Head:
Satan's Best Lies are Lined with . . . Facts
Facts are about having accurate evidence
and winning arguments: BEING RIGHT.
The Facts often Blind you from the Truth.
Living Life Lovingly . . . from the Heart:
Truth is the Harmony and Integrity
of your Whole Way of Being:
Heart, Mind, & Soul:
BEING TRUE

* * *
*

Being in your Head means you focus upon facts, instead of Truth. Being in your Head means Being Right, instead of Being True. Being in your Head means you have ceased to pray! Being in your Head means dancing with darkness. Being in your Head further *feeds* a problem, rather than *fixes* it. To discern between facts and Truth (see page 219) will expose the devil's deceptions and keep you in your Heart—and out of your Head. The truth is His Mercy, and not mental machinations, *is* the underlying Source of all health, healing, and happiness. Solutions from the Heart will ever be effective in unraveling Life's most important issues, while Head solutions will always fall short.* And when it appears that Head techniques may have "worked," this is only because the Light gives liberally *in spite* of foolish imaginations—not *because of* them.

Better than the Head approach of *figuring* and *coping* . . . is the Heart approach of having *faith* and *hoping*—thus, you connect to the powers of Heaven. With *mind power* alone, you can only contrive a strategy to *cope* with problems that never resolve to complete closure; in contrast, with the healing help of Heaven, you can be lifted up to a brightness of *hope*, an unfailing *hope*, that will completely *dispel all darkness* and turn *adversity to advantage*—as sure as the Sun will rise.

RETURNING TO INNOCENCE

We begin our lives in innocence. Beings of goodness, love, and light. Observe a young child . . . pure innocence: no prejudice, no grudges, and no anxiety—just joyful, playful, uninhibited happiness. From birth, not even a shadow of darkness exists in these clean, clear creatures called "bundles of joy." In a newborn babe, . . . there is only love and light. That's a child! And we all began that way. We began our lives in pure innocence, . . . this was the immaculate "motion" in which we were "set." The momentum of Light and Goodness was our guiding energy from the beginning.

Recovering your own Inner Innocence is the key to Changing Your Stripes. Regardless of where you are in Life's journey, whether personal progress is great or small, in one moment of commitment you can turn and face the Truth within, and immediately put your feet on the path of Recovery—now! Of commitment W. H. Murray said, *"Until one is committed there is hesitancy . . . a chance to draw back, always ineffectiveness; the moment one definitely commits oneself, then Providence moves too."* Murray adds this soul-searching query:

* * * * *

I want to know what you ache for, and if you dare to dream of meeting your hearts longing.

* * * * *

---

* By failing to include the reality of Heart and Heaven in its approach, the secular therapies are hopelessly Head-heavy, and puts all their ontological "faith" in "forces" that supposedly brought about Big Bang. Now, if "forces" did not combine to bring about a Life-Creating Bang, then the other secular alternative is that "something" came into existence from "nothing," a.k.a., "creation ex nihilo"—an assumption much more mystical than creation by a Creator. Secular science's first article of "faith" is that human life evolved from dolphins. IF evolution of the species did occur, then man's ancestors came out of water! Thus, we were "dolphins" BEFORE we were "monkeys." Now if the supposed single cell organism that Big Banged into existence, began its evolving in the dirt—billions of years ago, then possibly mankind actually evolved from "corn" and maybe the movie, "The Children of the Corn," has deeper meaning than we first imagined (*wink*).

The Creator has given to all humanity a Gift of Guidance. What it means to be human is to inherently know the way to personal fulfillment and ultimate refinement. You possess all you need, to succeed, with one possible exception: You may not have a *driving desire* to walk in the Light. If you lack this desire, you will be stuck in a self-defeating trap: how can you grow the flower of your fulfillment, if you won't *plant* the seed, and even if you *do* plant the seed, how can that *flower flourish* if you have no desire to *nurture* the seed?

You will find and fulfill your heart's desire in the Light. The whisperings of Light will illuminate the way to *desire* and *recovery*. But only those who move from the shadows into the warming rays of the Sun will clearly hear the voice of Light.

* * * * *

The Voice of Light is heard in the Light.
Walk in the Light and I am warmed by peaceful radiance.
Walk in the Light and I hear the Whisperings of Light.

* * * * *

You will continue to be *who you are*, until you become someone *new*. Until you Change Your Stripes, you will bring the *old animal* with you wherever you go! And as you encounter *new situations,* you will tend to act according to the *old patterns* of the *old creature*, . . . repeating *old ways* that do not work and do not bring happiness. You can try to run from your troubles . . . but you cannot run from yourself. All your problems are portable, you bring them with you wherever you go; hence, the same *old creature* relocates to *new relationships* with energetic hopes and optimistic anticipations, only to find the same *stale issues* arising again and again.

Wherever you go, you take yourself with you. It's the *same old you* . . . pretending to be *new*—because the clothes are new and the place is different, and the hairdo is new. But what is not *new*, what has not Changed is . . . your Heart. Thus, the same old issues will continue to arise unless you allow an "Outside Force" to bring you back to your original Course—your primal "motion" of purity and honesty.

Without this fundamental change from your core, *portable problems* will eventually *re-surface* as you face future situations. Robert Louis Stevenson said:

* * * * *

You cannot run away from a weakness;
you must at sometime fight it out . . . or perish.
And if that be so, . . . why not now,
and where you stand?

* * * * *

Superficial scenery and cosmetic appearance may change . . . while root problems remain the same. Life's most perplexing problems are not solved by running around, but by going through—persistence will ultimately win over avoidance. To effectively face your *weakness* and take a *stand*, the best questions need to be set and secure, like a Lighthouse beacon shining the way. The best questions begin by examining the condition and quality of your Heart. Like dew on morning grass, superior solutions spontaneously appear as you push aside the puny logic of your Head, and yield to the powerful yet gentle impressions of the Heart. If you're unfamiliar with the dialogue of Light, entering into this lifting and illuminating communion . . . may require the initial planting of a seed.

So, the central question echoes again: how can you grow the flower of your fulfillment, if you won't *plant* the seed; and even if you *do* plant the seed, . . . how can that *flower flourish* if you fail to *nurture* the seed? If you don't seize this seed, and plant this seed, and nurture this seed, you will never succeed in Recovering the True You. Your *old broken-record routine* will tend to play its annoying tune over and over again, until you Change Your Stripes!

The saying goes, "You can't change a tiger's stripes!" Indeed YOU alone cannot bring about this *change*. YOU cannot "make it happen" by the force of mental will (p. 286); instead, you must "let it happen," . . . yield to the Light of Innocence and allow the Creator to recover you, redeem you (see page 288).

This Recovery is a most precious process . . . for *who you become* while in this life is the only possession you will take with you at the time of transition.

* * * * *

The Greatest Prize for Life's labors is not realized in material possessions or impressive accomplishments, but in the progress of personal character. You labor for your own becoming, this is your richest reward. Who You Become is your greatest possession; make it your Masterpiece!

* * * *

The key to Changing Your Stripes IS NOT a matter of willful choosing; the power to *change from your core* does not reside in mental will power; the miracle of Recovery unfolds by unwavering faith, and not by willful figuring. Becoming a New Kind of Creature is a miracle that happens as you release your mental will, and yield to the moral will written in your Heart—it is the power of the Creator that makes you a New Creature.

* * * * *

Recovering the You that is True begins to unfold as you get out of your Head, and consistently hear and heed the impression of the Heart. The only Change that matters is A Change of Heart: A Recovery and Redemption that happens only with the Help of Heaven.

* * * * *

As Heraclitus discovered over two millennia ago "It is in *change* that we find purpose." With the dawning of a bright new day, as you embrace the Light, a new *way of being* is reborn. A *way of being* that brings with it . . . a new *way of seeing.* Through eyes of innocence a world of simplicity, unity, and opportunity opens to view. Changing Your Stripes and Becoming a New Kind of Creature means that from this day forward, you sow the seeds of Love and Light . . . making tomorrow's harvest very Bright.

~ 4 ~

Index:

Where Do I Find That?

* Section Heading

* Section Heading

* Section Heading

* Section Heading

* Section Heading

The subject in this poem stands red-faced, veins-popping and teeth-clenched, trying to achieve self-control; willfully trying to steer his destiny, for he is the master of his fate . . . or so he assumes—his aim is upon SELF-MASTERY:

INVICTUS

by William E. Henley

Out of the night that covers me,
Black as the Pit from pole to pole,
I thank whatever gods may
for my unconquerable soul.

In the fell clutch of circumstance,
I have not winced nor cried aloud.
Under the bludgeonings of chance
My head is bloody, but unbowed.

Beyond this place of wrath and tears
Looms but the Horror of the shade,
And yet the menace of the years
Finds and shall find me unafraid.

It matters not how strait the gate,
How charged with punishments the scroll,
I am the master of my fate;
I am the captain of my soul.

ACKNOWLEDGMENTS

The principle of being true to the truth was instilled within me at an early age by those to whom I dedicate these writings. The experiences of my lifetime verify the teachings and example of my goodly parents and my loving family.

Thanks to friends and family who participated in the "proofing project" (you know who you are). If there are any mistakes herein, it's their fault (*wink*).

I give tribute to great teachers who have impacted my life profoundly: To the late Reed R. Bradford for teaching me the most important things in Life first, then a little sociology. Though he was criticized for teaching "religion" in sociology classes, his teachings were true to the mission of Brigham Young University. In contrast, criticized for teaching a little "sociology" in religion classes (hah), I thank Wilford E. Smith for writing the key recommendation that got me into my Doctoral program. To the late Lyal E. Holder, a master teacher, who taught me what it means to learn and the art of facilitating that discovery.

My appreciation also goes to Chauncey Riddle, a brilliant philosopher and humble man of God, who taught me to begin all intellectual inquiries by asking the best questions. My thanks to Richard Williams, social psychologist extraordinaire, who taught me (among other things) to NOT reify *activites* into *things*, and faithfully wrap word-descriptions around reality. To Darwin Thomas, for teaching me how keep my writings focused upon the topic at hand—avoiding the temptation of tangents (albeit clever and intriguing)—and for being the doctoral committee chairman that made my Ph.D. degree happen.

My appreciation goes to C. Terry Warner for providing me with the foundation and framework for dozens of key concepts expressed herein; specifically, the tell-tale signs of betrayal, wordless emotional lies that we live, and reinforcing the importance of the "only change that matters." I also thank Terrance Olson for refining the key concepts of self-deception and betrayal, as well as teaching me the core truth that a *way of seeing* is inseparable from a *way of being.*

And finally, an eternal "thank you" to the Creator for the miracle of Life and for graciously giving us all the Gift of Guidance—that we might know the way to happiness here, and hereafter.

In contrast, the subject in this second poem asks an entirely different question of Life (see Invictus, p. 286). Yielding before his Maker, he strives for the highest form of MASTERY:

THE SOUL'S CAPTAIN

by Orson F. Whitney

Art thou in truth the master of thy fate? The captain of thy soul?
Then what of him who bought thee with his blood?
Who plunged into devouring seas and snatched thee
from the raging flood?

Who bore for all our fallen race
what none but him could bear,
the God who died
that man might live,
and endless glory share?

Of what avail thy
vaunted strength,
Apart from his vast might?
Pray that his Light
may pierce the gloom,
that thou might see aright.

Men are as bubbles on the wave,
as leaves upon the tree,
O' captain of thy soul, explain!
Who gave that place to thee?

Free will is thine--free agency,
To wield for right or wrong;
But thou must answer unto him
To whom all souls belong.

Bend to the dust thy head "unbowed,"
small part of Life's great whole!
And see in him, and him alone,
The Captain of thy soul.